An Untold Story

An Untold Story
The Roosevelts of Hyde Park

by
Elliott Roosevelt
and
James Brough

FOUNDED 1838
GPPS

G. P. PUTNAM'S SONS, *New York*

B
Roosevelt

Copyright © 1973
by Elliott Roosevelt and James Brough

SBN: 399-11127-1

Library of Congress Catalog
Card Number: 72-97308

PRINTED IN THE UNITED STATES OF AMERICA

c.4

Contents

*Illustrations will be found
following page 160.*

Introduction

For almost as long as I can remember, I have been reading about a man and a woman, scarcely recognizable by me, who are identified as Franklin and Eleanor Roosevelt. It used to be the fashion to picture them both as legendary beings of heroic size, immune to frailty or human passion. To each of us within the family, they emerged as total strangers, not the father we loved and the mother we respected.

But history—or at least the historian who creates it—demands idols. It seemed inappropriate for me to attempt to correct the distortions and restore my parents to humanity. If Father was depicted in book after book as unbelievably great and Mother as unfailingly gracious, then the principal damage done was to credibility.

There was another doubt in my mind. Perhaps it was important to the American tradition of log cabin democracy to remember that even a President remains a man, though the tendency grows increasingly strong to make him out to be a demigod, beyond the reach and touch of the people who elect him.

As the father of his country, George Washington is a lay figure; his foibles, his false teeth and his expense account give him reality. Abraham Lincoln, the rail-splitter plagued with self-doubt and family problems, is a source of inspiration; the single-minded crusader for freedom, regardless of color or creed, is not.

Recently, I became increasingly perturbed over a twisting of facts which has led far too many people to regard Father as a cardboard puppet, manipulated by anyone with the urge to try, dependent on Mother for strength and wisdom. She, in turn, is looked upon as a latter-day Joan of Arc, incapable of error or sin. Neither portrait contains the faintest element of truth. Mother, whose idolators are largely responsible for this mangling of the record of yesterday, would have been among the first to acknowledge that.

These pages are an effort to set the record straight, to present the story of two real human beings and the relationship between them: how in completely separate ways they came to greatness through tremendous physical and mental anguish. This is the way it was. I trust only that it may serve as a lens to clarify for history the intricate personalities of the man who became the thirty-second President of the United States and the woman who, after his death, earned her place as the First Lady of the Western world.

E. R.

The truth is found when men are free
to pursue it.

—Franklin Delano Roosevelt
February 22, 1936

Washington

1916

1

EARLY that summer, as I recall, even the three of us older children had reached the conclusion that the family was growing too big too fast or else that the narrow little house had mysteriously become too small. Anna could scarcely wait for her classes at the Misses Eastman's to be over and Jimmy to start on vacation from the Potomac School so that we could be on our way again to Campobello, where there would be plenty of room for all of us, since Father had the house there enlarged in time for our annual vacation.

In Washington, which struck us as a dull place to have to live in, we had been sadly overcrowded for three months now, ever since the arrival in the third-floor nursery of yet another baby brother. That, of course, had meant the return to our household of Blanche Spring, to whom Mother had turned in every pregnancy from the time of Anna's birth ten years earlier. The stocky, little trained nurse was "a very lovely person," in Mother's words. All her pregnancies had been unpleasant, so she was deeply attached to Miss Spring.

"She adored babies," Mother once said, "and she tried to teach me something about their care." The self-confidence of Anna Eleanor Roosevelt had not developed very far in those days, and her abilities to look after a family were sometimes put to the test. Two days after the new baby was born, I developed a heavy spring cold, with the glands standing out on the sides of my neck. Nothing would do but to have another nurse brought in to take charge of me, feverish and in bed in the room over Mother's.

"It was a *trying* experience," Mother said later in that well-measured, high-pitched voice of hers, whose flutterings conveyed more meaning than her words.

Making room for Miss Spring threatened to burst our seams. With Franklin junior, whom we called Brud, toddling around, we added up to a family of seven. We had four servants, the same number that Mother brought down from New York in 1913, along with a governess and a nurse. Others came in every day to help with the cleaning and cooking, including Albert, who combined the duties of handyman and chauffeur. For the summers, when Father was frequently left alone in the house, we could call on the services of Millie and Frances, both black, who had been bequeathed to us by Auntie Bye.

Johnny, the baby, was certainly thriving in the hands of Miss Spring. We all were fat newborns by today's standards, not one of us weighing in at less than 10 pounds at birth, with something of a record set by myself at 11 pounds and more. But Johnny promised to outdo his brothers and sister. The nursery scales registered 14 pounds 13 ounces, and he was only three months old but already showing signs of the temper which made him something of a terror so far as Mother was concerned.

She had not particularly cared for the house from the day we moved in, and we had been living there for three years. It was one more home, like our New York house on East Sixty-fifth Street, which had come to her ready-made and fully furnished. This Washington place was a sublet from Auntie Bye, born Anna Roosevelt in 1855, who was Theodore Roosevelt's older sister and Mother's aunt. Auntie Bye was another woman to whom Mother habitually turned in times of need. Mother knew the house well from visiting there as an orphaned girl seeking counsel and comfort from a favorite relative.

It was decidedly old-fashioned but comfortable enough until Franklin junior and now Johnny arrived. Its location could scarcely be more convenient, just six blocks down windy Connecticut Avenue to the Navy Department, where Father was enjoying himself to the hilt as Assistant Secretary under the watchful eyes of his boss, Secretary Josephus Daniels. Father, for reasons of economy, invariably walked to the office, as often as not in the company of the wizened little man he had brought to the job as his own assistant and fellow conspirator, Louis Howe.

Our house stood on N Street, which ran into Connecticut Avenue, where the Victorian Gothic monstrosity of the old British Embassy dominated the view; some of Father's more intimate friends lived or worked there, engaged in every kind of diplomatic maneuver to draw the United States into their country's war against Germany.

Number 1733 was one of a red-brick row, indistinguishable from its neighbors, with an unfenced, handkerchief-sized lawn in front and a miniature garden in the rear, where we occasionally ate breakfast if the weather turned hot and humid, with the dishes served on a wrought-iron table in the little rose arbor. The street's massive shade trees made the rooms gloomy, even with the sliding double doors between them on the main floor pulled open to give us children more space to roam in. The house had never been wired for electricity. Gas sconces stood out from the walls and chandeliers from the ceilings, lit by a servant with a taper at dusk. One of the first of my admonitions I remember is Mother's "You must never, *never* play with the gas."

Dark wallpaper and heavy carved mantelpieces contributed to the general effect of genteel but somewhat joyless respectability. So did the ugly walnut furniture, which our irrepressible grandmother, Sara, characteristically proceeded to rearrange the first time she came to dinner. "Moved chairs and tables and began to feel at home," Granny noted in her diary after she had seen the new premises of her son and daughter-in-law.

In later years, Mother was careful to leave the impression that she had always been resentful of such acts of Granny, but there was no such feeling at that time. She leaned on her mother-in-law for help, advice, and sometimes consolation. Mother was so incredibly unaware and inexperienced in every kind of situation that she welcomed many of the things, always intended as kindnesses, which Granny insisted on doing for her.

Father relished living in the unimpressive, cramped little house, just as he enjoyed virtually everything else in life. It had earned a footnote in history, which was a subject in which he steeped himself. Number 1733 was the Little White House for a brief period when Auntie Bye lent it to her brother, Theodore, after McKinley was shot at the Pan-American Exposition in Buffalo and the first

Roosevelt to become President delayed moving into the White House itself out of consideration for the ailing widow.

There was another reason for his being fond of N Street: It was an address with a certain distant echo of the sea, which was a boyhood love he never lost. The house had been the home of sleepy old Admiral William Sheffield Cowles of the United States Navy after he met and married Auntie Bye when she was living in London in the nineties as the hostess of James Roosevelt Roosevelt, Father's half brother, twenty-eight years older than he, who was then First Secretary of the American Embassy there. Our neighbors included retired admirals and other naval officers, aging generals and old-time Congressmen, who took their morning constitutionals along the sidewalk; their wives made the rounds for afternoon tea. The *Social Register* listed most of N Street's residents in those days when Washington was a quiet, small town beginning to burst at the seams, just like our household, with a population problem. But its growing pains were the effect of the Great War.

My own feelings of vague hostility usually began at breakfast time, when the whole family except for the two youngest gathered as a daily routine in the dining room at the back of the main floor. I could trace my discontent to the food, which was delivered on a creaking dumbwaiter from the kitchen downstairs, to be served by one of the maids. Nothing tasted anywhere near as delicious as the dishes we were used to in Granny's house at Hyde Park, which everyone but Mother regarded as our real home. The meals we children put away there must have been one reason why we all grew up so hefty.

We ate soup-platesful of fresh strawberries, grown in the garden or in Granny's massive greenhouse, doused in sugar and cream from the farm so thick that you had to spoon it out of the pitcher. We tackled hot cereal or porridge, eggs and bacon, mountains of homemade muffins and rolls. Granny—and Father—had such pride in the bounty of Hyde Park that fruit and vegetables and fresh-laid eggs were shipped down to us in Washington.

As a household manager, though, Mother did not compare to Granny. She ran into constant problems with finding and keeping servants. The meals were wholesome enough, but plain and uninspiring because she had little interest in planning menus, and the cooking was decidedly mediocre.

Mother was invariably up and dressed by the time the children came down. Her beautiful red-brown hair would be parted high and gathered in a chignon pinned up on her head. She favored practical wool skirts and shirtwaists, on which she wore her single piece of everyday jewelry, a brooch from which hung a little gold watch. She firmly believed in punctuality as a virtue, and the watch was often consulted.

Father's idea of the importance of timekeeping in no way coincided with hers. He carried a watch on a gold chain fastened through a waistcoat buttonhole, but throughout his life I rarely saw him look at it. He was much more leisurely about his morning routines. He liked to linger in his separate bedroom, reading the newspapers, sipping a first cup of coffee. While Mother was seeing us settled at the breakfast table, he was likely still to be shaving, using a cutthroat or the open razor with a replacable blade, which he kept to the end of his days.

Breakfast could seldom wait for Father. Anna, whose pale-blond hair hung to her shoulders, had to be off to the Misses Eastman's, Jimmy, in knickerbockers and long black socks, to the Potomac School. Mother sat herself at one end of the table opposite Father's empty chair. This was a position of status which she never enjoyed at Hyde Park, where her place was halfway down the dining-room table, with Granny in command at its head. Mother rang the little silver bell which she kept beside her teacup to signal the maid to start serving.

Father came downstairs at the same brisk pace that took him everywhere. He was considered a stylish dresser, from his high collars to his Peel shoes, bought in London. His English-cut, dark business suits lasted him for years, but they kept their impeccable fit.

"Good morning, Babs," he would say, kissing Mother lightly on the cheek. "Good morning, chicks. How are we all today?" As he sat down and spread his napkin, the silver bell tinkled to call the maid.

He seemed permanently to be overflowing with energy, but never more so than in the mornings. He invariably awoke in a high good humor, ready and eager to tackle anything the day might bring. I do not remember a breakfast time when there wasn't a smile on his lips and in his eyes. The austere look which came when he peered down through the pince-nez he wore ever since his Harvard days was assumed only during office hours, in keeping with his role as a hard-driving go-getter in the service of his country.

This was the year that daylight saving time was introduced as a wartime measure in England, so he might have touched on that in table conversation, since he thought it was a "bully" idea. He possibly talked about Charles Evan Hughes, whom the Republicans had nominated on June 10 for the Presidency on a platform of "straight and honest" neutrality. Mother and Father both had been dinner guests of Justice and Mrs. Hughes before the candidate started attacking Daniels and the Navy Department, prompting my father to ask, "Does Mr. Hughes not know what the Navy knew, that the Navy in March, 1913, was a hollow shell? . . . All it needs now is boosting and not knocking."

Whatever he spoke of over breakfast, Mother would glance at her watch to be sure we were running on time. On a typical morning, the front doorbell would ring before we finished. Louis Howe was stopping by to pick up Father to walk down the avenue. Father's first move on being appointed to the department had been to send to New York for Louis. "Dear Ludwig," he wrote, "here is the dope. Secretary—$2,000. Expect you April 1, with a new uniform."

Not even his best friends, and Father rated highest among them, called Louis imposing. He weighed little more than a wizened one hundred pounds. His rumpled clothes, forever gray with cigarette ash, hung loosely to his spare body. His long neck was encircled by a two-inch-high collar, seldom very clean. As he entered the dining room, there was a warm smile on his incredibly wrinkled face, which was pitted and scarred from a childhood accident. When he spoke, his voice was astonishingly deep and dignified.

"Good morning, Boss. Good morning, Mrs. Roosevelt."

Mother made no pretense that she liked him. She felt somehow excluded from the intimacy he and Father shared, the affectionate bantering that went on between them, the secrets they kept exclusively to themselves. She found it hard to tolerate Louis' table manners, which were careless and often crude, but she could not ignore her duty as hostess.

"Would you care for some breakfast, Mr. Howe?"

"No, thank you. But I would like some coffee, please." The little bell rang again. Louis took his black and steaming. He pulled out a pack of Fatimas—he switched to Sweet Caporals in the years ahead—and lit one of the hundred or so he smoked a day. His nicotine-stained fingers trembled, and he broke into an asthmatic cough at the first draw. Mother frowned.

"Do you think you should see a doctor about your cough?"

Louis smiled again. "It's an old friend. I once saw a doctor in Albany who gave me two months to live. That was nearly ten years ago."

After Sis and Jimmy had left for school, the conversation might turn for a minute or two to the war. Father, only half-jokingly, used to say he was afraid that he might "do some awful unneutral thing before I get through" which would bring America in with both feet on the Allied side. Twenty-one years later, Mother wrote that she was attracted by the staunch pacificism of William Jennings Bryan, the silvery-maned spellbinder who had been a dinner guest of my parents before he resigned as Secretary of State to protest President Wilson's increasingly strong policies toward Germany. But at this time, she seemed to agree completely with Father.

"I think we have a little too much patience with Germany, don't you?" she wrote to Granny, whose opinions on the subject were even fiercer than Father's.

Father's special concern was the war at sea. He had argued for months that the British fleet ought to challenge the Kaiser's battleships in a major engagement. That had come about, without a clear-cut victory for either side, in the Battle of Jutland in the first days of June. One of his concerns now was the menace of German submarines; this was the year when the U-boat *Deutschland* reached New York in July and was sunk on her return voyage. He assuredly talked of this to Louis.

"There may be a submarine or two over here pretty soon," Louis said. "What are the plans for Campobello? What happens if one of them turns up there?"

We regarded Campobello Island as an integral part of our family life in spite of all its blowing fogs and rocky barrenness. Almost every summer Mother took us children, the governess and some of the servants there, to stay in the house which Granny bought for us next to hers. "Campo," as everyone in the family called it, could be reached only by boat, a choppy half-hour's crossing from Lubec or Eastport on the Maine coast. The nightmare of German submarines in the Bay of Fundy did not seem at all ridiculous. Nobody knew what they might do when they had sunk the *Lusitania* and killed one hundred twenty-eight Americans aboard just over a year ago.

"Oh, I fancy we shall be safe enough," Father said. "I can't believe that the Germans will want to capture Campo, but if they do, we'll be ready for them." But Campobello was Canadian territory, and

Canada was already fighting Germany. "Come on Louis. It must be time for us to be on our way." He gave Mother and me a quick kiss on the cheek, which I promptly returned in the same manner, as all of us children did. A kiss was a family custom which we continued into adulthood. "I always kissed *my* father," Pa used to say.

He must have loved striding down Connecticut Avenue every weekday morning with Louis hurrying along at his side, the two of them looking uncannily like Don Quixote and Sancho setting out to battle with giants. Government girls on their way to their typewriters turned their heads to watch. Society gossips rated Father to be among the handsomest men in town, long-muscled, superbly fit from weekend exercise. His good friend Nigel Law, Third Secretary at the British Embassy, who had arrived aboard the *Lusitania* in November, 1914, thought that he was "the most attractive man whom it was my good fortune to meet during my four years in America."

On his way to the front door with Louis, Father paused to pick up his straw hat, which in summer replaced his winter bowler. At that moment, another caller was lifting the hem of her long skirt to climb the front steps. She wore a lace jabot at the neck of her blouse, encircled by a black velvet ribbon. She was fair, slender, full-breasted and smiling. Lucy Mercer had lived in this same row of houses, at Number 1761, as a child before her family's fortune was dissipated. Now she returned on most mornings of the week to work for Mother as a very social secretary and guide on the finer points of Washington's social protocol, which she knew like the back of her slim hands.

Louis raised his hat. "Good morning, Miss Mercer."

"It's the lovely Lucy," Father said, calling to Mother.

Then the Assistant Secretary of the Navy and his indispensable companion turned into the narrow street to head to work. The domestic explosion which was kept secret from the world for close to half a century still lay in the future, two years away, but the mechanisms that produced it were already ticking.

2

My mother, who became generally recognized at the First Lady of the world after my father's death in 1945, was a repressed, painfully introverted girl of twenty when they were married in March, 1905. Father, who had reached his twenty-third birthday two months earlier, was a self-made extrovert, by no means repressed, but almost equally sheltered and emotionally immature.

Granny, a widow for more than four years, was dead set against the marriage, being certain that her only son was far from ready for such a momentous step, which threatened to take him from her. But this response was scarcely surprising. She had felt much the same about everything he sought to do that would remove him even temporarily from Hyde Park as he grew up, unless it fitted her ideas of what was good for him, and that included going off to school at Groton. The pattern was fundamental in the relationship between mother and son; she had breast-fed him until he was two years old.

The young bridegroom was in many respects more boy than man. He retained a boyish delight, consistently encouraged by Granny, in collecting stamps, ship prints and wild bird specimens. The birds were shot in the woods and fields around Hyde Park with the gun his father, James Roosevelt, gave him at fourteen, then mounted for display in the house. He had a boy's brand of courage in blithely ignoring a succession of crash landings on an already badly bruised hip so that he could win a high-kicking contest, which was a bizarre pastime at Groton, and then write to tell Granny all about it, because she expected that kind of pluck in him. Courage was something else that grew in him. His experiences with the opposite sex had been limited, it would seem, to teasing the girls at summer picnics—he was a gay young blade in white duck trousers, fiercely striped shirts and a dashing boater—to mild flirtations on dance floors and at fashionable parties on Beacon Hill during his student days at Harvard. His dates, which never developed into anything serious, were restricted to the Hyde Park neighbors' daughters, such as Mary Newbold, whose parents may well have been disappointed when he announced that he was engaged to Anna Eleanor, his fifth cousin once removed.

He seldom failed to keep Granny informed, in his customary

bantering way, about the girls he met. During his sophomore year at Harvard, a dentist had to extract a front tooth. After a week of talking "with a lithp" and looking "like a thight," as he wrote his mother, he had a new tooth put in and was "proposed to by three girls." He added, joshing her, "My best friends don't recognize me and say, 'Who *is* that handsome fellow?' "

Granny never could have imagined his marrying so young. He found his real contentment, she thought, in the company of his male friends, all wealthy young men in the same social circle, like his Harvard companions, Lathrop Brown, Livingston Davis and the rest. "He had never been in any sense a *lady's* man," she said, so she had no one in mind as a future bride for him. He had never even talked to girls with any earnestness "except on that memorable occasion when he had taken a young lady driving in a dogcart on Long Island and found to his consternation that she had fainted."

Only a few years later, when we lived on N Street, much of that aspect of him had drastically changed. He was as debonair as ever, with an equal zest for living, but now he knew that men and women alike admired him, and he responded in kind. Old Admiral Cowles, our landlord, shook a finger at him: "The girls will spoil you soon enough, Franklin, and I leave you to them."

Father used to joke with his friends about what he called "the saloon, the salon and the Salome," which were three distinctly different categories of social diversion available in Washington. The "saloon" described any house where drinks were poured generously. The "salon" was anybody's home where artists and savants gathered to talk. The "Salome" was Father's term, as one of his later aides reported, for "a mansion where the music was soft, so were the sofas, and the ladies were very pretty. Franklin knew them all."

The change in Father came about partly as a result of his growing belatedly into manhood and all it signifies in terms of human needs. But the far more important factor influencing him was the change in Mother's attitude toward him which occurred in the intervening years.

Eleanor could only consider young Franklin a great, unbelievable catch when he proposed to her when they both were on a visit to Groton to see her brother, Hall, who had followed him in school there. The exact words they used to each other are unknown; neither of them ever told us children. According to one account, by a latter-day friend of Mother's, Father promised her that "with your help" he "would amount to something some day," while she supposedly replied, "Why me? I am plain. I have little to bring you."

Knowing the nature of my parents, I seriously question whether those words, or anything remotely like them, were exchanged between them. Those phrases have a spurious ring to them, like so much and so many of the legends which were carefully created around Mother and Father as time went by.

If he was no more than a boy in terms of experience with women at the time of their marriage, Mother was no more than a child in her knowledge of men. Only two members of the mystifying, unapproachable other sex had genuinely touched her heart until then—her father, Elliott, for whom I was named, and her brother, Hall. For the rest, she knew only old family friends and relatives, most particularly her two uncles on her mother's side, who were both drunkards.

Mother was born in New York City on October 11, 1884, the eldest of three children of Elliott, who was Theodore Roosevelt's younger brother, and Anna Hall, whose fragile beauty and blood lines made her a queen of old Manhattan society. The birth, which went smoothly in spite of concern about Anna's health, was one of the happier moments in an otherwise tragic year for the Oyster Bay Roosevelts. Eight months earlier, the death of the Roosevelts' mother, Martha, had been followed within a few hours by the death after childbirth of Theodore's wife, Alice Lee. "There is a curse on this house," Elliott exclaimed, and Mother grew up believing he was not far wrong.

A sense of Victorian Gothic guilt colored much of her thinking throughout her younger years. She tended to remember deaths in her family—and they were many—instead of births and the simple everyday rewards of living. She would insist, without a shred of evidence in any photo album, that she "must have been a more wrinkled and less attractive baby than the average." On the contrary, early photographs show her as an unusually solemn, but by no means unattractive little girl, round-faced, with her luxuriant hair tied back in a pretty ribbon, much the same style which she liked for Sis at a similar age.

Although Mother regarded herself as having been almost exclusively her father's daughter, I think that she was more the product of her mother's stern upbringing. Anna Hall was strictly disciplined in mind and body by a father who kept a resident clergyman like a pet in his house so that he would have someone to talk to and who forced her to walk several times a day with a stick held in the crook of her elbows across her back in order to improve her posture.

Great-grandfather Valentine Hall, after a misspent youth, became a penitent and a gentleman of leisure, with no talent or inclination for business, since he lived on his parents' money. Their donations to him were generous enough for him to build Oak Terrace, a dismal, drafty Victorian mansion on the Hudson River twenty miles above Hyde Park, just north of the village of Tivoli; he also had a New York town house on West Thirty-seventh Street. Both residences, in their furnishings and atmosphere, would have made worthy homes for Mr. Barrett of Wimpole Street, with prayers said twice a day to correct the sinfulness of mankind.

There was another, totally different side to this priggish tyrant with the tightly buttoned suits and the carefully curled hair. He doted on his wife, Mary, a beauty and a belle, and treated her as a child. He chose all her dresses and personal jewelry, teaching her nothing about business, not even how to write a check. He died when Anna was seventeen, the oldest of six children who were in charge of a widow who knew literally nothing about running a household or how to avoid conceiving unwanted offspring.

Within three years, Anna met and was married to Elliott. "He is such a tender, sympathetic, manly man," Auntie Bye, his older sister, told her. Elliott adored his "tall, slender, fair-haired little beauty," though the rigors of her training had left her cold as ice, to judge by some of the tales we heard as small children about Grandfather Elliott, told by an old servant, Rebecca, who had worshipped him.

He had every bit, and perhaps more, of the dash and daring which is associated with his brother, Theodore, who was two years older. Elliott, in fact, signposted some of the paths which the future President followed in his struggle to build himself up as a man after a sickly childhood plagued by asthma. Elliott had graver problems of health to overcome. From boyhood on, he suffered from seizures of dizziness and head pains so severe that they made him scream. Yet at sixteen, sent off to the Texas hill country, he became an expert horseman and rifleshot. His letters home to Theodore stirred his brother's later love of the West and the outdoors.

Theodore rated himself and his younger brother, who had once defended him from school-day bullies, as "almost equal" as athletes. "He rows best; I run best; he can beat me sailing or swimming; I can beat him wrestling or boxing. I am best with the rifle, he with the shotgun."

When Elliott was married to Anna, he had recently returned from an expedition to India, hunting tiger and elephant, then on through the Himalayas to Tibet, drawing on part of an inheritance of $125,000 to pay for the trip. In that, too, he paved a way for Uncle Ted, who became identified as a great African safari man. So Elliott, largely overlooked by history, emerged as a major influence on one President and, through Mother, had an indirect role in the making of another.

She remembered her father calling her "a miracle from heaven." Yet she was careful to point out that "he had a physical weakness which he himself probably never quite understood." She gave the impression in her own writing, as well as to people who wrote about her subsequently, that his weakness was alcoholism. She spoke of his dominating her, of his being "the love of my life for many years after he died," which happened two months before her twelfth birthday. "I never doubted that I stood first in his heart," she said, because "he was the only person who did not treat me as a criminal."

What she omitted to do was to bring out the truth that he died of a tumor of the brain, which had originated in his childhood. For the greater part of his short life-span—only thirty-one years—he had suffered constantly increasing agony, while he kept up a façade of gaiety as a hunting, shooting, polo-playing sportsman. His "problem" with drinking was that he turned to alcohol as the only possible means to alleviate the pain. In the slow process of dying, it was his anodyne.

Mother mentioned this to me when I had grown up, but to the world at large she persisted in presenting a picture of a loving, yet weak-willed father who drank himself to his grave, leaving her a weeping orphan, consoling herself by daydreaming about him. As children, one of the stories she often told us about him had her sitting in a carriage outside the Knickerbocker Club in New York, with three fox terriers, waiting by the hour while he got drunk inside, then going home alone. It was, she said, a traumatic experience, which may have explained why, on the subject of alcohol, she made no effort to conceal her prejudices.

Throughout the time when we were growing up, she genuinely

saw herself as a kind of Little Nell, which was the pet name her father had for her, after the sweet, shamefully victimized heroine of Charles Dickens' *Old Curiosity Shop,* a book which he made her read when she could not have been old enough to comprehend a fraction of its meaning. Without a doubt, there were enough parallels between her real circumstances and the vicissitudes of poor Little Nell to leave an indelible scar. Significantly, the books she remembered best from her childhood were the novels of Dickens, in which virtue, after long ordeals, invariably wins out in the end.

Elliott's brain disease put him in and out of sanitariums and nursing homes; at one point, Theodore suspected that his brother was insane. During his periods of exile, Mother's upbringing became as severe as Anna's had been. Anna's ideas of a suitable education did not go much farther than having her daughter repeat Bible verses, an echo of Great-grandfather Hall's regime. At the age of six, Mother could neither read nor begin to write. More than that, she recalled "I could not sew and could not cook and knew none of the things a girl should know."

The bitterness of her existence caused Anna frequent headaches; one of her daughter's few physical contacts with her came about when she was invited to sit at the head of her mother's bed and stroke her forehead. They slept in the same room. Mother, skillfully depicting the scene and the pathos involved, described "the thrill of watching her dress to go out in the evenings." Anna "looked so beautiful," she said, "I was grateful to be allowed to touch her dress or her jewels or anything that was part of the vision which I admired inordinately."

Perhaps there was an element of sheer exaggeration in her words, as there was in her description of herself as an inveterate youthful liar, who would practice her pitiful deceits to win attention or escape a scolding. The fact is that she was a painfully shy, introverted girl who would have resorted to untruth, in my opinion, only to avoid being noticed. Trying to disappear into the woodwork was a habit she kept long into marriage and her own motherhood.

Whatever her feelings for Anna were, and she did not speak of loving her, there was never a mention of sorrow over the icy, scornful woman who "was always a little troubled by my lack of beauty" and who made her feel guilty for that and a dozen other things. Mother was eight when Anna died of diphtheria in 1892. Any chance or possible hope of intimacy and a normal mother-daughter relationship between them was lost. "Death meant nothing to me," Mother said.

Anna by then had borne two sons, one named for his father, the other christened Gracie Hall. A year later, Elliott junior died of scarlet fever. Mother's sense of loss was no stronger than it had been for Anna. She wrote to her father, in a vein she could only have found in her mother's sanctimonious instruction, "We must remember Ellie is going to be safe in heaven and to be with Mother who is waiting there and our Lord wants Ellie boy with him now, we must be happy and do God's will and we must cheer others who feel it to. You are alright I hope."

Mother and her brother Hall, who was two years old, went to live with Great-grandmother Hall. A dozen years of widowhood had changed the once-spoiled bride. She had seen her younger children grow up totally out of her control. She had given up trying to keep them in check and turned for consolation to her dead husband's fundamentalist views about religion. Determined that her two grandchildren should be kept in line and given the discipline her own children lacked, she reared Mother to accept every word in the Bible as literal truth.

Mother brought up the point years afterward, when she had gone to Father for a serious talk about the kind of religious instruction we children should be getting; she fancied that he did not give enough thought to the subject.

So far as her Grandmother Hall was concerned, "If the Bible said that Jonah was swallowed by a whale, he was," she said, "regardless of the fact that a whale does not have a large enough throat to swallow a man."

Father gave her one of his quizzical looks. "What you were taught never hurt you, did it?"

"No, I suppose not—even though it never gave me any chance to think these things out for myself."

"Well," he said, "since it didn't hurt you, why not let the children have the same kind of teaching and then think things out for themselves when they grow up, just as you did?"

The household of which Great-grandmother Hall was the nominal head could well have served as a model for *Bleak House*. She spent most of the day in her bedroom, coming downstairs principally to receive callers in the blue-damasked drawing room of the brownstone town house. The rest of the place was the domain of

Pussie and Maude, two of her daughters who remained at home, and her older son, Vallie, while Eddie, the younger son, visited there from time to time. A cook, a butler, a laundress and a housemaid, who doubled as lady's maid, constituted the domestic staff.

In one way or another, her children were sorrowful examples of Great-grandmother Hall's problems and her inability to cope with them. They all squandered money away, sometimes by heavy gambling and disastrous losses. Pussie fell in and out of love with hysterical frequency. Her brothers were dashing young lions of New York society, rich amateur athletes of championship caliber, taken up by Diamond Jim Brady and his set, until the pressures of living up to Great-grandmother's holier-than-thou standards began to tell on them. Eddie spent less and less time at home; he preferred going off on monumental drinking bouts. Vallie stayed home to drink, rampaging with a gun through the mansion at Tivoli, where the family spent its summers, taking potshots across the lawn at his sisters. At Oak Terrace, with only oil lamps to light the cavernous rooms, they often went to bed by candlelight. The furnace was never lit; on chilly nights log fires warmed the downstairs and wood-burning stoves glowed in the bedrooms—there were fourteen of them. Mother's lifelong preference for cold houses was one more fraction of her inheritance.

Her forbidding grandmother cut down sharply on Mother's contacts outside the immediate family. She had previously been allowed frequent visits to see her Uncle Theodore and his exuberant brood at their home, Sagamore Hill, at Oyster Bay on Long Island Sound. Now she saw Roosevelt cousins only at Christmas parties. They were the only boys of her own age she ever met.

If she were asked, I am sure that she would have said that she sincerely loved Great-grandmother Hall, because that was the answer a dutiful child was taught to make. In fact, real love between them did not exist. That was clear when, as a child, I used to be taken from our house on East Sixty-fifth Street by Mother out to Fifth Avenue, where she would hail a hansom cab, and we would ride down to Gracie Square to pay a call on Great-grandmother.

"She expects us at three," Mother would say, "and we must not be late."

At a few minutes before the appointed time, we would be on Great-grandmother's doorstep. "We'll stay no more than forty-five minutes," Mother would say, and forty-five minutes later, on the dot, we would bid good-bye to the portly old woman for whom none of us felt a glimmer of affection, only a sense of somewhat awed respect.

Between her Bible-bound grandmother and two frivolous aunts, whose chief concern as blossoming belles of New York was to find themselves husbands, Mother in her early teens had no one to confide in or learn from about questions of physical love. Her mother had derided her daughter's solemn, old-fashioned ways and nicknamed her Granny. Aunt Pussie, in a fit of temper, told her that, compared with the beautiful Hall girls, Mother was an ugly duckling who would probably never have a beau. Her Roosevelt relatives had the same thought. In an often-quoted letter, Theodore's second wife, Edith Carow, wrote to Auntie Bye after one of Mother's visits to Sagamore Hill, "Poor little soul, she is very plain. Her mouth and teeth seem to have no future. But the ugly duckling may turn out to be a swan."

Auntie Bye came as close as anybody to being the confidante Mother needed in those years. She was almost a cripple, with a spine so malformed that it gave her a look of a hunchback, thickened at the shoulders. The only physical features to be counted in her favor were her wonderfully kind eyes and her shining red-brown hair. As her two brothers, Theodore and Elliott, and her only sister, Corinne, married, she was left the old maid of her branch of the Roosevelts. Yet they all depended on her. It was Auntie Bye who brought up Theodore's first child, Alice, when his first wife died. It was Auntie Bye who played the key role in determining Mother's future after she had been left an orphan.

Mother and Alice Roosevelt, who became Alice Roosevelt Longworth and is still a shining light of Washington society, were both condemned to wear orthopedic braces when they were children. The dark suspicion existed among the Oyster Bay Roosevelts that there was some inborn weakness of the bones that could afflict any child. It might make an interesting subject for medical study today. Alice, anyway, soon rid herself of her leg-irons and took to leaping up stairs two and three at a time. Mother, on the other hand, who wore a brace to correct curvature of the spine, blamed weak ankles for her reluctance to join in ice skating and various other kinds of athletics and for her apathy toward ballroom dancing.

I believe that the disability of Auntie Bye, who nevertheless produced a perfectly healthy son after her marriage to William

Sheffield Cowles, lingered on in Mother's memory. She looked for things to go wrong in her own children because she was convinced that she came from a fated family. As a child, I was put into leg braces. Consequently, when I stumbled into the embers of a fire at a beach picnic at Campobello at the age of three, unnoticed by the nursemaid who was supposedly in charge of us, I could only sit there, with hot coals caught between the irons and my legs.

"He only cried a little and nurse says they are only skin burns," said Mother, writing to Father about the incident. Sometimes there were mishaps while she was away.

When the time came for Mother to go away to school, Auntie Bye made the choice. Thirty years earlier, she had been a pupil of Mademoiselle Marie Souvestre when she taught at Les Ruches in Fontainebleau, near Paris. Then the Franco-Prussian War, more than a hundred years ago, had impelled Mademoiselle to leave her homeland and open a school for girls, Allenswood, in a suburb of London. Mother was fifteen when she was first enrolled there and nearly eighteen when she left. Apart from vacations, when she occasionally met a Roosevelt cousin, she was virtually removed from the company of men. But she always carried with her a packet of her father's letters, rereading them like a missal.

By this time Hall was at Groton and giving evidence of dazzling ability as a scholar. As a boy and as a man, he had a mental brilliance which both Mother and Father recognized as far superior to their own. Inevitably, the orphaned sister and brother clung to each other; each of them was the only close relative the other had. Home again from Allenswood, she made a commitment to herself that she must spend at least one weekend in every school term with Hall at Groton. He had been her playmate, cast, for instance, as Man Friday while she was Robinson Crusoe, forcing him, as she wrote later, "to do many strange things." Now she looked on him, by her account, as she would a son. She lavished her affection on him as perhaps the one true love.

She was firmly set in her self-chosen rôle of Little Nell when she "came out" as a debutante and made a bashful entrance into New York and Washington society. In Washington, it was again Auntie Bye who took her in hand and had her stay at the house on N Street. She was so "aghast at this obligation" of making afternoon social calls with her aunt that the experience was etched in her memory. Ten years later, when Mother rented the house and returned to

Washington as the wife of the Assistant Navy Secretary, she felt so intimidated by that obligation that she sought her aunt's help once more. There is little doubt in my mind that it was Auntie Bye who recommended Lucy Mercer as a secretary for her.

At dances and debutante parties, Mother began to see more and more of her dashing cousin Franklin, who often came down from Harvard to the same parties which she so bashfully attended. They had known each other in the past, of course, at Hyde Park, Sagamore Hill and other relatives' houses. He had not been invited to Oak Terrace. "No one," Mother explained, "was ever invited to come for a meal or to stay with us who was not so intimate that he knew the entire situation." After they were engaged, Father, as an "intimate," went up to Tivoli, where he found Vallie on his best behavior. Father fancied that "I seem to have a good effect on him."

As adolescents, we children, in particular Sis and I, used to speculate about our parents' marriage, in the fashion of most young people. What had brought them together? Were they ever deeply in love with each other? The latter question was hard to answer when we saw the distance which had developed between them.

We concluded that Mother set out to win Father more than he tried to woo her. He must have taken enormous pleasure in bringing her out of her shell, to the best of his considerable ability to do such things with anyone. The girl who had cringed on the dance floor suddenly enjoyed going to dances. He made parties fun for her for the first time. Suddenly, and amazingly to her, she had a beau. She was stunned by the thought that here was a handsome man who would not only look at her but seek her companionship. She poured out her heart to him, undoubtedly the best listener she had ever met. As a token that he was put on the same pedestal that her father occupied in her memory, she signed letters to him "Little Nell."

On Father's part, we decided that there was a strong element of pity as well as love. Beyond that, he felt secure with a girl whose lack of worldly experience exceeded his. A more sophisticated woman, in all probability, would have scared the daylights out of him at that stage of his development. He had cast an eye on several young ladies, but nothing serious had come of it. One dazzling object of his affection was Frances Dana, a granddaughter on one side of her family of the poet Henry Wadsworth Longfellow and on the other of Richard H. Dana, who found instant literary fame with *Two Years Before the Mast*. But she was a Catholic, which made marriage impossible by Granny's Protestant standards. Frances went ahead and became the bride of one of Father's Harvard classmates, Henry de Rham. Father kept in touch with both husband and wife.

In accordance with the day's standards, he seldom met his future bride without a chaperone. Until they announced their intention to be married, they did not so much as kiss, according to Mother. "You never allowed a man to give you a present except flowers or candy or possibly a book. To receive a piece of jewelry from a man to whom you were not engaged was a sign of being a fast woman, and the idea that you would permit any man to kiss you before you were engaged to him never even crossed my mind."

Father had been reared by Granny under the same austere, passionless code, which he accepted unquestioningly. For entirely different causes, he, too, had never lived in a house in which a man and a woman shared a loving, physical relationship.

His father, James Roosevelt, was a sporting country squire, who had been a widower for four years when he first met his distant cousin, Sara Delano, at the home of the Theodore Roosevelts in 1880. He was fifty-two years old, with a son, Rosy, by his first marriage. Sara was exactly half that age, the same age actually as Rosy, but James immediately set about courting her, "a sly old chap," as he was described.

Sara was one of the five beautiful, stately Delano sisters, a daughter of Warren Delano II, who made, lost and then rebuilt a fortune in the China trade. She had not lacked admirers, but none of the younger men appealed to her. At twenty-six, according to Victorian standards, she ran the grave risk of becoming an old maid until she became the bride of the aging squire. "James," she wrote contentedly in her diary, "is too devoted to me."

He was a man not unlike her own father, with a fortune, comfortable but not overpowering, made largely from coal mines and railroads; he invariably kept five hundred dollars in gold in his house in case of need in an emergency. None of his grandchildren was born in time to see him, but portraits and photographs show him adorned with muttonchop whiskers and a certain twinkle in his eyes, dressed in English tweeds like a character out of Anthony Trollope.

He had a warm heart and quiet sense of fun, both of them handed down to Father, which were two qualities that Granny could not aspire to. She was obedient to his wishes, but the compelling emotions of joy or grief or fear were unknown to her in any strong measure. Perhaps she saw the difference in their ages as a protective barrier, shielding her from sexual attention which she did not enjoy. On top of that, he had a weak heart. Every spring he took her to Germany, to the celebrated spa at Bad Nauheim for the sake of his health. He always came home full of praise for "the cure," vowing that he felt much improved.

On January 30, 1882, in her big carved walnut bed at Hyde Park, Granny bore her first and only child. She had performed her wifely duty; she was ecstatic over her baby; but one was enough. On every shred of evidence, she made no attempt to bear another child during the next eighteen years before her husband died. His health had been failing rapidly for some time by then. She had planned to spend the winter of 1900 in a cottage she rented for them in Aiken, South Carolina. But before they could leave, he suffered another heart attack and died on December 8. Father did not go to Aiken for another thirty years or so, and then for altogether different reasons.

In some senses of the word, he had no father, only a man old enough to be his grandfather, who, no matter how hard he tried, could not keep up with his growing son. They enjoyed a happy companionship, nevertheless. Father used to tell how he once filched two Seidlitz powders from Grandfather's medicine cabinet and hid them in the china chamber pot under the bed of his staid German governess. In the middle of the night, when the chinaware had been put to use, the terrified woman ran screaming for Granny with a tale of effervescent woes.

Grandfather had no trouble in guessing the cause of the eruption. He summoned his son into the little octagonal room which had been added off the dining room at Hyde Park; he used it as his study. "Consider yourself spanked," he said. According to Father, Granny was never told what happened. Judging by her reactions to the story, which was something of a favorite of Father's, Mother wished that she hadn't heard it either.

Granny could see no valid reason for her only son's wanting to be married to Eleanor Roosevelt and any number of peremptory reasons why he should not. "Franklin gave me quite a startling announcement," she confided to her diary on the day he broke the news to her of the engagement.

"I know what pain I must have caused you," he told her, "and you know I wouldn't do it if I really could have helped it—*mais tu sais, me voilà.*"

The prospective bride dashed off a note to "Dear Aunt Sallie," saying that she realized "how hard it must be" for her. She felt in no way sure that the marriage would be permitted to go through.

Granny played for time, hoping that what appeared to her to be a temporary infatuation would wear off. She took Father, who was still at Harvard, and his roommate there, Lathrop Brown, on a cruise to the West Indies in the hope that absence would wither the romance. In fact, with that aim in mind, she encouraged her son —and his friend—to meet and entertain a number of eligible girls who were aboard with them. Auntie Bye invited Mother to take refuge with her in Washington, though she returned briefly to New York to serve as maid of honor on Pussie's long-awaited wedding day. The bridegroom, Forbes Morgan junior, was quite a few years younger than the amorous bride. In her first volume of memoirs, Mother, who had an uncanny knack for camouflaging thoughts she had about herself so that they appeared to concern other people, wrote of that marriage, "We knew she was temperamental and wondered how they would adjust themselves to the complicated business of married life."

The cruise failed to bring about the results Granny had counted on. As soon as it was over, she and Father went down to Washington, he to go around for tea with Mother at Auntie Bye's, Granny to try one more move in her campaign. She took Father to see her old friend, Joseph Choate, whom Uncle Ted had called back from London, where he was the United States Ambassador to the Court of St. James's, to confer about the Russo-Japanese War. Would he take Father back to England with him as his secretary? Sorry, Ambassador Choate told Granny, but Father was too young for the job.

Granny, who could be magnanimous in defeat, left Father behind when she went back to Hyde Park. She confessed to "feeling pretty blue" now that he was "gone." "I feel as if the time were not likely to come again when I shall take a trip with my dear boy . . . but I must try to be unselfish and of course, dear child, I do rejoice in your happiness and shall not put any stones or straws even in the way of it. . . ."

Mother continued her own campaign to endear herself to her

Aunt Sallie. It went on without interruption long after she and Father were married on March 17, 1905, in the twin, interconnecting brownstone houses of her cousin, Mrs. Henry Parish junior, and Mrs. Parish's mother, Mrs. Livingston Ludlow, Numbers 6 and 8, respectively, on East Seventy-sixth Street, just around the corner from Fifth Avenue. An altar was set up before the fireplace in the Ludlow drawing room, just as had been done for Pussie's wedding.

Father's gift to Mother was the gold pendant watch, with her initials set in diamonds, which she was to find so useful in the future in keeping us running on time. Granny's gift was a collar of pearls, which Mother wore, feeling, she said self-deprecatingly, "decked out beyond description." That night, when the bride and bridegroom had taken the train for Hyde Park, Granny noted her impressions of the day in careful sequence: "Took Mrs. Peabody out in the electric to do some errands. Had all the ushers to lunch. Left at 2.30 for 76th Street. Franklin is calm and happy. Eleanor the same. All the family at the wedding. . . . About 200 at the ceremony, a large reception afterward. Theodore Roosevelt, President, gave Eleanor away."

After graduating from Harvard the previous June, Father was at Columbia Law School, studying for the profession that Grandfather James had wanted him to follow. Father, in fact, would have gone into the Navy and not to college if he'd had his choice. He needed to complete the scholastic year at Columbia, so a week later the young Roosevelts moved into an apartment in the Hotel Webster on West Forty-fifth Street. Hall moved in with them.

Mother explained earlier that "I want him to feel he belongs to somebody." As a married woman, she felt that she should provide a home whenever he wanted it for the brother whom she treated more as a son. She was delighted to find a room for him in the hotel suite so that he could spend his holidays from Groton with them. "He seemed to fill the entire apartment," she reported happily.

It was her good luck, she knew, that only minimal housekeeping was required of her, since she had forgotten what little she had learned from the servants at Oak Terrace. At that time and for many years to come, she leaned on Granny, the resolute mistress of Hyde Park who with Father's help managed every detail of the household, the farm, and the estate there in the meticulous fashion of her late husband.

Mother yearned to be loved by her mother-in-law, her "dearest Cousin Sallie," as she usually called her in what was a complicated relationship in terms of genealogy. Her letters were almost fawning: "I must write and thank you for being so good to me yesterday. I know just how you feel and how hard it must be, but I do so want you to learn to love me a little. You must know that I will always try to do what you wish, for I have grown to love you very dearly during the past summer. . . ."

Whatever Granny believed, Mother tried to believe, or at least make a show of believing. Granny had her share of prejudices, and anti-Semitism was one of them. In my opinion, Mother never shared those sentiments, though she was repelled by the flashiness of a few *nouveau riche* New Yorkers. Yet there was an era when her remarks to Granny seemed to be evidence of real scorn for all Jews. What she was doing was playing up to Granny, making another attempt to ingratiate herself with the older woman, who, no matter what, usually regarded her daughter-in-law as "poor little Eleanor." That, ironically, was precisely the impression of herself which Mother set out to create in her chosen role of Little Nell.

Perhaps the honeymoon gave both man and wife a hint of what the future would hold. They had gone into marriage with no true knowledge of what is needed for an enduring physical relationship. Instead, they shared only the superficial, romantic view of love, which I think led rather rapidly to disillusionment. The difference in years between Father's parents had made normal, vigorous relations out of the question for them. "Well, you know," Granny once told my brother Franklin, "we were Victorians. I knew my obligations as a wife and did my duty." If she had brought herself to talk about marriage to Father in his adolescence, that was the point of view which she inevitably expressed.

Mother had only her Hall aunts, with their accounts of erratic romances, or her embittered grandmother as her source of information, or possibly Auntie Bye, a cripple who, it was feared, could not bear a child. In what I find to be one of the most touching and revealing passages which she wrote in her lifetime, Mother said, "I know now that it was years before I understood what being in love was and what loving really meant. I had very high standards as to what a wife and mother should be and not the faintest notion of what it meant to be either a wife or a mother, and none of my elders enlightened me. I marvel now at my husband's patience, for I realize how trying I must have been in many ways. I can see today how funny were some of the tragedies of our early married life." That was written in 1937, when it seemed that the damage which had been done could never be amended.

She went into marriage with exactly the same feelings that Granny expressed: Sex was a wife's duty, never a source of joy or, as it can be at its best, of ecstasy. She had, in her own words, "an almost exaggerated idea of the necessity of keeping all of one's desires under complete subjugation." That thought would be completely alien to Father, who was beginning to develop a lusty love of life in all its rich variety.

When the term at Columbia was over, they sailed on the *Oceanic* for a second honeymoon in Europe. Mother was terrified of being seasick, but this was one thing that she soon conquered. She gave a hint of the kind of pleasure she found in Father's company when she wrote to Granny, "Thank you so much, dear, for everything you did for us. You are always just the sweetest, dearest Mama to your children, and I shall look forward to our next long evening together, when I shall want to be kissed all the time."

Where she was striving to tie herself to Granny's apron strings, he was eager to loosen them. He was a duly attentive husband—"I've never been so well looked after," Mother said—but in all probability she already sensed that he was not, and could not be the idealized Sir Lancelot that she dreamed her father to be. She resented it if he looked at any other woman, but she kept her feelings strictly to herself.

At their hotel in the Dolomites, Kitty Gandy, who owned a New York millinery shop, was a fellow guest. She "promised *me* a new ostrich feather hat for next winter," Father joked, to Mother's concealed disdain. "She was a few years his senior," she reported later, "and he did not know her very well at that time, but she could climb and I could not, and though I never said a word I was jealous beyond description and perfectly delighted when we started off again and drove out of the mountains."

When they returned home, for Father to spend one more year at Columbia, she was pregnant. Meanwhile, Granny had rented a house for them at 125 East Thirty-sixth Street, just three blocks from her own at 200 Madison Avenue. She furnished it completely, down to kitchen pots and pans, and she engaged three servants for them. She wanted to replace its gaslight with electricity until Father demurred at the cost of installing the wiring as a needless expenditure for her. Mother was to be under the complete care of Granny.

Hall moved in, too, on a permanent basis, and was told to look on the house as his home while he continued in boarding school.

The expenses of running the household, paying the rent and the servants' wages would have been far beyond the young couple's means if Granny had not constantly subsidized them. She was generous to a fault, in the old-fashioned phrase of those days. Whenever Father needed help, he had only to ask for it, and he usually had no need to ask, because Granny anticipated what he or Mother wanted and was ready with a check, cash or a gift in kind.

As a law student, Father's income amounted to roughly $5,000 a year under the terms of Grandfather's will, but the trust fund of $100,000, which was its source, was controlled by Granny. Mother's own inheritance produced about $7,500 from another trust fund, this one invested mainly in New York Central Railroad stocks and bonds, which was administered by the bank where Henry Parish, of Number 6 East Seventy-Sixth Street, was a vice-president.

Cousin Henry was a tall, thin, gentle soul, dominated by his snobbish, straitlaced wife, Cousin Susie. Mother regarded him as "the kindest person I have ever known." He painstakingly showed her how to keep accounts when she was in her teens, which was the only lesson she had in handling money until after her marriage. But where the Halls squandered their fortunes, the Delanos husbanded theirs. Granny taught Father to watch every penny, not to hoard but to spend wisely, and to note every expenditure. As a meticulous bookkeeper, she imposed similar standards in running Hyde Park, where the cost of a gallon of paint or a hired man's hourly wages was carefully recorded for scrutiny by her or by Father.

One of the first workaday contributions Father made toward organizing the household was to educate Mother in the matter of accounts. He set up books for their household expenses and taught her how to maintain them, while Granny and Cousin Susie Parish, two equally strong-minded women, gave her the benefit of their advice on housekeeping. Out of her income, plus something like three hundred dollars a month which Father contributed, she was to pay all the household bills and buy clothes for herself and, later, for us children. This was a typical Delano arrangement.

Mother used to claim that "it was a good thing for me to be perfectly miserable for three months before every one of my six babies arrived." Like most young girls—she was only twenty-one—she had been afraid that she might prove to be barren in marriage and, accordingly, a bitter disappointment to Father. He very definitely wanted children, though perhaps not so rapidly as they came along. That winter, feeling sorry for herself but determined not to show it, she put herself into Granny's willing hands and enjoyed being completely dependent. "A very pleasant contrast to my former life," she thought, "and I slipped into it with the greatest of ease."

In the mornings, she religiously took a long walk with Granny for the sake of her health. In the afternoons, she went driving with Granny in her town brougham. They usually ate one meal a day together, sometimes including Father if he came home to lunch from law school. Granny was overjoyed with her timid, awkward young daughter-in-law. "I thank you, darling," she said, "for being what you are to me already."

One can only guess at Father's state of mind. Accustomed as he was to Granny's skills in domestic affairs, he could only notice a sharp difference in his own household, run by servants and not by Mother, who knew nothing about such things as planning a menu or cooking a meal. It may have been symptomatic of the concern he felt about the relationship which was developing between them that, for the first time on record, his nights were disturbed and he walked in his sleep.

As the time of her confinement drew near, Mother's anxiety came closer to the surface. "I had never had any interest in dolls or in little children," she said, "and I knew absolutely nothing about handling or feeding a baby." Possibly it was Granny who found and engaged Blanche Spring. At breakfast on May 3, 1906, the stocky little nurse called Granny, who hurried around to East Thirty-sixth Street, arriving ahead of the doctor. By lunchtime Anna was born, "beautiful little girl," Granny noted, "ten pounds and one ounce."

One of the legends concocted about Mother has it that when Miss Spring left at the end of her assignment, Mother, yielding to Granny's persuasions, hired a permanent nurse, a young, inexperienced girl from the Babies' Hospital, and bitterly regretted yielding on this point. The truth is that no alternative ever entered her mind then or for many years later. Mother was keenly aware of her limitations. When Sis as a three-month-old baby suffered convulsions at Hyde Park, Mother sensed that the doctor who attended her "felt a great contempt for the ignorance and foolhardiness of any young woman who would have a baby without knowing even the rudiments of how to care for it."

A new nurse, an older Irish woman, was added to the staff at East Thirty-sixth Street. On one of the nurse's weekly days off, Mother was holding a small dinner party. She gave Sis her evening bottle and put her to bed, but the baby began to howl. She was still crying when the guests arrived. Mother, in a panic, telephoned the doctor.

"She may have a little wind," he said reassuringly. "Are you sure you got up all the bubbles after her last bottle?"

Mother had completely forgotten that essential final step in feeding a baby. "Franklin," she said, "you will have to start dinner without me." The hostess bubbled the baby and soon got her off to sleep. But Mother was so upset by now that she continued to bob up and down stairs all evening until Sis woke up and started in howling again.

"After this experience," Mother said, "I registered a vow that never again would I have a dinner on the nurse's day out."

Shortly after Anna's birth, Mother had to undergo an operation which, in medical practice of those days, was rated as severe. It used to be thought that the patient's condition arose from purely physiological causes, but today psychological tension is recognized as at least a contributory factor. That was possibly the case with Mother. The family physician, Dr. Albert H. Ely, performed the surgery in my parents' house. Granny's diary recorded the event: "My dear Eleanor was operated for hemorrhoids. . . . Pretty serious, and she was very weak."

She was, in fact, worse off than that. The doctor feared that she would not come out of the ether. As she came slowly, even reluctantly, back to consciousness, she could hear him asking, "Is she gone? Can you feel her pulse?"

For once, she acknowledged to herself that she was in considerable pain, yet she kept that a secret until much later. She simply refused to speak to anyone who came to her bedside, and that included Father. "I imagine that they probably thought that I was far more ill than I really was, and worried about me unnecessarily," she remembered. "My disposition was at fault rather than my physical condition!"

Within a year, she was pregnant again, and Father's only income still came from the trust fund and Granny's generosity. He continued at Columbia, frankly bored with the prospect of further studies. He never graduated or took a degree, but he was able to pass his New York State bar examinations. That fall, he went to work for the notable old downtown firm of Carter, Ledyard and Milburn as a "full-fledged office boy," in his own words, with no salary for the first year.

The firm was trustee for John Pierpont Morgan, and its clients included the Astor estate and the American Express Company. Contact with those dazzling names was restricted to senior attorneys. Father's humbler duties consisted of running errands, doing research in the law library, and gossiping with juniors like himself about their hopes and dreams. He ultimately was promoted to head clerk in charge of municipal court cases and then to the company's admiralty division, which he enjoyed if only for its association with the sea.

The most important thing that happened to him in his three years as a law clerk was the gradual broadening of his horizons. For the first time in his previously sheltered existence, he rubbed shoulders with men far removed from his class of society, people more colorful, less restrained than anyone he had known at Hyde Park, Groton or Harvard. He was starting a new phase of his social education and relishing it.

Inevitably, some of the effect spilled over into his role as a husband. His taste for male companionship increased, inside and outside the office. He spent more and more time with Hall, who was nineteen, each of them finding in the other the brother that Father never had and the younger man had never known. Father took to playing Saturday night poker with "the boys" over Mother's as yet unspoken but explicit disapproval. He was easing out of Granny's bonds and gradually adjusting to the new set of restraints which Mother, on her own admission, wanted to put on him.

"I feel quite lost and sad without you," she wrote him once, when she had been left at Hyde Park while he stayed overnight in New York, "and it was horrid coming home last night, so I don't think we will try this experiment again, do you think?" Then she softened her admonition with a plaintive, "Incidentally, I hope you miss me dreadfully, too!"

If they were separated for longer periods, as when she stayed with Granny on Campobello and he went to work at the law office, she chided him, "I was horribly disappointed with your hasty little scrap of a note yesterday after not getting anything for two days."

In mid-December, Miss Spring returned to stay in the house. Mother began making up lists of jobs for Father to tackle. What to say to Granny . . . what to tell Anna's nursemaid . . . what telephone calls to make . . . what bills should be mailed. She found a different worry this time when her labor commenced: Suppose the baby turned out to be another girl and she would never have the son which Father and Granny were hoping for?

My brother James was born early in the morning on December 23, 1907. "Weighs ten pounds five ounces," Granny's diary reported. Jimmy rapidly caught pneumonia, and his food seldom agreed with him. Miss Spring's stay was extended, and one of the living rooms was turned into a bedroom. To make more room, Hall had to be moved into Granny's house. Our family was experiencing its first chronic case of overcrowding as a consequence of having babies. Granny had anticipated the problem and solved it in her own fashion by buying a lot on East Sixty-fifth Street and having twin houses built, each six stories tall and interconnected like those of Mrs. Parish and Mrs. Ludlow, except that ours could open into each other on almost every floor, and their front doors led off a single entrance hall. Granny drew a little preliminary pen-and-ink sketch of what she had in mind, complete to a curl of smoke coming out of the chimney: "A Christmas present to Franklin and Eleanor from Mama. . . ." Father, who liked to build things himself, pored over the plans with Granny. Mother left everything to the two of them, having no interest in the project.

Our family moved into Number 49 and Granny into Number 47, which was as close to us as a Siamese twin. A few weeks afterward, Father found Mother weeping in front of her bedroom dressing table. "What on earth is the matter?"

"I don't like living in a house which is not in any way mine," she said sobbing. "It does not represent how I want to live."

"Don't be such a goose," he told her. "You'll feel differently in a little while." He left her alone to calm down. She realized that she was acting like a fool, but she thought nevertheless that "there was a good deal of truth in what I said."

Soon she had taken up the habit of many a disgruntled wife and was jotting down in her diary, which she kept briefly, the hours at which Father came home at night. Poker playing at the Knicker-bocker Club, with its sharp associations with her father, delayed his return until 4 A.M. Two weeks later, "F. went to Harvard Club dinner and got home three-thirty a.m. Dined with Mama."

3

The year 1910 saw the major event in my own life: I was born on September 23. Otherwise, history indicates that these were twelve months of comparative calm. In the White House, Uncle Ted's handpicked successor, William Howard Taft, conducted himself with portly dignity, as did the Emperor Franz Josef in Vienna. George V came to the throne in England, Hitler reached his twenty-first birthday in Linz, and Franklin Delano Roosevelt entered politics.

The precise moment of entry was at three o'clock on a sunny August afternoon when he strolled across the gravel path which linked Granny's house in Hyde Park with that of her stepson, Rosy, a few minutes' walk over the trim lawns. Tom Leonard, a house painter and Democratic committeeman for the district of Hyde Park, was at work on a ladder, redecorating a room in Rosy's house. Father had been advised to see him.

The housekeeper announced him, "There is Mr. Franklin, who wants to see you," and the painter came down the ladder.

"Hello, Tom."

"How do you do, Mr. Roosevelt?"

"No, call me Franklin. I'm going to call you Tom. I want to enter politics, and Mr. Perkins, the county chairman, told me I'd have to see you."

Leonard did not want to take up too much time, so the conversation was brief. "The town caucus meets next Wednesday night in the town hall. I think it would be fine if you could be there."

"I'll be there," said Father. "I'll come up from New York."

On the following Wednesday evening, Father stood up and said a few words to outline his desires. The house painter and his colleagues were sufficiently impressed to want to help the young man, who still looked almost like a boy for all his twenty-eight years. "He was always willing to be advised and to consider it," Leonard recalled. "I don't think he ever did an intentional wrong."

The process of political indoctrination continued at the local policemen's clambake in Buckingham Woods. Father, exercising the broad, confident smile which became world-famous, circulated among the police, their wives and children. "You made a definite hit," Leonard assured him.

There was never any question that he would be anything but a Democrat. This was another inheritance from Grandfather, who was also born and reared in that faith, though he had voted for McKinley, not Bryan, in 1896. The Dutchess County Roosevelts had been Democrats for as long as anyone could remember, which put them in the minority in the district. The last state senator that the party had managed to elect was the Roosevelts' neighbor, Tom Newbold, and that was thirty-two years ago.

But Grandfather had remained active, a regular attendant at town caucuses, with a way of stalking out of meetings if he disapproved of the men who were picked. Although his son took after Sara in his looks and general appearance, a lot of people thought he was much more like James in his personality and the ability to get along with everybody.

Mother, who has been portrayed as having steered Father in most decisions in his career, spent the summer in Campobello while he planned the course he would follow during a round of talks with Dutchess County leaders of the party. The family had become too big to camp out as it had done in the past in Granny's house on the island. So she bought Father his own place, right next to hers, complete with furnishings. It was a rambling, shingled house with nearly three dozen rooms of various sizes, bought at the bargain price of five thousand dollars, as offered in the will of its previous owner, Mrs. Hartman Kuhn, who knew and admired Father from his childhood on and wanted him to have the place when she died.

"I shall weep," Mother wrote him from Campobello, if he could not make time to get up to see his family. From time to time she had Blanche Spring as a house guest—she already had an English nurse and a German girl for the children—though "Mama always seems to dislike my doing things with her." Possibly Granny would have liked Mother to do more things for herself. "I broke it to Mama Miss Spring was coming up and put it all on you," said one letter to Father, who was often drawn in as an intermediary with Granny, much against his will, since Mother could not bear the thought of confronting Granny or anyone else.

She kept up her flow of instructions to him. Find two cleaning women for the New York house. . . . Have a housemaid do out the library. . . . Telephone the chimney sweep. . . . Bring up some magazines. . . . Buy a gift ("some nice book not more than five dollars") and send it to a friend. . . . Check the doctor's bill. . . .

Toward the latter half of the summer, Mother left Campobello to await my birth in New York, while Sis and Jimmy with their nurse went back to Hyde Park with Granny. With my arrival in the world, Mother had borne four children in as many years, each of them preceded by long spells of pain and nausea. Ten months earlier, she had grieved over the first Franklin junior, dead from pneumonia at the age of seven months and nine days, "the biggest and most beautiful of all the babies," as she remembered him.

He had been christened only three weeks before that in the bay window of the old drawing room at Hyde Park, wearing the long lace robe which had been Father's and was used for all of us children. He showed signs of having a cold, and Sis and Jimmy both came down with influenza during the next few days. The two nurses, Nellie and Emma, were there, of course, to look after all three children.

The christening took place on October 10. "A sweet sight," Granny wrote in her diary that day, "but my heart sank a little because Baby looks so delicate and exquisite." Four days later, Mother left Hyde Park for New York. "I was beginning to go up and down between New York and Hyde Park," Mother said obscurely in her 1937 volume of memoirs. The point is obscure and of only possible historical interest now, but it would seem that Father did not go with her.

On October 23 Granny's diary reported, "Eleanor came up, and she and Franklin saw the doctor." That was on a Saturday. In the course of the following week, Mother returned to Manhattan. She was there on the following Friday when Granny, lunching at the house of some friends, the Olins, received a frantic telephone call from her housemaid, Annie. The baby was close to death. "I *flew* home," said the diary entry. "Dr. Gribbon was here, holding precious Baby. He got there just in time, as the little heart had almost stopped. I telephoned E. She and F. came at 8.30, bringing Miss Spring. Dr. Gribbon stayed until eleven."

The next morning, Father, Mother and Dr. Gribbon took the sick child on the nine-thirty train to Grand Central, to consult a specialist, who diagnosed serious heart trouble. Granny waited only one day to join them on East Sixty-fifth Street. "I could hear every cry all night from my room, where I lay useless," wrote my grandmother, who has consistently been depicted only as a selfish martinet.

Just before seven o'clock on the following day, November 1, Father called the room where she waited. "Better come, Mama. Baby is sinking."

"I went in. The little angel ceased breathing at seven twenty-five. Miss Spring was asleep in her room. . . ."

In her memoirs, Mother remembered the date as having been November 8. She recalled seeing the group of people who gathered around the coffin at the burial in St. James' churchyard in Hyde Park as she thought, "How cruel it seemed to leave him out there in the cold!"

She brooded over her lost baby, reproaching herself bitterly for having done so little about his care. She felt that she had neglected him as a mother, known too little about him, and she blamed herself for that. "I even felt that I had not cared enough about him," she said subsequently, "and I made myself and all those around me most unhappy during that winter. I was even a little bitter against my poor young husband, who occasionally tried to make me see how idiotically I was behaving."

Her morbid mood continued when she discovered that once more she had conceived. "Certainly no one could have behaved more foolishly than I did practically up to the time of Elliott's arrival," she said, "and I should have known better." The meaning of that oblique reference is unfathomable. She passed a quiet summer on Campobello, so far as we know today. Did she expose herself unnecessarily to physical exertions which she thought could be harmful to her health? Is there a hint that she was tired of bearing children in such swift succession? If that were true, she knew of only one recourse. When Sis was a young woman, Mother confided to her that she had gone into marriage totally ignorant of any method of contraception whatsoever. Not a single female relative had ever told her that ways and means were available to forestall pregnancy. The only security Mother knew was in abstinence.

Of myself, she wrote, "He suffered for a great many years with a rather unhappy disposition, and I think in all probability I was partly to blame" because of the "idiotic" way she had behaved in the months before I was born. But if anyone was to be blamed, surely it was Grandmother Hall or the bevy of beautiful Hall aunts who had allowed an inexperienced girl to grow up unaware of what really happened when a man and a woman were married.

Father pressed ahead with his new political ambition. A lot of young men of his class had similar ideas for themselves, sparked by the achievements of Theodore and his ideals of the duty of men of goodwill to enter public service. There are parallels to be found in the excitement aroused when John F. Kennedy was President, temporarily drawing some of the best brains in the country toward the White House.

Not that Father could have appealed as a "brain" to the beleaguered party machine in Dutchess County. The leaders saw his Harvard background as a political handicap. His habit of throwing back his head to focus through his pince-nez they interpreted as a sign of arrogance. They mistook the idealism, which had germinated in his school days, for a streak of self-righteousness.

They invited him to stop by at Poughkeepsie headquarters so that they could take a closer look at him. He turned up, as Grandfather might well have done in his place, wearing a dark riding habit. "If you run," he was told, "you'll have to take off those yellow boots and put some pants on."

They had decided to run him for the State Senate seat which Tom Newbold had once held. Mr. Newbold, an aristocrat by Dutchess County standards, would help him. So would gusty Judge John Mack, an old-line politician with a law office in Poughkeepsie and a reputation for helping to keep loyal Democrats out of jail. The judge frankly assessed Father's chances of winning in this staunch Republican district as being five to one against.

They figured that his name might be an asset. Uncle Ted was the dominant personality of the United States. A Democratic Roosevelt, as John Gunther once wrote, would be a dramatic drawing card. In the party councils, too, they shrewdly realized that Granny would pay all her son's campaign expenses and could be counted on to contribute to the war chest.

Two weeks after my arrival, Father was given twenty-four hours to make up his mind whether or not to accept the nomination. Mother stayed in New York while he undoubtedly talked the whole thing out with Granny, who went with him to the Poughkeepsie hall to hear his acceptance speech. He burned his bridges by resigning from Carter, Ledyard and Milburn, much to the dismay of old Mr.

Ledyard, who undoubtedly thought that his young law clerk was out of his mind.

Mother was kept informed by Father of his plans, but it did not occur to her that she had any part to play in them. She disagreed that women should go into politics or even have a vote. Pussie was the only champion in the Hall family of women's suffrage. She made the mistake of trying to convert Mother, who had her mind firmly made up about most questions in those days. At least one violent argument broke out between the two of them, which probably concluded with tears on both sides, leading Hall to reprimand his usually reserved sister for lack of self-control.

When Father took up the challenge of contesting a State Senate seat which the Democrats had won only once in the fifty-four years of Republican Party history, he had no car of his own. Granny was a traditionalist, body and soul, who considered that horseless carriages in no way compared with a brougham and a handsome pair of horses as a stylish means of transportation; she kept horses and a carriage stabled in Manhattan up until well after World War I.

Father's campaign plans called for him to show his face in every town, village and crossroads store in the Twenty-sixth District. So he went to "Hawkey" Osterhoudt, who ran an automobile hire business as well as a piano store in Poughkeepsie, and rented a gaudy red Maxwell touring car, with Hawkey as chauffeur. He nicknamed it the Red Peril.

Only four weeks remained until election day. In the acceptance speech to which Granny listened with great pride, Father had said, "I need not tell you that I do not intend to stand still. We are going to have a very strenuous month." That they did.

His ambition was to talk personally with every one of the Republican farmers in the three counties which made up the district, men who had voted the straight ticket for half a century because they disliked the smell of Tammany Hall, its record of big-city graft, and its stranglehold on the Democratic Party everywhere. His companion on the road and star of the traveling show was Richard Connell, running for reelection to the United States House of Representatives. As a prop in his fustian oratory, the Congressman would whip out the Stars and Stripes from under his Prince Albert coat as he thundered, "The same old flag that waved at Lexington, the same old flag that Sherman carried on his march to the sea. . . ." It was from Connell, incidentally, that Father borrowed the opening phrase which he made as much his own as a radio station's call letters: "My friends."

In sun and rain, the team of Connell, Roosevelt and Hawkey ranged through the hills of the Hudson Valley in the flag-decked Red Peril at a perilous 22 miles an hour, the first time anybody had campaigned by automobile in the state of New York. They covered more than 2,000 miles, mostly over rough dirt roads, averaging ten speeches a day, meeting trains, attending rallies or simply setting up drinks for everybody in a roadside tavern. They scared horses, hit a dog, fixed a flat and made one appearance in the wrong state when they overshot the Connecticut border. Father's education was progressing by leaps and bounds in meeting his fellow men face-to-face under every kind of condition and in picking up the grass-roots techniques of campaigning from an old, seasoned professional.

The political apprentice went through most of the campaign with a marked limp, the result of being knocked off the step of a New York trolley car by a passing ice wagon when he went down to visit Mother, who stayed at East Sixty-fifth Street.

Mother thought Father looked thin, tense and nervous. "No lines as yet in his face," she remembered, "but at times a set look of his jaw denoted that this apparently pliable youth had strength and Dutch obstinacy in his makeup." The unmistakable message was that she had once regarded him as pliable but found him to be obstinate in the five years they had spent together.

Republicans dismissed him as a pushover, a "rich young man," as they tagged him, who had the gall to run around in that open car, with almost nothing in the way of a party organization to back him, on "a vaudeville trip for the benefit of the farmers." Most local newspapers largely ignored him—the leading Poughkeepsie paper mentioned him only twice; that only prompted him to spend four hundred dollars on paid advertisements of his own devising.

His message was warmhearted, vague, but lightened with a touch of humor. "Government," he said, "is not like a doughnut. It cannot have an empty space in the middle but must be an entirety." Dozens of times he repeated, "I want to represent you, the people of these counties, and no one else. I am pledged to no man, to no special interest, to no boss."

On the Hyde Park estate, Moses Smith, the grizzled old tenant who had known Father since childhood, listened to him talk and fancied that the most telling point he made was in advocating a standard-size barrel, of ninety-six-quart capacity. Farmers needed it for uniform measurement of their produce, but it did not yet exist. They suspected that the candidate could speak their language, even if he did have a Harvard accent.

Mother traveled up for one meeting before the campaign ended. She had never heard him make a political speech before. Instead of the quick, often teasing pace she was used to, he spoke slowly and deliberately, driving his words home, pausing to let his message sink in. Typically, she confessed that now and then she was personally worried that he would not be able to get through to the end.

On a cold, wet November morning, the young Roosevelt learned that he had won, with an unprecedented majority of 1,140 votes of the more than 30,000 that had been cast. He ran far ahead of the party ticket, and there had been a Democratic sweep, gaining control of both houses of the legislature in Albany. Victory was owed to a powerful combination of forces—Father's energies and Granny's money. She had bankrolled him to the extent of more than $1,700, five times as much as any other candidate spent in the district.

She paid the rent of $1,500 for six months, the extent of the legislature's term, on the big brownstone house at 248 State Street in Albany, which my parents chose without her. A week later, eleven days before Christmas, she went up with them and expressed her approval of their choice: "A very large, fine house. Can be made comfortable." She immediately set about planning how the furniture might be rearranged. Mother's memories were imprecise. "I suppose I must have gone to Albany and looked at the house which we took on State Street, though I have no recollection of doing so."

On New Year's Day, we moved out of New York into our new temporary home. In the party, there were three servants, a new English nurse for Sis and Jimmy and the Slovak wet nurse for me. Granny, of course, came, too. Father was already at work, while Democratic leaders mulled over the implications of his unexpected success. Tom Lynch of Poughkeepsie, a trustworthy supporter from the beginning, showed where his sentiments and dreams for the future lay by putting in storage two bottles of champagne, which he vowed would stay unopened until the day Father was nominated for the Presidency of the United States.

"Big Tim" Sullivan of the Bowery, a Tammany boss, had a different idea. "You know these Roosevelts," he said. "This fellow is still young. Wouldn't it be safer to drown him before he grows up?"

But Father's method was to teach himself as he went along, mainly by listening to other people talk. The instructors he sought out included the likes of "Big Tim," who was forever ready to help a constituent in time of need. The Tammany man, like the rest of the party veterans in Albany, gritted his teeth and put up as best he could with the "awful arrogant" newcomer.

"Poor old Tim Sullivan never understood about modern politics," Father once reminisced, "but he was right about the human heart."

On the afternoon of the day we moved in, Father had arranged a reception for as many of his Twenty-sixth District followers as wanted to stop by. "Come and see me" was a standard invitation of his. While Mother fretted in silence over the chaos and hired caterers plied the guests with refreshments, farmers and their families from three counties wandered through the rooms for three hours. "Dirt or disorder makes me positively uncomfortable," Mother admitted.

She had the consolation that for the first time she was living on her own, with Granny and the dominating Cousin Susie Parish out of reach. When Granny returned home in the middle of the week, however, Mother wrote to her almost every day, but the craving was starting in her to be independent of her mother-in-law and, it would seem, of Father, too. To all outward appearances, she was the epitome of a dutiful wife.

Making social calls and entertaining at home kept her increasingly busy. She hurried home every afternoon for tea with Sis and Jimmy, then to read to them or play with them until their bedtime in the room they shared with the English nurse over the library. "I tried having little Anna lunch with us, but after spending a solid hour over the meal on our first attempt, I returned her to the nursery." Jimmy had apparently developed a heart murmur, which meant that the nurse had to carry him up and down stairs.

The library became the meeting place and informal clubhouse for a group of party rebels, led by Father, who decided to go to war with Tammany bossism. Until the Seventeenth Amendment to the Constitution was ratified in 1913, United States Senators were chosen not by popular ballot but by majority vote of the various state legislatures. Tammany's candidate was "Blue-eyed Billy" Sheehan, a Democratic boss whose long career had been shadowed by scandal. Father, who consistently proclaimed his faith in "free, fair, decent" politics, set out to block the nomination of Sheehan, who actually was a New York neighbor of ours, living across the street at Number 16. It was the kind of fight that set well with Father's beliefs. It would have the added advantage of spreading his name far and wide.

Hostile newspapers quickly labeled him "the college kid," who, as the *Morning Telegraph* sneered, was convinced that "the way to win imperishable fame was to get out and kill a political boss every morning before breakfast." More sympathetic reporters pictured him as the Galahad of the insurgents. The lines were drawn, and the battle made lively reading.

The Albany insurgents met daily, at ten and at five, with late sessions sometimes interrupted for dinner before they resumed and then continued far into the night. Mother saw it as her obligation as the hostess to sit through the evening sessions in an atmosphere thick with intrigue and cigar smoke. When she concluded that the talking had lasted long enough, she would serve beer, cheese and crackers from the pantry as a strong hint that the time had come for everyone to go home.

The sessions continued over a period of nearly three months, holding the rebels together to keep them from being picked off by Tammany threats of vengeance or promises of bribes. Convinced that Sis and Jimmy were slowly choking to death in their bedroom above, Mother had them moved up a flight to a room on the top floor, which, as she said, "simply meant an extra flight of stairs up which to carry Jimmy, and down, several times a day."

Her interest in the tricky craft of politics, in which she was to develop outstanding skill, was sparked by the long weeks of library meetings and the conscientious visits she made to the public gallery of the Capitol to hear something of what was going on there. She was not sure that she enjoyed herself, but in her opinion a wife should be interested in whatever interested her husband, whether it was politics or prime ribs of beef for dinner.

She did know that she found the company of many of the men who were in the habit of dropping in at the house repugnant to her. At the head of her list of aversions stood the name of Louis McHenry Howe. The gnome of a man, as usual, was wearing at least three and probably four hats in serving as many employers. Nominally, his job was as second-string correspondent in the Albany news-gathering bureau of the New York *Herald* at a salary of twenty-five dollars a week. He also fed news of the legislature to another New York paper,

the *Telegram*. Perpetually on the verge of destitution, he had worked
on and off for four years for Thomas Mott Osborne, the indepen-
dently wealthy, crusading mayor of Auburn, New York, as a kind of
confidential agent, writing him long reports on the inside plots and
counterplots of the legislators.

In his guise as a political reporter, Louis spent a lot of time
winning the confidence of Osborne's opponents, then carefully
sowing discord among them. The role of secret investigator and spy
appealed strongly to Louis, partly because he interpreted it as a
private war against Tammany in the interests of better government,
which he believed in with all the fervor of his incredibly agile mind.
The forty dollars a week he received from Osborne did not begin to
compensate him for his labors. From his dingy office on State Street,
he ran a letter-writing factory, bombarding out-of-town politicos,
sympathizers and newspaper editors with items bearing his
employer's signature. He helped in fund raising. He set up in-
telligence files on people and organizations, for use against the
enemy, in favor of allies and potential friends. Every day of his life,
totally-frustrated to date, he schemed how to thwart the opposition,
how to promote the causes which he held dear.

Not merely money and certainly not the wish for fame, but love of
behind-the-scenes power motivated him. He could scrape by on
enough for a skimpy meal and five or six packs of cigarettes a day,
with something left over for his wife and daughter at home in
Saratoga. Grace Howe was used to chronic insecurity. "The child
and I," she told him, "can tag along after the bandwagon and get on
as the chance comes."

Her notion of something closer to heaven was for Louis to latch on
to a state job at maybe $2,500 a year. Her hopes were temporarily
dashed when Osborne fired him with a week's notice. Louis' intense
pride made it impossible to tell his boss that a doctor had just
predicted that asthma and chain smoking were likely to kill him
within two months. But he pleaded with the mercurial Osborne to
be allowed to continue working for him without pay. The mayor
relented and took him back on the payroll. Louis went off and on
that payroll for the next three years.

Osborne was an ally of the insurgents. Louis came to our house in
a dual role as Osborne's man and roving reporter, giving *Herald* and
Telegram readers the inside story of what the rebels were planning to
do next. It was an easy step for him to act as an adviser and

informant for Father's group, then go beyond that and file a flattering article to the *Herald* about Father, who was, Louis predicted, a man to watch.

Louis, in turn, was a man after Father's own heart as he taught himself the cuts and thrusts of partisan politics in a bitter interparty struggle. Louis was older by eleven years, but his life had been jammed full of such experiences so that he could as well have been a centenarian.

He had been a menopause child, sickly from the moment of his birth in Indianapolis, but both his parents had money enough to take him to the doctor for almost daily checkups, to give him his own pony cart, to provide him with books, which he read by the dozens as a precocious, sheltered schoolboy. In the financial panic of 1873, the family lost everything and fled to Saratoga. In that playground of the rich and mecca of gamblers, his father landed a job as a newspaper reporter and ultimately raised the funds to gamble himself by buying the weekly Saratoga *Sun*, which he rapidly turned into a loyal organ of the Democrats.

At seventeen, Louis went to work for his father; plans for sending him to college collapsed for reasons of his ill health and the shortage of family cash. By then he was compelled to wear the clumsy truss which he could not leave off for the rest of his days. Nevertheless, to overcome his introverted upbringing and his physical disabilities, he had taken to golf, tennis, fishing, tobogganing, and, most of all, cycling. A fall headfirst on a gravel road gave him the facial scars which drove him to bragging that he was "one of four ugliest men in the State of New York." When we came to know him better, we recognized that as a cover-up for his deep-down sensitivity.

He fell in love with the theater in those distant days when the brightest names of Broadway played in Saratoga Springs every summer season. He mastered the art of makeup and the craft of stage lighting. He directed and produced wildly ambitious amateur performances. On top of the poetry which he had been composing since childhood, he started writing plays. He took a few turns as an actor himself, longing to play heroes but condemned by his looks to appear as the low comic.

As a young reporter, only outwardly hard-bitten, he married Grace Hartley, a plain but pleasant girl from Fall River, Massachusetts, who shared his interest in dramatics, stamp collecting and antiques. He designed and made some of the ornaments which adorned the house her mother bought for them, and he filled their yard with flowers. But the Republican hold on Saratoga slowly drove the *Sun* into bankruptcy. Grace had gone back to stay with her mother in Fall River when their daughter, Mary, was born. Her visits there grew longer and longer because Louis, doing odd jobs as a racetrack reporter and free-lance feature writer, scarcely earned enough to feed his family.

With his creased face and scanty hair, he looked a hundred years old when he first came into contact with Father. He had more skills at his fingertips than half a dozen other men combined. He could write anything from a poem to a fast-breaking news story. He had a solid reputation with his editors for tireless research and astute political analysis, which made him an uncannily accurate forecaster of election results. He was equally adept at playing poker and probing the vanities of his fellow men. Forty years of hard knocks had left him with ingrained contempt for superficiality and profound cynicism about everything but the measurable facts of life, yet his sense of irreverent humor stayed intact.

He could not spell too well or come close to balancing a checkbook. He was close to being flat broke, his health was precarious, and he had just endured the loss of the first son born to Grace. Edward Hartley Howe died of meningitis within a week of his birth in November, 1910. In the baby book his father prepared for him, only one page contained an entry, inscribed by Louis: "There are no records of the little brother's life set down within this book because they are written in our hearts and nothing can ever wipe them out."

It could well have been Louis Howe who prompted Father into inviting Blue-eyed Billy and his wife to luncheon at our house. That was the sort of audacity which was typical of him. After coffee had been served, Father invited the target of the insurgents' plotting into the library. The small talk with Mrs. Sheehan seemed to last forever to Mother. When their guests finally left, she turned hopefully to Father. "Did you come to any agreement?"

"Certainly not," he answered, surprised at her question. He had no intention of backing out of the battle. He believed, sincerely but only vaguely as to details, that government must be returned to the hands of the people. "Special interests" had to be curbed, and those included Blue-eyed Billy. In the final outcome, the insurgents did beat Sheehan, but the power of Tammany, which put up another of its leaders as a compromise candidate, was only dented. Consequently, the political careers of most of the party rebels were over and done with in a matter of two more years. As Alfred B. Rollins, the biographer of Louis Howe, has noted, Father learned at least two lessons: In politics self-righteousness is not enough; you must recognize power wherever it exists. Louis had known those truths ever since he was a boy reporter. What he needed desperately now was a man of potential power who needed him, someone on whom Louis could stake whatever remained of his future.

He first addressed Father as "Beloved and Revered Future President" in a telegram he sent on the July day when Woodrow Wilson, governor of New Jersey and former Princeton professor, was nominated for the Presidency of the United States. Until then, Father had been plain "Mr. Roosevelt" to Louis, who worked alongside him, rounding up New York State delegates who would support Wilson in advance of the Democratic convention in Baltimore.

Father, who had joined in opening the campaign headquarters of his favorite candidate, took more than a share of credit for ensuring the nomination, which came on the forty-sixth ballot. He wired Mother: "ALL MY PLANS VAGUE SPLENDID TRIUMPH." She had initially gone with him to the convention city, where they rented a house with two other couples. But they found the place stripped of everything but the bare essentials, even cups and spoons. "I never slept in more uncomfortable beds," she said.

On her own admission, she understood nothing of the interminable struggle which she saw on the floor of the convention hall. The weather was unbearably hot, besides, and Father was too occupied with politicking to spend much time with her. She went back to New York, collected us children, and took us off to Campobello. Father wired her there.

Physically and in spirit, they were together less and less. The previous summer, she had gone up to the island with the family early, leaving him to stay alone with a skeleton staff of servants until the legislature recessed in Albany. Then he came to join us, but he left again when the lawmakers reconvened in September. In the spring of the present year, he established what was to be a pattern of getaway trips by taking young Hall with him to Panama. After three years at Harvard, his brother-in-law was ready for graduation, with a Phi Beta Kappa key. "They had, from all accounts, a delightful time," Mother said.

She reserved most of her criticism for Granny, complaining about her not to Granny's face, but to Father. For instance, there was an upset over housing arrangements, when we were to stay at Number 47 instead of opening up our own house in between leaving Campobello and going on to Albany. Finding room for two sets of servants was the nub of the problem, though Granny wanted to squeeze them all in somehow. Mother was grimly opposed to that, as she let Father know. Depending on what was looked for in it, the letter she wrote him demonstrated either a burst of independence or shrewish exasperation:

"I think she had better decide another time before speaking, and as I wrote you it would be foolish to get new servants and put them in her house as Lydia is going. I expect to let Emily go also as I overhead a conversation which made me decide that she talked too much even though she might seem nice to me. . . . After Cousin Susie is in town, I'm sure she will love having us stay there if we want to anytime, and I would rather do that than go to Mama's now!"

Now that Wilson had been nominated, Louis, still employed as a part-time agent by Osborne, joined Father again in working toward the next necessary goal: getting their man elected. Their political logic told them that if they helped him, he would surely help them, sooner rather than later. Father had been genuinely impressed by the New Jersey governor when he paid a call on him in Trenton during his first term as a State Senator from Albany. In Father's opinion, Wilson "figured it out that Western civilization would attempt to destroy itself through the natural sinful activities of modern man unless by the grace of God the decent people of Western civilization resolved to support the doctrine of the Golden Rule." That kind of sweeping view of history was irresistible to Father. As the twentieth century grew older, it turned out to be an astonishingly accurate analysis.

Young Senator Roosevelt had his own problems besides striving to get a Democrat into the White House for the first time since 1892. He was fighting for his political life in his own district, where he would be up again for election in the fall. Tammany was out for revenge. His leadership of the insurgency had lost him the support of some Poughkeepsie party leaders. He set his hopes on making

another automobile crusade—this time in his own car, which
Granny had bought for him. Then early in September, he caught
typhoid fever and was bedridden in the house on East Sixty-fifth
Street. Louis Howe's hour had struck at last.

My parents had traveled down together in the steamer from
Campobello and brushed their teeth with water, probably from
island wells, in their staterooms' pitchers. We children were settled
in at Hyde Park, then Father and Mother went down to the New
York house for an overnight stay. It had been rented out for the
winter before, and only a caretaker was living there.

Father felt too ill that evening to do anything but put himself to
bed. Mother, however, thought that she should take an old family
friend, Ronald Ferguson, who was visiting from Scotland, out to
dine in a restaurant. It was a major challenge for her. "He was a very
charming man," she recalled, "and though I dreaded the thought of
taking him out alone, once embarked on that dinner I enjoyed it
very much."

The next morning, Father was no better. The doctor whom
Mother called could not diagnose the cause of the low fever. Unwilling to take on servants, she nursed him for a week, giving him
medicine which left his condition unchanged, serving him meals on
trays which the caretaker prepared. As the days went by, she
realized that her own strength was fading, but it did not occur to my
determined mother that she, too, might be ill.

A week and more later, Granny hurried into town to see what was
wrong. "Now that you are here," Mother said, "I think I will have
my hair curled and go to bed." Granny's good-night kiss on the
forehead of her daughter-in-law told her that Mother was feverish.

"I think I probably am," she replied stoically, "but I shall be all
right in the morning."

"Let me take your temperature," said Granny. The thermometer
registered 102. On Granny's insistence, the doctor was recalled, and
Mother was sent to bed. Tests taken the next day disclosed that she
had typhoid fever, contracted, it was guessed, from the Campobello
water in the steamer's pitchers. That solved the undiagnosed mystery of Father's illness; he, too, had picked up typhoid.

"I proceeded to have a perfectly normal case," Mother said, "and
with my usual ability to come back quickly, I was up and on my feet
while Franklin was still in bed and feeling miserable. . . ."

At this time, Louis' situation was more than usually despairing.

When Wilson was nominated, Louis had quit his newspaper jobs, believing that he would go to work full time for Osborne. But the fitful mayor had finally dismissed him, paying him nothing for his trouble in garnering Wilson votes for the Baltimore convention. Howe wrote to Father in this crisis, "If you can connect me with a job during this campaign, for heaven's sake help me out."

Father had a job open for a nimble lieutenant right on his own doorstep, and he was equally desperate. Without someone to run his own campaign, he would be doomed to defeat in a three-way race against Jacob Southard, a progressive Republican, and George Vossler, the candidate of the Bull Moose Party set up by Uncle Ted in August after he walked out of the Republican convention in June. Father had Mother telephone Louis at his ocean-side shanty in Horseneck, Massachusetts, where he had taken refuge from financial storms. Howe came running.

Closer contact with Louis only increased Mother's hostility toward him. He could not be persuaded to put away his cigarettes even in the sickroom; she felt that the smoke fouled the fresh air which she firmly advocated as part of the treatment for any illness. She fretted over the amount of time he spent closeted with Father in strategy conferences from which she was excluded. She derided his inability to balance the checkbook on the bank account Father set up for him.

"No need to worry," Louis habitually said, "there's still money in the bank. I don't need any more." Finally, he came up with an overdraft. Father discovered that as a bookkeeper Louis always added the amount of the checks he wrote instead of subtracting it.

This was one of the comparatively rare occasions when Father paid Louis—he drew $50 a week—out of his own pocket. Otherwise, he did his best to find outside sources of income, always modest, for his alter ego. On one early occasion, he tried to cajole a friendly Albany lobbying group into paying Louis a weekly $10 as a retainer, as well as handing over $250 for mailing expenses. Only when the lobbyists proved balky did Father resign himself to forking out his own cash to Howe.

Within a day or so of being engaged, Louis was tirelessly campaigning for Father all over the three counties. "Keep the temperature down and get on the job," said a bulletin to Father from the little man who respected nobody. "I'm having more fun than a goat, and Southard will know he's been to a horse race before we're done."

To install himself at the center of the action, Howe established his headquarters at the shabby old Morgan House in Poughkeepsie. He found a boardinghouse near Vassar College for his long-suffering wife, their daughter and their second-born son, Hartley, who was one year old. Kiddens and Bubkins were his names for the two children, whom he played with whenever his travels permitted.

Grace had plenty of cause for nagging Louis, and sometimes she did just that. "I married you for better, for worse," she would tell him. "I couldn't go through another entire winter like last winter." Yet they had a strong affection for each other. That fall, he took her with him, with her hat tied with a veil under her chin, in the open car he used to crisscross the Twenty-sixth District. He buttonholed party leaders and voters alike. He flooded the three counties with letters extolling the new boss' record on agriculture, labor and boss- ism. He wrote brilliant, full-page newspaper advertisements, which were submitted for Father's approval: "Here is your first ad. . . . As I have pledged you in it, I thought you might like to know casually what kind of a mess I was getting you into."

He made no attempt to pinch-hit for Father as a campaign orator. Louis realized his own strengths and weaknesses to the nth degree, and public speaking was not one of his talents. At his own insistence, the youthful Senator was billed to appear personally at every major rally. As things turned out, he had not recovered in time to show up at any one of them.

"Your man Howe is a corker," said one admiring letter to Father. "He is the quaintest political promoter in America." Exactly how quaint was proved on election day: Roosevelt, 15,590 votes; Southard, 13,889; Vossler, 2,628. It was an astounding victory for Louis and for Father, who outran every candidate, including Woodrow Wilson. Final returns gave the lantern-jawed governor 6,301,254 votes. Uncle Ted picked up 4,127,788, against Taft's 3,485,831. People with an eye to the future did not overlook the fact that Eugene Debs, the unflagging Socialist, more than doubled the number of supporters he had attracted to the party platform in his two previous bids. Six percent of the poll, nearly a million votes, went his way.

In Hyde Park and Poughkeepsie, the Democratic faithful gave full credit to Howe, who wanted no accolades, only a permanent sponsor. Father acknowledged his indebtedness to the goblin of a man who had won the election and Father's respect simultaneously.

From that November day when the returns rolled in until the end, Father and Louis were two halves of a single political being, as essential to each other as the two parts of a tennis ball—and with just that kind of bounce.

Neither one of them had to wait long to be rewarded. The gamble they each had undertaken in backing Wilson for the nomination paid off within weeks of the convening of the new legislature in Albany. For much of that period, Father left Louis to handle his affairs in the State Senate while he set out to impress the President-elect with the claims of the New York Independents, not forgetting himself, who were confident that the times were changing and that Tammany had become a dinosaur. On his first trip to Trenton, New Jersey, he succeeded in missing his train and rode on a later one to Princeton with Wilson. Anyone who knew Father would be surprised to hear that he did not grab the opportunity to mention his own ambitions. Like Uncle Ted in his day, Father had his eye on the Navy Department.

He was in Washington for the Inaugural in March, when Josephus Daniels, whom Wilson had just appointed Secretary of the Navy, offered him the job of Assistant Secretary. Mother knew what was in the wind as she waited in New York. "It never occurred to me," she reported, "to question where we were to go or what we were to do or how we were to do it."

Father had met Daniels at the Baltimore convention nine months ago. The new "Dear Chief" of the Navy Department, as Father was soon to address him in a whirlwind of interoffice memoranda, spoke of that Baltimore meeting as a case of "love at first sight." However, the softhearted provincial newspaper proprietor from North Carolina took the precaution of checking out in advance the appointment he had in mind. He went to Elihu Root, elder statesman of the United States Senate, who had been Taft's manager at the riotous Republican convention. Root talked like an oracle. Thinking sadly of Uncle Ted's Bull Moose breakaway which cost Taft the election, he warned, "Whenever a Roosevelt rides, he wishes to ride in front."

That did not deter Daniels. When he broached the subject with Wilson himself, he was asked sharply, "How well do you know Mr. Roosevelt? How well is he equipped?" The President-elect was only probing. I fancy that, so far as he was concerned, Father had already been appointed to a job of his liking as a result of their train ride together from Trenton. That was the way Father, and Louis, liked to get things done.

In every sense of the word, Father was a man marked for political advancement. On the way down to Washington, aboard a Pennsylvania Railroad train, William McAdoo, another party bigwig to whom he had been introduced during his frantic days in Baltimore, sounded him out concerning two other jobs, Assistant Secretary of the Treasury and Collector of the Port of New York.

But Father had no doubt about what he wanted. On Inauguration Day, when Daniels came up to him in the lobby of the Willard Hotel, Father's love was the Navy. The young "boss eater" had already collected—to Mother's quiet despair—nearly ten thousand books and pamphlets on naval affairs, and he had read all but one of them. He was greatly influenced, too, by the parallels between his own career and that of Uncle Ted, who had once sat at the same desk in the same job that was offered to Father, which proved to be a stepping stone to the White House for Theodore.

"It would please me better than anything in the world," Father told Daniels. "All my life I have loved ships and have been a student of the Navy, and the assistant secretaryship is the one place, above all others, I would love to hold."

He immediately resigned his Albany seat, giving Louis the task of winding up all matters there. While Mother lingered in New York, in no hurry to enter into a new way of living, Father moved into the Powhatan Hotel in Washington like a duck taking to water. He was thirty-one years old, the youngest man to hold the appointment in the Navy's history, when he was sworn in on March 17, 1913, the eighth anniversary of their wedding.

Mother had the news indirectly. She opened a wire addressed to him, which would be a routine action for her, since she habitually read any correspondence of his which she saw around on his desk. She wrote pointedly to him that evening, "A telegram came to you from Mr. Daniels, so we know you are confirmed and finally launched in your work!" She added an equally sharp postscript: "Many happy returns of today, dear. I ordered your 17th of March present as we couldn't do anything else together!" The significance of those exclamation marks was not lost on Father. In a letter he sent her that day, he confessed that in all the excitement he had forgotten their anniversary.

Two days after Father took office, Daniels went home to attend a banquet in Raleigh. As Acting Secretary, my enthusiastic father happily told reporters, "There's a Roosevelt on the job today. You remember what happened the last time a Roosevelt occupied a similar position?" That had been a mere fifteen years ago. If their memories needed jogging, Daniels' own newspaper, the *News and Observer,* would have helped them. It ran Father's picture under the headline HE'S FOLLOWING IN TEDDY'S FOOTSTEPS.

By then he was already urging Louis to hurry down to the capital, where the job of private secretary to Father waited for Howe's special talents as his share of the reward for their efforts to get Wilson into the White House. The salary of $2,000 a year—shortly to be increased by another $1,000—was the biggest regular money Louis had ever earned. "It will break me," he joked to Father.

Within two weeks, the team was reunited. Until he mastered departmental detail, Father lightheartedly complained that he had to accept on faith the mountains of documents he signed, "but I hope luck will keep me out of jail." Louis, ferreting his way through the intricacies of red-taped organization, pretended that his duties consisted entirely of "blotting Franklin's signature." At least, the "Franklin D. Roosevelt" firmly written with a steel-nibbed pen satisfied Granny, who had advised him "not to write your signature so small, since it gets a cramped look and is not distinct. So many public men have such awful signatures. . . ."

Louis would have grinned sardonically to read that from Granny. He was well aware that, whereas Mother disliked him, Granny detested him. She refused to allow him in her house if she could help it. To her, he was the uncouth epitome of everything she had attempted to shield Father from. But Louis took it all in good part. The two fellow conspirators, Louis and Father, had no secrets from each other. In high good humor, they could joke together about the two women who, in their different fashion, seldom gave up trying to mold the junior Cabinet minister into the man they wanted him to be.

4

The prospect of going to live in Washington appalled Mother. To add to her own doubts about her ability to handle the duties of the

Assistant Secretary's wife, she had the word from Auntie Bye that she would have to prepare herself to make endless mandatory calls on other government wives, attend countless functions as protocol demanded, entertain constantly at home as Washington custom required.

She had hurried up to see her aunt, who was deaf and almost doubled over in old age, at the Cowles' old home, which stood off a tree-shaded street in Farmington, Connecticut. By the fire in the library-sitting room, the older woman pictured life in the capital as it had been before her dozing husband, the admiral, retired.

"You will find that many of the young officers' wives have a hard time," said Auntie Bye, "because they must keep up their position on very small pay. You can do a great deal to make life pleasant for them when you are in Washington, and that is what you should do."

Mother, who listened carefully whenever she was told what she "should do" by her aunt, made a vow to follow her instructions to the letter. Keeping up appearances on comparatively small pay was something she was certainly familiar with, and so was Father. He received his new salary of $5,000 a year in cash installments every two weeks.

"I don't know where it went," he told a colleague, "it just went. I couldn't keep an account with myself. And after about six months of this, certain complaints came back from home about paying the grocery bill. And so I began taking my salary by check and putting it in the bank and taking perhaps five dollars cash for the week and putting it in my pocket—trying to, anyway."

He schooled himself to make ends meet without having to turn too often to Granny, though it was she who paid his insurance premiums. "I enclose an insurance card on my life but your pocket," he wrote to her. The first car he bought in Washington was a secondhand Marmon. He assiduously refrained from hiring cabs whenever a streetcar would do, even when he was carrying luggage to go off on a trip or toting a golf bag to catch the Connecticut Avenue trolley up to the Chevy Chase Club. Most of his suits and shoes dated back to his Harvard days. He wore jackets until they were threadbare, then saved them as hand-me-downs for his sons. He refused to throw out a single pair of the English shoes, which were a weakness of his. He thought that paying more than two dollars for a shirt was an outrage.

As a hopelessly addicted collector of books, prints and ship models of the American Navy, he bought cannily and thriftily, an interminable browser in the shelves and trays of old shops and an expertly cool bidder at auctions. One of the bargains he acquired was a trunkful of letters, among them the love letters of a naval officer of our eighteenth-century fleet. Louis, on call twenty-four hours a day, acted as his scout in buying for these collections, which did not stop at naval memorabilia but ranged from time to time to chapbooks, children's books, miniature editions of the classics, and stamps. The two men, with still another interest in common, spent hours debating whether a stamp they had seen and judged as being worth perhaps five dollars might be picked up for a quarter or thirty cents if the philatelist knew less then they did. Father's collecting instinct did not stop there. He had a compulsion to save every letter, bill or scrap of paper that came his way.

Obviously, our New York house would have to be rented at a worthwhile price if our domestic style there, with four servants and two nurses, was to continue in Washington. With Mother staying behind to do the groundwork, Father set about finding a tenant and was delighted when Thomas W. Lamont, the Wall Street banker, signed a lease.

Not until that fall did we join Father, when we moved into Auntie Bye's house on N Street. He had already made himself at home in his job and in Washington society. He had a long list of friends, including the best man at his wedding, Lathrop Brown, who had been elected to Congress from a Manhattan district, and he was rapidly making more. He was never short of invitations to attend a party or dine out. At one dinner party, he had been reprimanded for his cheek as an adolescent might be by a middle-aged woman guest, the wife of a naval officer, who was overwhelmed to discover that Father was her husband's civilian boss, the second-in-command of the Navy.

One of the few divergences between Father and Louis lay in their attitudes toward socializing. Louis scorned it; Father had a whale of a time. He saw a side of it which, for different reasons, was shut out of Louis' experience, as it was from Mother's. Louis, who had brought Grace and their two children into a modest apartment a few blocks from N Street, was too acutely aware of his physical appearance to want to mix with people he was likely to regard as butterflies. Mother was so painfully uncertain of herself that social life other than among her family and close friends was an ordeal.

She could not rid herself of fear of the coming season and the burden of obligations it would place on her. But Father found enormous fun in meeting anybody.

Washington was on the threshold of visible and invisible change. The social rounds still had to be made and visiting cards deposited. Horse-drawn carriages continued in use, but electrics whirred up and down the avenues, and automobiles were no longer a sight to turn anybody's head. The White House, which Cousin Alice Roosevelt Longworth, Theodore's eldest child, had found furnished in "the late Grant and early Pullman" period, had been handsomely done over. Little Henry Adams, who was a friend of Auntie Bye and Uncle Ted, watched what he thought of as the deterioration of quality in the living from the windows of his house across Lafayette Square from the home of Presidents. His was one of the carriages which occasionally appeared outside Number 1733 N Street soon after we had settled in. Only five feet four inches tall, he was frail as a reed, and he refused to leave his horse-drawn victoria, but he had the children out to sit with him on the worn leather seat.

The bored wives of newcomers to the city often complained that it could be the dullest place on earth in summertime, when the steamy heat put an end to concerts, receptions, musicales, the theater and most other activities. But there was plenty of not entirely parochial fun to be had at picnics on the green banks of the as yet unpolluted Potomac, walks across its bridges to the cool Virginia woods, swimming at the beaches and public pools, dancing the new fangled tango and hesitation waltz at secluded country inns. For Father, too, there were the pleasures of a clubman at the Metropolitan and the Army and Navy, which he passed on his way to the office.

Mother took us children to Campobello as usual for the summer before she embarked on the dreaded tasks of an officialdom wife. She had a foretaste of what was in store for her when Father, who came up for a short vacation, ordered the battleship *North Dakota* to anchor off Eastport over the Fourth of July weekend. In advance, he had drilled her and the children down to my three-year-old self in Navy protocol: who walked ahead of whom, what to do when he stood at salute, whose hand to shake, what parts of a ship were off limits to women and children.

When the time came for Father to take us on a tour of the ship, Sis, Jimmy and I swaggered aboard, suitably attired in blue sailor suits.

We all had a splendid day, but Mother was worried that we might disgrace ourselves. As the Assistant Secretary's wife, she accepted the responsibility of entertaining the senior officers at tea, bridge and dinner, and the job stretched out for days when thick fog kept the *North Dakota* securely anchored.

Back at his desk, Father assured her that no more battleships were scheduled to stop by, but "I may come up in a destroyer later, but that means only three officers." She would welcome him aboard a destroyer or with a whole fleet, she replied, if it might bring him sooner to Campobello, "but of course the destroyer will be easier to entertain." She could rarely detect when he was teasing her.

From N Street, she set out as a slave of the social system every weekday afternoon shortly after luncheon, to make between ten and thirty calls by five o'clock, so that she could be home for tea. "The children," she remembered conscientiously, "were always with me for an hour before their own supper and bedtime." She limited most calls to a tight six minutes, timed by her pendant watch. She followed a rigid schedule. On Mondays, the wives of Supreme Court Justices; Tuesdays, Congressmen; Wednesdays, members of the Cabinet; Thursdays, Senators' wives; Fridays, diplomats. Other mortals were fitted in on whatever days were mentioned on their formal cards, which in the style of the period bore visiting hours, rather like those of doctors. "I am Mrs. Franklin D. Roosevelt," she recited, her voice fluttering with nervousness. "My husband has just come as Assistant Secretary of the Navy."

She combed hotels for Congressmen from New York, grumbling a little to herself because they changed quarters so frequently. She climbed flights of boardinghouse stairs; she stopped by at great mansions and rented row houses, missing nobody, just as Auntie Bye had instructed her to do. Mother consoled herself with the thought that she must be making some headway in conquering her fundamentally retiring nature because she could never have steeled herself for anything as challenging as this in Albany. She made her rounds in Washington only from a sense of fulfilling the obligation which had been imposed on her by Auntie Bye. Tallying the number of calls she made and adhering to her rigid timetable were what counted with her, not the conversations she could have had with those she called on.

"I could have learned much about politics and government," she said, "for I had plenty of opportunity to meet and talk with interesting men and women." But she had little or no personal interest. Her life "remained centered in the family."

Of course, she saw no cause to worry about us children when she was away, since we had the nurse and governess. She was blissfully unaware that, in the fast turnover of English nannies, at least one was a vicious tyrant who would push Sis to the floor and kneel on her to teach her better manners. The same good woman once forced Jimmy to gulp down the entire contents of a mustard pot because he could not take his eyes off her daubing her lunch with a thick layer of the scalding English variety. In New York, she had compelled him to put on one of Sis' dresses and parade up and down the East Sixty-fifth Street sidewalk with a sign on his back reading I AM A LIAR after he told her he had brushed his teeth and she disbelieved him.

My turn came later, after the birth of the second baby to be christened Franklin junior. I succeeded in upsetting him in his high chair and roared with laughter to see him on the floor. Nannie shoved me in a closet and locked the door in such a fit of temper that she broke off the key in the lock. Mother was out that day. I howled for a while, but nobody came to the rescue until Father arrived home. More than three hours had gone by. He was customarily patient over any domestic turmoil, reluctant to get involved. Jimmy recalls this occasion as one of the few times we children saw Father livid with rage.

"This frightened Elliott more than being locked in the closet," Jimmy says, "yet Old Battle-ax stayed on." She was our torment for years, long enough to repeat the closet treatment on Franklin junior, down to breaking another key in the lock. Mother finally dismissed her only when she found occasion to inspect the dresser drawers in the nurse's bedroom while the bane of our young lives was out. One of the drawers was full of empty gin and whiskey bottles. Secret drinking was a much more serious crime than child abuse. Old Battle-ax had swung at us for the last time. None of us victims was more pleased than Father, though he never intervened more than once.

A month or two after the family had been established in Washington, both our parents took off on an official inspection of disused Navy yards in the South. Father clearly did not look forward to spending all his free time only in Mother's company, because he had invited his much-admired first cousin, Laura Delano, to go with them. Though she was petite and almost fragile where Granny was tall and stately, she had the patrician manner of all the Delanos. She also had a constant eye for romance, including one affair with a close relative, but marriage was not for her.

An early love of hers was a Japanese merchant prince's son whom she met on a visit to her father, Warren Delano, in Canton, China. She was quickly shipped home to break up the affair. She saw no more of her admirer until 1941, when he turned up in Washington as a member of the diplomatic mission from Tokyo that was ostensibly trying to smooth relations with the United States at the very time the Japanese battle fleet was steaming on Pearl Harbor. At the specific request of her former love, Father invited her to Washington.

Father loved the companionship of Laura, whom we called Aunt Polly. Her sardonic tongue and quick mind appealed powerfully to him. Granny regarded her as being "just a little bit racy" but was extremely fond of her for all that, since she was a Delano and a favorite of her father, Granny's brother Warren. But Mother and Aunt Polly were forever at dagger points, and Polly's sharper blade could prick the skin of Mother's sensibilities. That may have been one reason for Father's wanting his cousin along.

She was obviously bent on enjoying herself without being rushed while Mother saw the whole trip as an endurance test. The train pulled into New Orleans early on a November morning. Father immediately led his party on a brisk walking tour of a largely deserted Navy yard, politely declining to ride in an offered car. He spent most of the day clambering up and down iron stairways, probing every corner, overlooking nothing. After a quick conducted drive around the city, he went off to speak at an official dinner; Mother and Aunt Polly rejoined him after they had been the guests of "a delightful retired Navy gentleman," who took them to dine in a restaurant, which could have been Antoine's by Mother's breathless description of its finery.

The group then was whisked off to the opera, followed by a private supper party which kept them out of bed until two. Three hours later, they were up again, to leave for Biloxi without any breakfast on the yacht of Ernest Jahncke, who became Hoover's Assistant Secretary of the Navy after 1928. To start the day, some warm champagne was served. "Of course, I could not drink champagne!" said Mother, reminiscing about the trip, which was developing even more distastefully than she anticipated.

"Hours went by before we got anything to eat or drink, and I was feeling faint and miserable in spite of the fact that we were steaming along on completely landlocked waters." Fear of succumbing to seasickness and losing her self-possession haunted her, though she set her mind on overcoming it, and she managed to do so finally by an effort of will. She may have had another cause for feeling physically out of sorts.

When they reached Biloxi, Father sailed off in a side-wheeler to be shown the harbor. After Mother and Polly had been driven in procession through the town, the three of them, half asleep, were guests at another banquet. Polly's escort was scarcely her style, a Southern gentleman who neglected to fasten any buttons on his flapping, high-buttoned boots. The ladies listened to a speech by Father, just as eager as he was to catch the overnight to Pensacola, where, according to schedule, the train would pull in at 5 A.M., but the car they were in would be dropped and shunted onto a siding; they could sleep late and debark when they were ready to. At 4:45, Father pounded on the door of the compartment in which Mother and Polly were fast asleep. "We are in the wrong car. This one goes on through. We have to be off in fifteen minutes."

Mother could be up and dressed in a wink as a matter of daily routine, but Polly always lingered. She still had not finished dressing when the train drew to a halt. Father hurried in to help her. The local Pensacola family delegated to meet them found them bleary-eyed and sorting out their hastily packed luggage. The announced plan was for the visitors to eat breakfast with them right away, then two hours later appear for a more formal meal.

"Not I," said Polly, with Delano firmness. "*I* am going to bed." Mother had no such thought, determined as she was "to do my duty as pleasantly as possible." Father had another day of counting every rivet left at the long-neglected base, which had once seen wooden ships built but was now almost a jungle. They spent the night aboard another train, bouncing along to Brunswick, his final call. At a stag dinner there, numb from lack of sleep, he made a speech which his audience seemed to think was too short, so to satisfy his listeners, he stood up and improvised another.

"If this is official travel, I have had all I want of it," said Polly on their way home. Mother fancied that her own years of making similar journeys had only just begun. Hindsight told her something more. "I realize," she said, "that the very strenuousness of some of these experiences built up a confidence in my ability to stand things which has stood me in good stead throughout the rest of my life." The severest tests she was faced with as a woman and a wife lay not too far ahead.

Soon after she was back in Washington, she learned that she was going to have another baby. Her nausea at the idea of drinking warm champagne as an early-morning eye-opener aboard Jahncke's yacht may have been a telltale sign. The practice she had followed to avoid pregnancy during the past four years, the longest span of freedom in her marriage so far, had been only spasmodic. At some time in November, a man-and-wife relationship was resumed.

Pregnancy, added to the social calls which made every day a day of holy obligation, proved too much for Mother to handle alone. She was in urgent need of someone to help her play her joyless part in society, a secretary who knew the ropes and would be able to guide her through the labyrinth of duty. I imagine that she must have gone again for advice to Auntie Bye. Aunt Polly probably had a hand in making the arrangements, too. Certainly, she was a key figure in the developments which followed once the choice of a secretary had been made, and Lucy Page Mercer began appearing at our house three mornings a week.

She and Mother worked together in the living room—there was no other space available. Lucy would curl herself gracefully on the carpet, spreading out for sorting the letters, cards, bills and invitations that flowed in, prompted by Mother's calls. Lucy was gay, smiling and relaxed. We children welcomed the days she came to work. Granny, who could be stinging in her remarks to and about people she did not care for, found only praise for her: "She is *so* sweet and attractive and adores you, Eleanor."

She was twenty-three years old, with a rich contralto voice, femininely gentle where Mother had something of a schoolmarm's air about her, outgoing where Mother was an introvert. As an adolescent living at Number 1761, she had been in and out of the neighbors' houses. She was nowadays welcomed in them as a guest. Though she was a paid employee, earning some thirty dollars a week from Mother, she was listed in the Social Register in New York as well as in Washington, a lady to her fingertips.

Her mother, Minnie Tunis, had been called the most beautiful woman in the capital, with the smoldering promise of passion in her dark eyes. She had inherited a fortune made in Viriginia real estate when she was twenty. Her first husband was an Englishman, whom she divorced for his adultery after she met Carroll Mercer. He was a native-born Washingtonian, a "cave-dweller" in local terminology, with a reputation for wildness. As a lieutenant in the United States Marines, he had been put on half-pay for two years for being drunk on an expedition to Panama. But by birth he was a Carroll of Maryland, and an ancestor, Charles Carroll, was a signer of the Declaration of Independence. That put Carroll Mercer in the top drawer of blue-blooded society, and Minnie had more than enough money to cut a broad swath, though money tended to run through their fingers, as it did through the Halls'. "Gentleman" was the description of Lucy's father entered on her birth certificate when she entered the world on April 26, 1891.

But the Gay Nineties turned gray for the Mercers when most of their money ran out some time before the century ended. Carroll enlisted as an Army captain, serving under Colonel Theodore Roosevelt when his Rough Riders charged San Juan Hill. After his discharge, the family moved into N Street, a considerable step downward from the style of previous homes the Mercers had lived in.

The breakup between them occurred there. Carroll departed, to live across the street from the Metropolitan Club, and Minnie took their two daughters, Lucy and the older Violetta, to New York to open up a business as an interior decorator. She apparently enjoyed other favors from what in those days were known as rich patrons. With the financial help of Carroll relatives, both girls were sent to Austria for education in a convent there. One anecdote about their arrival has it that the nuns were so shocked by the Mercer girls' flimsy nightgowns that they told them, "Only prostitutes wear such garments." The girls were bewildered. "What," they asked, "is a prostitute?"

Before Lucy came to work for Mother, Minnie returned with Lucy and Violetta to Washington, where the mother found a job in an art gallery, Violetta took up nursing, and Lucy followed in Minnie's footsteps as an unsuccessful interior decorator. The gossips, who had kept up with the checkered affairs of the Mercers in the pages of a locally published scandal sheet, *Town Topics*, heard that

Minnie had forgiven Carroll, "and all goes merry as a marriage bell."

In point of fact, Carroll, still a gay blade, was living as a houseguest of a friendly investment banker on K Street, while Minnie and the girls shared a genteel apartment in the Decatur on Florida Avenue. Carroll made the rounds of the Metropolitan Club, as did Father, and the Chevy Chase Club, which Carroll had helped found. His daughters kept in touch with him and were guests in the houses of his friends, the same houses to which Father and Mother were invited. Perhaps Lucy could have found a job at better pay, but working as a personal secretary was the next best thing to being a hostess in her own right. She filled in for Mother at luncheons and dinners as an equal among friends. Had they been asked, the snobs who abounded in the city would have said that socially Lucy occupied a rung or two on the ladder above the Roosevelts.

Early that summer, Mother followed the undeviating pattern of taking us to Campobello, where she planned to have her baby. Father was left behind in Washington, with two servants, Millie and Frances, in the house and Albert, the chauffeur, on call. Lucy also remained on the payroll, keeping up Mother's social business.

Dr. Albert H. Ely, the New York gynecologist who had delivered her four previous children, was supposed to be in Campobello in time for the confinement. Blanche Spring was with us, as usual, to take care of Mother. Granny was installed in her next-door cottage. Father darted between Washington, our summer home, and New York, where his endless wrestling with Tammany went on without interruption, this current bout involving the matter of political patronage. Louis, who sometimes tired of haunting the gloomy, parquet-floored corridors of the State, War and Navy Building, was off on a long vacation.

Father happened to be in Campobello when Mother came in to wake him in the night and tell him that her labor pains had started. He would have to sail across to the mainland to rouse Dr. Eben Bennett, the gray-haired country doctor in the little fish-cannery town of Lubec; he attended to our summer medical problems, which were frequent among us children. Father ran down to the dock where our schooner, the *Half Moon*, was moored, shouting down to the crewmen to bring her in. Granny heard him and came hurrying over with a robe over her nightgown. The services of Dr. Ely would have to be dispensed with.

An hour or so later, the *Half Moon* was back with Dr. Bennett, who seven years later, almost to the day, would make a similar journey, with Father not at the helm but lying paralyzed in his bed. For the first time, Mother's labor was prolonged. "I felt very guilty," she said, on account of the doctor's other patients. "I tried to make him leave, but he felt very responsible and insisted on sitting around."

On the evening of the following day, Franklin junior was born, the second to be given the name. There was only one scare in the early weeks. Miss Spring put a blue veil over his crib to shield him from the sunlight. He sucked on it while he was left alone. The trusted nurse returned to find his face dyed blue and was terrified that the dye had poisoned him. Less than a year later, Mother was pregnant for the last time.

She was still convalescing after Franklin junior's birth when a United States destroyer came cruising along the Maine coast. Father, asserting his authority, gave the officers and crew a sample of his skill as a pilot by taking the ship's wheel and nudging her through the Narrows, between Campobello and Lubec, where the tidal bore of the Bay of Fundy runs more than fifty feet high, the greatest anywhere on earth. That demonstration, a favorite of his and often repeated, was typical of many of the traits of his character—daring was one of them. Taking controlled risks was part of it.

"Gee! But these are strenuous days," he wrote Mother when he was back at his Navy Department desk. "Most of the reports of foreign cruisers off the coast have really been *my* destroyers." Either from the office or from the house, he kept her posted on what he was doing and what was happening around him, whether it was the surge of excitement caused by the war which had just broken out in Europe or humdrum domesticity. "Mr. Daniels feeling chiefly very sad that his faith in human nature and civilization and similar idealistic nonsense was receiving such a rude shock. So I started in alone to get things done and prepare plans for what ought to be done by the Navy end of things." And also: "Miss Mercer came in and cleaned up."

On August 14, three days before the baby came, he had reluctantly announced that he intended to get into the race for the United States Senate. With Louis taking it easy at his cottage on Horseneck Beach, Father had to make the decision alone this time. He gave Louis and Mother advance notice by telegram. He was going to run in the Democratic primaries in September as a progressive pitted against any Tammany nominee. He had "finally agreed to be the goat," he told a friend. Wilson stayed aloof, but it was his Ambassador to Germany, James W. Gerard, a wealthy stalwart of Tammany Hall, who was selected by the party leaders as Father's opponent. Louis came on the run to Washington to get the campaign wagon rolling again.

Mother's attitude was as disinterested as Wilson's. "I remember very little about the campaign," she said. She did not leave Campobello until near the close of Father's fruitless six weeks of trying to drum up votes against Gerard, who was so sure of winning that he refused to leave Berlin. Louis tried most of the tricks in his repertoire. To upstate newspaper editors, he sent out a boiler-plate page which claimed, falsely, that Wilson supported Father. He wangled endorsements from labor leaders whose union men worked in the Navy yards—but made the mistake of having the leaflets with the endorsements printed without a union label.

On primary day, Gerard overwhelmed Father by a vote of almost three to one. To prove he could be a party "regular," Father spent most of October campaigning for the Democrats, but in the November elections for Congress, the Republicans steamrollered most of their opponents, including Gerard.

On the surface, Father was glad to be back at his desk at the job from which he had the foresight not to resign. But his chief, Daniels, detected that he was "hurt." After a short stopover in Hyde Park, Mother was home, too. "Life," she wrote opaquely, "was beginning to assume more serious aspects, and when we got back to Washington that autumn many things had begun to change, though on the surface the social life went on as usual."

5

Life on the surface consisted, among other things, of us children being perfect little models of deportment when we were taken to weekly dancing class in the enormous, ornate ballroom of the British Embassy. Usually the governess, or sometimes Mother, dragged us up the street to join the other unhappy sons and daughters of officialdom and the diplomatic corps in learning, quite literally, to trip the light fantastic. But Jimmy and then I hated everything to do with the lessons, from the white gloves to the waltzes, from the Eton jackets we had to wear down to the prescribed black patent-leather pumps. Mother had firm ideas about dress and deportment.

The classes were sponsored by Lady Spring-Rice, wife of Sir Cecil, the British Ambassador, whose humor was unaffected by chronic ill health. "Springy" and his lady were close friends of Uncle Ted, who had introduced our parents to them. Father drew closer and closer to the British as the war spread farther and faster across the outside world, and his impatience flared over Wilson's delays in helping the Allies against Germany and the Central Powers.

We children ached for weekends to come, when Father made time to play with us. When he was home, which was too seldom in our prejudiced opinions, he would run upstairs to romp with us at bedtime. "Are you snug as a bug in a rug?" he would ask as we were tucked in.

In winter we would haul out our sleds, which he would tug through empty, snow-covered streets behind our secondhand Stutz, which replaced the secondhand Marmon, up the slopes of Connecticut Avenue, so that we could hurtle down, belly-whopping. If the hills were too steep and slippery, he would turn around and put the car into reverse, its most powerful gear. He combined his love of the strenuous life—something else he shared with Uncle Ted—and his delight in his children's company in games of field hockey, with teams recruited from the British Embassy, and baseball played with his friends and ours. Mother stayed home.

One of his recruits was Ronald Lindsay, who followed Springy as ambassador. Jimmy and Sis offered to teach him baseball, which he had no more than heard of before. "You slide for bases," they told him, "by diving for the bag." When he tried it, he finished with a bloody nose. Father launched into a lecture on playing fair, but Lindsay thought his wounds were all good fun and would not hear of Jimmy and Sis being bawled out.

The closest of Father's British friends was Nigel Law, the embassy's third secretary, a twenty-four-year-old bachelor, who was sent to Washington to join in the buying of American war matériel for his country. A strong mutual attraction existed between the two men. Nigel was invited to dinner on N Street a few weeks after he first came into town. Whenever Father was left alone as a summer bachelor, Nigel became his boon companion.

One June night, when they had gone together to a friend's wedding in New York, Father took Nigel on to the Harvard Club, where a victory in the annual boat race at New London was being celebrated in champagne. Hours later, the two of them paraded off with an army of other celebrants behind an improvised brass band. With arms linked and more champagne taken along for refreshment on the way, they crossed Fifth Avenue to the new Yale Club building, three blocks away. All but two Yalies were asleep, but from the balcony overlooking Vanderbilt Avenue those two invited the serenaders in for a drink.

Dawn was only an hour or so away when Nigel and Father checked into a hotel, asking to be called at 5 A.M. A taxi carried them to a Hudson River pier, where Father took charge. They boarded a torpedo boat of the United States Navy, which the Assistant Secretary piloted upstream to Hyde Park to introduce Nigel to Granny. "Our wash nearly sank some barges moored to the bank," Law remembered in a letter to Jonathan Daniels, Josephus' son and Lucy Mercer's biographer. Besides being a witty companion and partner in gaiety, he had another bond with Father: They were both attracted to Lucy.

So, without question, was another old friend and confidant, Livingston Davis, of Pride's Crossing, Massachusetts, whom Father brought into the Navy Department "as my second pair of legs," with the title of special assistant in charge of operations and personnel. Livy's boisterous adventures with Father went back to their Harvard days. He was a bluff, hearty individual, exactly my parent's type, and the polar opposite of Louis. With Livy, Father golfed, dined and wined, and shared confidences. Mother, needless to say, disliked and distrusted him.

On the surface, she was the quiet, sensible wife who completely subordinated herself to a dashing young husband who was destined someday for greatness. Josephus Daniels stood beside him one morning on the portico of the State, War and Navy Building, which faced the White House across Pennsylvania Avenue. The Secretary with the perpetually rumpled hair and string tie told his assistant, "You are saying to yourself, 'Someday I'll be living in that house.' " The words were meant as a joke aimed at a man, only a few years past thirty, who made little effort to conceal his ambitions or anything else that stirred his mind or heart. I doubt whether Father accepted the Chief's remark as prophecy, though nobody in his family had the least thought of where his destiny lay. He didn't discuss such things with us.

If Mother was uncertain of the future, she realized all too clearly what the recent past had meant for her. "For ten years," she said, "I was always just getting over having a baby or about to have one, and so my occupations were considerably restricted during this period." She restricted herself to doing what she ought to do in the light of her convictions. She was drawn not an inch closer to Louis, but because he was Father's associate, she had the Howes to dinner and went with Father to play a few rubbers of bridge with Louis and Grace. Louis then had no car of his own, so Mother, with the chauffeur driving, picked up Grace and Mary to take them shopping.

Between Granny's possessiveness of her son and the increasing involvement of Louis with Father, there was less and less room left for a truly shared life for my parents, even if either of them had wanted it. This was borne home pointedly to Mother shortly before her last baby was conceived. In the summer of 1915, we had not been long in Campobello when Mother received a telegram saying that Father had suffered acute appendicitis and had been taken to the Naval Hospital in Washington for an operation, which was an extremely serious surgical procedure in those times. She set off on a journey involving a sea crossing, an overnight train to Boston, then changes there and in New York. Granny, who had also been advised of the emergency, easily outpaced her to Washington from Hyde Park and reached Father's bedside a clear day ahead.

In a Pennsylvania Railroad car between New York and the capital, Mother was handed another telegram by a messenger who walked through the train calling her name. All it said was "FRANKLIN DOING WELL YOUR MOTHER-IN-LAW WITH HIM—LOUIS HOWE." Mother's reaction could have been expected by those of us who knew her intimately. "I could cheerfully have slain poor Louis, who was trying to be kind and relieve my anxiety, simply because I had to claim that wire and eyes turned on me from all over the car."

Two weeks later, Father came up to our summer home for a month's convalescence before he got back to the job of urging the building of a bigger Navy in preparation for the war which he was certain America would enter sooner or later. A month before the baby was born, he was smitten by a throat infection and went off with Granny to Atlantic City to recuperate.

Mother had only just given up her chores of dining out and entertaining at home, with Lucy's help in sending out invitations. On one such occasion, either Mother or Lucy slipped. It could have happened either before or after the birth, but it was quite typical of our family's social life. It was Sunday, so the cook was off. Mother, in a dressing gown, was fixing an early supper of scrambled eggs, the only dish she felt competent with then or ever. When the doorbell rang, Father answered it in his smoking jacket.

On the doorstep stood their guests, Navy officers in full dress, their ladies in long evening gowns. They had been invited for dinner, but Mother's calendar showed the date as being the following Sunday. This kind of situation was made to order for Father's sense of humor. While he set about stirring cocktails, she scurried upstairs to change, then downstairs into the kitchen to whip up more scrambled eggs. Their guests, she noted, "left quite early."

She hoped that the baby would arrive on their wedding anniversary, which was also Grandmother Hall's birthday, but she was disappointed. Miss Spring had to call the doctor after dinner on March 13, when Father had gone out to a meeting. Granny, for the first time, was absent for the birth of a grandchild. Father returned shortly before eleven o'clock, only minutes before Johnny made his appearance.

If he had been born four days later on the double anniversary, there would have been even more poignancy in the event. Because after his birth until the end of Father's days, my parents never again lived together as husband and wife.

Mother had performed her austere duty in marriage, and five children were testimony to that. She wanted no more, but her blank ignorance about how to ward off pregnancy left her no choice other than abstinence. Her shyness and stubborn pride would keep her from seeking advice from a doctor or woman friend. She said as much to her only daughter when Sis had grown up. It quickly became the most tightly held secret that we five children ever shared and kept. It did much to explain what we had seen develop in the disparate lives of the unbelievably complex man and woman whom the world was later taught to refer to as Eleanor and Franklin.

6

Men and women alike were impressed by the sheer physical magnetism of Father. On meeting anyone, the first impression he gave was of abounding energy and virility. He would leap over a rail rather than open a gate, run rather than walk. The coach at the early-morning exercise classes which Father attended with a young group of other government officials said he was muscled like an athlete. Old ladies maneuvered to have him take them to dinner. Young women sensed the innate sexuality of the self-confident Assistant Secretary, who liked to work at his desk in shirt sleeves.

Lucy, in a way, was physically his complement. She was as tall as Mother, but she took greater pains with her clothes and her general appearance. Beyond that, she had the same brand of charm as Father—everybody who met her spoke of that—and there was a hint of fire in her warm, dark eyes. In the new circumstances of Father's life at home, I see it as inevitable that they were irresistibly attracted to each other.

Mother, jealous in spite of herself when other women cast admiring looks at Father and he returned them, seemingly had begun to have qualms about leaving him as a summer bachelor when she made her annual departure with us "chicks." She could have convinced herself that he had enough work on his hands to keep him and Louis busy six days a week.

In this election year, the two of them concluded that Father must bide his time in politics and spike all attempts to boom him as a New York State candidate or revivify the rebellion against Tammany, at the risk of another defeat. So he contented himself by making campaign speeches as a trusted party regular, lashing out at the Republican candidate for the White House, Charles Evans Hughes. For the rest, Father and Louis concentrated on Navy business. They sat out long hours of committee hearings in the Capitol, in the effort to win an appropriation of nearly $500,000,000 for more warships and more Navy recruits. Father dreamed of another means of preparing for America's inevitable entry into the war: the rounding up of rich men's power boats into an armed flotilla to combat German submarines.

But there was still time for fun with Nigel Law and the other British bachelors who lived on Ashtead Place; for trips to New York; for golf at the Chevy Chase Club. In the interests of maintaining family harmony, he wrote Mother chatty letters about his off-duty hours: "Went out to Chevy Chase . . . a nice dinner . . . everybody danced afterwards, except self, who lost his nerve. . . ."

Possibly, Mother's doubts were not allayed. When the chauffeur wrecked our car on a Washington street, she took the opportunity to send one of her typical warnings to Father, to be read between the lines of an apparently guileless comment: "Isn't it horrid to be disappointed in someone? It makes one so suspicious!"

A polio epidemic hit the country that summer, leading Father to write a different kind of warning in return: Swat every fly in the house at Campobello, and do not think about bringing the children back by train or by automobile, since some New England villages were blocking out-of-town cars with children in them. He wanted to borrow the USS *Dolphin,* the onetime Navy cruiser now used by the Secretary's office, to evacuate us all from the island. But, for the time being, Daniels was unwilling to allow that, scared by a Congressman's allegation that such a trip would be only a cover for political campaigning in the Maine primary.

As soon as the votes there were cast in late September, the *Dolphin* was put at Father's disposal. Meantime, he had instructed Granny to have the fumigators in at Hyde Park, where we children were to stay quarantined until the epidemic wore itself out. She must arrange, he said, for us to ride in a car which had not been driven by her coachman, one of whose children had caught the disease.

We sailed home to the Hyde Park dock in great style with Father early in October, thoroughly enjoying this seagoing perquisite of office, heedless of his fears of what everybody then called IP. Infantile paralysis was primarily a child's disease, was it not?

"I went back to Washington," Mother recorded. "From a life centered entirely in my family, I became conscious, on returning to the seat of government in Washington, that there was a sense of impending disaster hanging over all of us." Readers of those words, written more than twenty years after the event, imagined that she was referring to Wilson's declaration, of April 6 the next year, that America was entering the war. But by "all of us," she meant not the country at large, but her family. She was talking about trouble much closer to home.

She would unburden herself to nobody as yet of her nagging doubts about him. Sharing confidences was not in her essentially secretive nature. Lucy would be the last person to be confronted by

Mother, who left arrangements unchanged for the woman she now distrusted to come regularly to the house. Only Father could be informed, by an endless succession of veiled hints, that Mother was jealous and increasingly watchful.

At that time, I witnessed just once an outburst of emotion in her; it was such a rarity that the memory is sharp and clear. I was bewildered when it occurred, soon after the polio danger was over and we children were back on N Street. Mother came up to kiss me good night and dissolved into tears on my pillow. I had not heard her cry before in this uncontrolled, hopeless way.

She was still sobbing when Father came in to look for her. "What's wrong, dear?"

"I can't bear to go down and meet our dinner guests," she said. "I'm afraid I cannot face all those people, Franklin."

"Oh, nonsense," Father said. "They'll be arriving in a moment. Do pull yourself together."

It took her awhile to dry her eyes and compose herself, but she did as she was asked. For years, I attributed the scene to her shyness. Later, I came to realize it was far more than that. Those were the early days of Father's involvement with Lucy. Mother was facing the breakup of the marriage, and she felt at the moment that she was powerless to do anything to prevent it from happening.

He seemed to us to be spending more and more time away from home on Navy business or on political affairs. He was in Manhattan with Franklin K. Lane, the Secretary of the Interior, on the November night when Charles Evan Hughes went to bed certain that he had been elected the next President of the United States. Father and Lane left Democratic headquarters in the Biltmore Hotel at midnight, sharing Hughes' conclusion. The final result, showing that the President had been given a second term by something less than 600,000 votes, offered Father and Louis good cause for self-congratulation on their keeping out of the race in New York State, where Wilson lost by more than 100,000 ballots.

For some reason, Father called the day after the election "the most extraordinary of my life." He added, "I hope to God I don't grow reactionary with advancing years." But for the following two years, when the crisis over Lucy Mercer was coming slowly to the explosion point, he practically ignored New York politics. He turned time and again to the idea which Uncle Ted urged on him, of enlisting as an officer in the Navy and going to sea.

Lucy enlisted as a yeoman (F) in the summer of 1917 and was assigned to duty in the Navy Department. If the serial number given to her was any indication, she was Number 1106 among the women enrolled since the previous March, when the department ruled that the law did not stipulate that yeoman clerks must necessarily be males. The uniform was a drab affair of a tubular skirt, a shapeless belted jacket and a flat sailor hat, but she wore it whenever she turned up to work at our house.

"Some protective instinct makes us all attempt to keep our everyday lives on an even keel," Mother said, "though we feel the world rocking all around us." This comment, introduced in her account of American preparations for war in that era, can be only a deliberately obscure reflection of her own internal struggle. One of the exceedingly few welcome changes she found was the abrupt end to the fatuous round of social calls which the war brought about. She had time to spare now for worthier causes.

She attended one meeting called by Daisy Harriman, a widow whom the gossips had erroneously picked as a prospective bride for Wilson after his first wife died. The idea under discussion was to form a Red Cross motor corps, but since Mother could not drive, she decided that this was not a field for her. She took up knitting socks, scarves and sweaters for servicemen to occupy any idle moment that came along. Every Saturday, she turned our house into a kind of warehouse for the handing out of free wool provided by the Navy League and the collection of finished items from volunteer knitters. Lucy, with no more afternoon calling lists to occupy her, was drawn in by Mother to help out in the wool trade.

With Josephus Daniels' placid wife, Mother also enrolled in the Red Cross canteen, leaving her bed at five o'clock some mornings to go down to the tin shed in Union Station to serve postcards, candy and cigarettes to troops passing through. She joined in censoring the cards they wrote; suspicion of spies and sabotage pervaded the capital, matching her own somber feelings.

The canteen job put Mother in the company of Mary Patten, the eldest of three maiden sisters who were renowned as Washington's greatest gossips. "Don't telegraph, don't telephone, tell-a-Patten" was the maxim followed by anyone eager to spread scandal at short notice. It was more likely that Mary's tongue was already clacking about Father.

To carry on an affair clandestinely with Lucy would be completely alien to his nature. From his boyhood on, Granny drummed into him the concept of *noblesse oblige,* which she defined as, "People of social position like ourselves should behave *nobly* toward others." He did not flaunt his growing fascination with the graceful, charming girl whom many another man had fancied himself in love with. But he made no secret of his admiration for her, nor hesitated to discuss her with his friends, especially with Nigel Law and, I imagine, Livy Davis.

With a mounting sense of insecurity, Mother continued to watch and wait, letting Father know in her own guarded way that her suspicions were beginning to harden. She kept the household staff and us children longer than usual in the sweltering city. He was at his Navy Department desk soon after nine o'clock most mornings, and he did not leave it sometimes until well after midnight, but over the weekends he tried to combine Navy business with some needed breaths of fresh air.

In the middle of June, he requisitioned the *Sylph*, the gleaming white, 124-foot yacht formerly used by McKinley, Uncle Ted and Taft, which was now at the disposal of the Secretary of the Navy's office. Father had in mind a weekend's cruise down the Potomac, to escape for a couple of days the problems of mobilizing the Navy and enmeshing the missions of American warships with those of the British and French fleets. He took along as his guests his golf partner, John McIlhenny, and his wife; two officers of the Marine Crops; and Nigel Law and Lucy.

Something made Mother miss the sailing from the Navy Yard. Always a paragon of punctuality, she had to be picked up downstream by a boat sent ashore from the yacht at Indian Head. It is inconceivable that she was not invited among the party. But it is possible that she decided at first that swimming and playing in the sun on the Virginia shores of Chesapeake Bay were not for her, then at the last moment changed her mind in order to watch over Father.

Whether it was part of a plan or the result of some event that occurred during the next forty-eight hours aboard the *Sylph*, Lucy's enlistment in the Navy as a yeoman (F), third class, followed one week later. On July 15, Mother reluctantly left for Campobello, evidently after an open quarrel with Father. It was her duty to go; it was her desire to stay to protect her marriage. He must have snapped at her to remind her that the family had to get away from Washington's nerve-racking heat.

"You were a goosy girl," he wrote from his office the day after we made our departure, "to think or even pretend to think that I don't want you here *all* summer, because you know I do! But honestly *you* ought to have six weeks straight at Campo, just as I ought to, only you can and I can't! . . . I am unreasonable and touchy now—but I shall try to improve."

Tension between them flared repeatedly in the coming weeks. The morning after his chiding letter, Washingtonians snickered over a tongue-in-cheek story in the New York *Times*, headlined HOW TO SAVE IN BIG HOMES, which reported that Mother's domestic food-saving program had been adopted as a model by Herbert Hoover's new wartime Food Administration. "Each servant has signed a pledge card, and there are daily conferences," wrote the woman reporter, who went on to quote Mother as saying, "Making the ten servants help me do my saving has not only been possible but highly profitable. Since I have started following the home-card instruction, prices have risen, but my bills are no larger."

At home with a head cold, Father resented our being made to look like fools. He dashed off another letter to her, biting in its sarcasm. "All I can say is that your latest newspaper campaign is a corker, and I am proud to be the husband of the Originator, Discoverer, and Inventor of the New Household Economy for Millionaires! Please have a photo taken showing the family, the ten cooperating servants, the scraps saved from the table and the handbook. I will have it published in the *Sunday Times*. Honestly, you have leaped into public fame, all Washington is talking of the Roosevelt plan, and I begin to get telegrams of congratulation and requests for futher details from Pittsburgh, New Orleans, San Francisco and other neighboring cities."

Mother did not think that it was entirely her fault. She replied, "I do think it was horrid of that woman to use my name in that way and I feel dreadfully about it because so much is not true and yet some of it I did say. I will never be caught again that's sure and I'd like to crawl away from shame." But she would seldom admit defeat once she had set any course for herself, and saving food was one of her pet causes. She henceforth kept an empty chair at our dining-room table "for Mr. Hoover," as we children were taught to say, to symbolize our dedication to curbing our appetites.

The weekend after writing his blistering comments, Father boarded the *Sylph* for another overnight cruise. His principal guests on this trip were Rear Admiral Cary Grayson, the current White House physician, with his wife, Altrude, who was another volunteer knitter. Charles Munn, a yachting enthusiast and an old Harvard friend of Father's, brought along his wife, Mary, a pretty young bride whose voluntary job was to collect the knitted garments from our house. Nigel and Lucy again made up the rest of the party. She and Mary Munn had been deputized by Mother to handle the Saturday woolens collection while we were in Campobello. Yeoman Mercer evidently had no trouble getting weekend leave.

Father was careful to report to Mother the names of all his guests on what he described to her as "a funny party, but it worked out splendidly . . . a bully trip . . . and they all got on splendidly." They swam for relief from the July heat, lunched aboard the admiral's flagship before seeing the fleet pass in review in the York River, and shared the joke when the band of one auxiliary vessel elected to play "Alexander's Ragtime Band" instead of "The Star-Spangled Banner."

Lucy evidently worked directly for Father at the Navy Department, since Mother had given him instructions on how she wanted the Saturday warehousing to be run in her absence. Her feelings about his association with Lucy began to emerge in an angry letter sent before that weekend on the *Sylph*. "Your letter of Thursday is here and one from Miss Mercer. Why do you make her waste all that time answering those fool notes? I tore them and the answers up and please tear any other results of my idiocy up at once. She tells me you are going off for Sunday and I hope you all had a pleasant trip, but I'm glad I'm here and not on the Potomac."

She had left him with another chore to supervise. At last, we were going to move during the coming fall into a house big enough for our family of seven. Auntie Bye was having the place on N Street redecorated to be ready for new tenants. Our new address would be 2131 R Street, but she would still be collecting rent from us because she owned this much more spacious house, too. More than likely, Lucy offered to help in the overall decorating work that was being done, since that had been a specialty of hers before she entered into the Roosevelts' orbit. Perhaps Auntie Bye detected a certain warmth between Lucy and Father and concluded that what gossips of the Patten school were saying was true: that Nigel, as an act of friendship, had agreed to be Father's stalking horse on public occasions.

The Washington summer brought on Father's almost annual throat infection, requiring him to go into the hospital for four days. Granny, who was visiting Lake Placid, prepared to hasten down to be with him, but on this occasion Mother beat her to it. She lingered on in Washington, leaving us in the hands of the nurse and governess. The running quarrel broke out again, but the true cause of the breach that was widening between our parents was not mentioned. Mother arrived with a long list of complaints to make. She was lonely for his presence in Campobello, and she wanted no one else there with them. She was tired of the string of excuses he had been making for not leaving Washington. He did not even bother to read the letters she sent "for you never answer a question and nothing I ask for appears." She even chided him for neglecting Granny by not taking the trouble to go to Hyde Park: "I know she will feel badly about it."

She concluded by delivering an ultimatum. He simply must be in Campobello before the month was out. If he was not there within two weeks— She underlined her intention to retaliate with a note sent on her journey back to our summer place: "Remember I *count* on seeing you on the 26th. My threat was no idle one." Her biographers have made something of a mystery of the nature of the warning she held over Father's head. There was no mystery; she threatened to leave him.

Father was not ready yet for a confrontation, and neither was she. He came up to spend a few days with us, as he had promised to, and on his leaving, Mother told him effusively that "the chicks and I bemoaned our sad fate all through breakfast." In his subsequent letters to her from Washington, he continued to report on where and how he was spending his time, not omitting the name of Lucy.

The quarreling over the subject which nobody wanted brought out into the light spread to include Lucy. Ostensibly, it was about something quite trivial. The two women clashed over a check which Mother sent to pay Lucy for her volunteer work in the wool and knitting business. Evidently seeing this for what it was intended to be, an effort to humiliate her, Lucy refused to accept it. Mother insisted. The check, which was returned, was mailed again to Lucy, whose determination was apparently equal to Mother's. She let something more than two weeks go by, then had the final word by unequivocally declining to cash the much-traveled bit of paper.

She had one more task to perform for Mother before their ways parted. The Navy League, supplier of the free Saturday wool, had forever been critical of Josephus Daniels, whom big Navy men called a pacifist. He, in turn, considered the league to be a front for war profiteers and "an unpatriotic organization." He forthwith ordered all league representatives barred from Navy ships and bases. This was another fight to stay away from in the judgment of Father, who had been assiduously courted by the league as an ally in its dueling with his Chief. The "wool Saturdays" had to end, for safety's sake. "*You*," he wrote Mother brutally, "are entirely disconnected, and Lucy Mercer and Mrs. Munn are closing up the loose ends."

Two days afterward, another letter to Mother reported "no news," except that Daniels was trying to organize something similar to the league's comforts committee, but under the Red Cross control. Father did not mention that Lucy's father had been admitted to Sibley Hospital, dying from nephritis and heart disease. Forty-eight hours later, Carroll Mercer was dead, to be buried, as *Town Topics* blithely put it, "with some semblance of his former state, attended by old cronies who served as pall-bearers."

Almost immediately, Lucy was discharged, with an outstanding record for good conduct as a yeoman (F), "by special order of the Secretary of the Navy." The date was October 5. There is solid ground to speculate on the following sequence of events. She was deeply in love with Father, and she hoped that they would be married. She was a working girl, helping to support her penniless mother, yet, at twenty-six, she had rejected every other man. Though she was a Catholic, that was no insuperable obstacle, though she could no longer receive the sacraments if she married a divorced man. Her mother had been a divorcée at her second marriage. The man Lucy married would not necessarily have to obtain a divorce and undergo conversion to her faith. There was the distant possibility of annulment, or if he were divorced, he could remain a Protestant and agree, in the standard procedure, that any children of their marriage would be reared as Catholics.

The unmentionable subject of a possible breakup of our parents' life together, still without explicit reference to Lucy, rose close to the surface when Mother and Father spoke with Granny one week later. With a sense of disaster approaching, Mother had completely changed her attitude toward the older woman, now that she might urgently require her help. Far from criticizing her domineering ways to Father as she had done only months ago, she was again addressing her as "dearest Mummy" and telling her, "You will never know how grateful I am nor how much I love you, dear."

As the three of them sat before the massive fireplace at the far end of the library in Hyde Park, the question Granny and Father heatedly discussed was family responsibilities and the future of the whole estate. "I should like you to promise me, Franklin," she said, "that it will be kept in the family forever, just as my family has held on to Delano property."

Father, bone-tired from overwork and internal conflict, could not agree. Clearly, he had doubts about the continuance of his immediate domestic patterns, without thinking about "forever." The argument had not been resolved when Granny saw her son and daughter-in-law off on the train to Washington. She returned home and, after reflecting for an hour, began to see fresh significance in Father's angry words. Though she wondered whether he would read it, she set down her thoughts on paper.

One highly significant passage read: "The foolish old saying 'noblesse oblige' is good and 'honneur oblige' possibly expresses it better for most of us. One can be democratic as one likes, but if we love our own and if we love our neighbor, we owe a great example, and my constant feeling is that through neglect or laziness I am not doing my part toward those around me."

Even more to the point, she wrote: "Do not say that I *misunderstood*. I understand perfectly, but I cannot believe that my precious Franklin really feels as he expressed himself. Well, I hope that while I live, I may keep my 'old-fashioned' theories and that *at least* in my own family I may continue to feel that *home* is the best and happiest place and that my son and daughter and their children will live in peace and happiness and keep from the tarnish which seems to affect so many. . . ."

With the approach of winter, Mother worked longer and longer hours as a volunteer, principally at the Red Cross canteen, scrubbing floors, making up sandwiches, anything to keep her busy. Often on her drive to the railroad station, she picked up Mary Patten; "I came to know her very well," Mother said. There were constant dinner parties to be arranged in our big R Street house. She remembered her weeks as being so crowded "that sometimes I wondered if I could live that way another day." She carried her knitting with her everywhere, brooding over a deep urge to get away from everything and everybody by volunteering to serve in canteens near the battlefields of France. But her primary obligation, she still felt, was to "stay with my children and do what work I could at home." She tried to push the thought aside, but she could not.

Father was equally anxious to escape overseas. He had become less discreet about his love of Lucy. They had been seen driving together by more people than his cousin, Alice Longworth, who invited them to her house for dinner, happy to plot against Mother. They had other gossiping friends who realized by now that something much more serious than a summer bachelor's flirtation had developed.

In December, their cover, Nigel Law, sailed home in a blacked-out convoy to recruit extra staff for the embassy. *Town Topics* missed an opportunity to impress its readers with inside knowledge in the arena of scandal. Its coy paragraphs said, "The gossip in Washington concerning a charming young girl highly placed in the official world and an equally delightful young man, close akin to the loftiest of British nobility, may or may not be true. . . . It would be an ideal match, as the young couple's ideas entirely harmonize. As the girl has recently gone into retirement because of family bereavement, the affair may reach a culmination sooner than expected."

Perhaps it did, but not in the fashion *Town Topics* readers had been led to expect. Father was desperate to get out of Washington. An active war record would serve him well if he ever wanted to return to politics after his past disappointments. More important, I believe the romantic side of his character drew an impelling picture of himself going to war, with the woman he loved waiting for him not far behind the front lines. But his big Navy associates discouraged him from volunteering, and Wilson advised Daniels, "Tell the young man that his only and best war service is to stay where he is."

The "young man," father of five and thirteen years married, acted in the manner of someone starting to wind up his domestic affairs. He sold the *Half Moon*, which had been a past joy, to the United States government. He set about letting our New York house again. He devoted more time to us children, taking us cruising with him aboard the *Sylph*. Then, in the summer of 1918, he obtained Daniels' permission to sail for Europe to conduct an inspection of Navy facilities. He went straightway into Livy Davis' office; for months, the two of them had lunched or dined together several times a week, with Lucy one of the inevitable subjects to discuss.

"Pack up your old kit bag, Livy," said Father exuberantly. "We're going to see the war."

He chose to make the Atlantic crossing in the USS *Dyer*, a brand-new destroyer rushed into service without a shakedown cruise to guard slow-moving convoys against German submarines. With the enthusiasm of a boy setting off on vacation, he designed his own uniform for seaborne adventuring: riding breeches, flannel shirt and leather jacket. He exulted in every minute of it, from a storm that smashed the dishes to an engine breakdown and alarm bells signaling a U-boat attack, which did not materialize.

In Paris, he met Livy, who had crossed separately in a troop transport. This was the companion whom Mother described as "lazy, selfish and self-seeking to an extraordinary degree with the outward appearance of being quite different." She may have read his diary, which Father preserved along with almost every other document which touched his life. That diary recorded the gaiety of a trip which the history books overlooked.

King George V invited the dashing Assistant Secretary to Buckingham Palace and told him, "In all my life I have never seen a German gentleman." At a dinner honoring the war ministers, Father met Winston Churchill, then Minister of Munitions, but Winston, always preoccupied with his own affairs, soon forgot about it. He spent a weekend with the Astors at Cliveden and splurged on a pair of silk pajamas, price three guineas, for the occasion.

In Paris, he visited President Raymond Poincaré, attended a dinner for Herbert Hoover, then moved to the front, overruling a Navy officer's attempts to keep him behind the battle lines. At Verdun, he came under German shelling. It was all "bully," but nothing was bullier than inspecting the Naval Railway Battery with the ramrod-straight Admiral Charles Plunkett, its commanding officer. Plunkett seemed to be the answer to Father's pressing desire for a change of scene, perhaps looking toward the beginning of a new life. The admiral promised to take him into the outfit, which fired huge naval guns mounted on railroad flatcars, with the rank of lieutenant commander.

Father wrote to Mother, "The more I think of it, the more I feel that being only thirty-six my place is not at a Washington desk, even a Navy desk. I know you will understand."

With Father away, she had accelerated her preparations for independence. She took driving lessons from the new chauffeur, Huckins. She still yearned to get overseas herself, yet she knew nobody would help her take what could have been an irrevocable step—certainly not Daniels, who would regard a divorce as a tragedy and political suicide for Father. "I had not acquired sufficient independence," she said, to go about obtaining permission to serve overseas.

Above all else in importance as she viewed it, she wooed her mother-in-law, to put her firmly on Mother's side if ever she could find the nerve, or the proof, to confront Father. "I wish we could always be together," she wrote. "Very few mothers I know mean as much to their daughters as you do to me." A month later: "I wish you were always here! There are always so many things I want to talk over and ask you about and letters are not very satisfactory, are they?"

For quite different reasons, Father would hold the same thought. Now that they were physically apart for the first time since their intimacy began, Lucy had occasion to write to him. Out of the habit of a lifetime, if not from sheer sentiment, Father saved the letters from the woman who loved him.

Livy's diary told of a breakneck pace as he and Father inspected Navy bases, ships and flying boats. They got drenched with rain. They snatched sleep when they could, or else sat up half the night fortifying themselves with scotch and playing pitch-penny. Father could not shake off a feverish cold, so he ignored it. Three days before they sailed for New York in the troopship *Leviathan*, Livy noted, "Franklin in bed with floo." Livy caught it, too. In midocean, the ship became a floating hospital, the officers, crew and overcrowded servicemen decimated by pneumonia, and the dead were buried at sea.

Livy's diary for September 19, the day the *Leviathan* docked, said, "Saw FD for first time. Looked rotten." Mother saw it differently. Alerted by Daniels' office that Father had double pneumonia, she left us children in Hyde Park and called Dr. George Draper to meet her and Granny on the pier in New York with an ambulance. They all would go back to Granny's house at Number 47 because our own home had been rented.

"When the boat docked," she recalled, "and we went on board, I remember visiting several of the men who were still in bed. My husband did not seem to me so seriously ill as the doctors implied, but Dr. Draper went with him in the ambulance and we soon had him settled in his mother's house."

A great deal of mystery has been generated about the climactic confrontation which finally took place between Father and Mother over Lucy Mercer. The one source of information quoted ad infinitum is Cousin Alice Longworth, who reported that one day she was indulging in a pastime of hers and doing imitations of Mother to amuse her Aunt Corinne, Theodore Roosevelt's youngest sister. "Auntie Corinne looked at me and said, 'Never forget, Alice, Eleanor offered Franklin his freedom.' And I said, 'But, darling, that's what I've wanted to know about all these years. Tell.' And so she said, 'Yes, there was a family conference and they talked it over and finally they decided it affected the children and there was Lucy Mercer, a Catholic, and so it was called off.' "

My own knowledge, my observations of, and talks with Father and Mother, together with all the weight of available evidence, make it possible to date the day when Mother and Father dared face the reality. It was September 20, when he lay in bed with pneumonia in Granny's bedroom. Mother, unpacking for him, found Lucy's letters. She had no compunction about reading them. They were the concrete evidence she had lacked and long waited for. She immediately called on Granny as the ally who would back her to the hilt.

Mother would have preferred a divorce. That was her first thought, and her first tactic was to offer it. She had grounds in the state of New York, which recognized only adultery. The letters were her proof. But Granny held ironclad views about *noblesse oblige* and broken homes. If divorce were the answer, she would cut off Father's money as punishment for his offense. He could never afford to support two establishments. And to be divorced for adultery would mean political suicide for a man who was already being talked about by a handful of people as a future President. If Louis Howe was consulted, as I am certain he was, the weight of his advice could easily be forecast.

So the course of embittered conversation changed. Plans for separation and divorce were "called-off," as Aunt Corinne said. Granny, as her part of the three-way agreement, would continue to lavish money on Father, as she did through all the White House years. Because he could see no alternative if he wanted to continue with any kind of career in or out of politics, Father agreed to give up Lucy. Mother, on second thoughts, preferred that choice. She had tasted enough of the personal pleasure of making a start on a career of her own to look forward to its continuance. And she knew enough of the strengths of the husband whom she no longer loved except as a sister to realize that he had greatness in him, which she could draw on.

Probably we children were talked of as the reason for maintaining the marriage, but at no time do I believe that this was the decisive factor. It was convenient for everyone concerned to pretend.

Mother set a price for her compliance when she laid down the rules in private with Father. This, she told him, meant that their marital relations could never be resumed. She was willing to have him as a partner in public life, not ever again as a husband.

Toward the end of the days of conferring, a telegram arrived for Father from Sis, then twelve years old, in Hyde Park. She had won a German shepherd puppy as a door prize at a Red Cross benefit in Rhinebeck, where Aunt Polly lived. Could she keep him? "Yes," replied Father.

"That telegram arrived at the turning point of her father's illness and caused him a great deal of amusement, for it was the first thing he had been really able to enjoy." So ran Mother's printed account of the events of those days.

She pictured him as being stricken again with flu in a household where only she escaped to nurse her family and three servants when we all were gathered again in Washington. If we children were asleep, she reported, she drove down to work for the Red Cross, leaving Father "in a little room next to mine." But, she added in a seemingly disconnected bit of philosophy, "Like all other things, the epidemic finally came to an end."

Father's dreams of wartime adventure as an officer and with a different wife were never realized. The next time he sailed for Europe, the Armistice had been signed, and his mission was to dispose of Navy equipment overseas. Mother went with him. A few days earlier, before the USS *George Washington* left port with them aboard, Granny had called on Josephus Daniels. What she had to say was not recorded, but it can be guessed at.

She kept her part of the bargain in human ambition, emotion and power that was struck in the house on East Sixty-fifth Street. Mother certainly kept hers. Father's future, however, was a different story.

Hyde Park

1920

1

Every Christmas, we could count on all the family being home together, and home to us children as well as to Father meant no other place but Hyde Park. "I come back on every possible occasion," he once explained to some neighbors, "with a true feeling that it is my home." For good reason, Mother had no such attachment to the house which Granny owned and ruled, "holding the fort," as Father said. Mother felt that she was treated as a guest, not always a welcome one.

From the windows of the small rooms off the nursery which were ours on the third floor, we could see the uncut forest which bordered the River Road across the field below the house. "When a man has been away a long time," Father once said, "it is sometimes necessary for him to get to a place where he can see the forest as well as the trees."

Jimmy had inherited Father's little room one flight down and the extra-long bed which Granny had ordered for him as a boy because she did not want his growth to be stunted. From the single window, the view stretched down an avenue of massive maples and elms to the old Albany Post Road and beyond that to fields where Indians camped before white men came.

The rule on Christmas mornings was that we could get up

whenever we wished, but we were not to disturb the grown-ups before seven thirty. Since, in our excitement, we woke long before daylight, we wasted precious little time admiring the landscape but concentrated, instead, on waiting for the magical moment to strike. In the downstairs hall stood the eighteenth-century grandfather clock bought in the Netherlands by Granny on her honeymoon. As it chimed the half hour, we were off en masse to Father's bedroom at the other end of the house, over the enormous ground-floor library. He would be awake and waiting for us, grinning broadly as he reached, perhaps, for an early-morning cigarette, lying propped up against two plump pillows in the carved oak double bed which had belonged to his godmother, Miss Nellie Blodgett.

We loved to visit his bedroom, with its clutter of souvenirs of yesterdays: naval prints; a framed photograph of the sorely missed *Half Moon*; family snapshots; the parchment signed by Wilson, appointing Franklin Delano Roosevelt to his former post as Assistant Navy Secretary, which hung over the door leading off to Mother's room. But of all our invasions of his bedroom, those on Christmas morning were the best of the year.

"Merry Christmas, Pa," we would chorus as we climbed on to his bed to exchange a kiss and receive a warm squeeze from his strong arms.

"Merry Christmas, chicks. And as Tiny Tim says, 'God bless us every one.' "

We darted across the rug to the high-manteled fireplace, which was built catercorner between a side window and the door leading to his dressing room and white-tiled bathroom. Tradition called for a stocking for each of us to be hanging there, filled with candies and small surprise presents as a preliminary treat. Father chuckled, sipping a cup of coffee from the tray which a servant had left on his bedside table.

By now Mother would have heard our laughter and come in to join us, in a dressing gown, from her room next door. If any of us had been old enough to realize the significance of the floor plan or to know about the ways of most other married people, we would have had a better understanding of the coldness which existed as a permanent condition between our parents.

The bedrooms had been added five years earlier as part of an expansion and general face lifting of the house. By then Father's political activities, and his constantly expanding collection of ship models and prints and books, made it patently clear that more room was needed downstairs. Granny was more than willing to pay for the considerable work it entailed, but she set one overriding condition in her talks with the architect, Francis L. V. Hoppin: "I'm old-fashioned and the rooms are old-fashioned, and we want to keep things as they are."

Just as they did with our twin town houses, she and Father planned every detail of the remodeling. He made a miniature model of the "new" house as they envisioned it in long talks by the fire in the old south parlor, which was to be cut in half to become Granny's "snuggery," where she would sit by the hour, reading and carefully maintaining her account books.

On the north end of the house, a servants' wing was built for Granny's regular staff, with eight single bedrooms for her butler, cook, houseman, lady's maid, and kitchen maid, as well as for the nurse and nursemaid installed there to look after her younger grandchildren. A laundress came in daily from her own cottage on the estate, which Father preferred to refer to as "the farm." A coachman and a chauffeur had quarters with their families over the coach house and the stables. "You could have three maids then for what you have to pay for one today," Mother said years afterward, when her awareness of social conditions led her to apologize for a style of living which she once looked upon as proper and necessary.

The *pièce de résistance* of the new addition was the paneled library, with huge fireplaces at each end, which stretched across and beyond the frame of the old house on its south end. Above the library, three bedrooms and two bathrooms occupied the space. Father's bedroom, with its fireplace and magnificent bay window with a door opening onto a play roof for us children, was matched by a bedroom for Granny, similarly equipped. Mother's solitary small room was fitted in between theirs; with no fireplace and a single window overlooking the roof; with a door in each wall opening into the much more splendid accommodations of her husband and mother-in-law; with no bathroom of its own.

Elliott "Tiny" Brown, an ex-center of the Princeton football team who weighed 250 pounds, was chosen by Father as the contractor. He completed the two new wings in the summer of 1915. Neither in Hyde Park nor in any other house we lived in do I remember Mother having me or any of her children visit her in her bedroom. She was not geared for any kind of intimate bedside chatting. Examining the upstairs layout of the rooms which Father and Granny designed leaves no doubt that even before 1915 he led a personal life which Mother seldom shared.

She would have some little inconsequential gift waiting for her on Christmas morning, and so would Granny, who would make her entrance into Father's room a minute or so after Mother. After more benign smiles from him, we children were packed off to dress or be dressed, ready for the next major event of the day, a sumptuous breakfast, served formally in the dining room

The whole house was filled with the scent of pine from the boughs cut by William Plog, the head gardener, who had lived in one of the cottages since 1898, when he started working for Granny. Under her keen supervision, the doorways and ceilings of the downstairs halls were all hung with Christmas greens, with a sprig of mistletoe over the library door. In the middle of that room a tree, handpicked by Father in accordance with another Roosevelt tradition, reached fourteen feet tall, a deserving subject for Currier & Ives.

A couple of days previously, it had been adorned with ornaments and wax tapers. All the children helped Father, who, standing on a stepladder, always placed the topmost candles. For fear of fire, which seemed to be born in him, he insisted on keeping a bucketful of water close by, with a big sponge tied to a long cane in case there were flames to be doused. Tapers were used by our grandfather, so his son accordingly spurned electric bulbs.

The day before, on the afternoon of Christmas Eve, the work people on the place and the house servants gathered for a party around the tree. Granny had bonus checks ready for everyone. We children were encouraged to muster a few pennies out of our allowances to buy a present for each child in the families of employees. Since Father's idea of spending money did not go much beyond ten cents a week, our giving tended to be restrained, possibly a dime-store ring for a girl like Florence Depew, daughter of Louis, who had been Granny's chauffeur for two years—I lost my heart to her.

There had never been a chair reserved "for Mr. Hoover" at Granny's table for breakfast or any other meal. Her increasingly plump figure testified to the portions and excellence of the food we were served. "Mama," Father would say in mock despair from his end of the table, "every time I sit down I put on five pounds." At her end, across the bowl of flowers which she arranged every morning, she smiled contentedly. Mother usually had little to say at breakfast in Hyde Park.

Sometime after ten o'clock, we all made our way, the pace depending on our respective ages, to the library, where presents waited on a separate chair for each of us. Huge logs crackled in each fireplace, scenting the air with the faint, sweet smell of woodsmoke. We chicks were a noisy, boisterous lot, rarely reprimanded by either Father or Granny and consistently spoiled by her. Of course, you always looked at your pile of packages and compared it, not always silently, with the size of your brothers' and sister's collection. Then, to our screams of delight and Father's laughter, we ripped off the ribbons and wrapping paper.

This was the time of day when relatives and friends stopped by, to share in the fun. Father's half brother, James "Rosy" Roosevelt, came over from his house across the lawns, bearded and fat and forbidding in his Victorian-cut clothes, limping with gout, clutching the arm of his second wife, Aunt Betty, a London Cockney, whom he married over her protests, after they had lived together for years. Granny tolerated Aunt Betty, though she thought much more of Rosy's first wife, who had been an Astor. Mother did not care for either Betty or Rosy, who, well into his sixties now, sometimes could not resist giving a woman's bottom a saucy pinch.

Our nearest neighbors, the Thomas Newbolds, arrived at the front door, to a warm welcome from Granny, to exchange presents and bring news of their children, Mary, Ann and Edmund. Our rich neighbors, Mr. and Mrs. Archibald Rogers, drove over from Crumwold, the estate he bought with the fortune he made as one of John D. Rockefeller's original associates. The Delanos showed up in strength: Uncle Fred, Father's favorite uncle, and his wife, Aunt Tilly, from Algonac, the family mansion on the opposite bank of the river, just above Newburgh; Aunt Polly from Rhinebeck, just eight miles away; and others.

Granny kept an eye on the time. All the strewn wrappings must be tidied up and the library restored to a semblance of order by shortly after eleven o'clock. Another rule was that on Christmas morning we went to church, no matter what, and the service began at eleven thirty. On that day in 1920, if I remember correctly, snow lay deep over the Hudson Valley. The big sled, with a matched pair harnessed up, drew up to the spotlessly swept steps of the terrace outside the double entrance doors. Bundled against the cold, we all piled in for the ride of a mile or so north to St. James', Granny an imposing sight in her furs.

She was a stickler for religion and an unremitting church-goer. Mother was her dutiful companion every Sunday that she was in Hyde Park, and we had no choice but to be scrubbed and dressed up in our Sunday best to go along, too. Father, frankly bored by many sermons and all sermonizing, made excuses to stay away. He found letters that had to be written or, in spring and summer, a game of golf to play on the bumpy links of the Rogers' place or up at Staatsburg. Christmas, though, was a day when, a vestryman as his father had been, he felt he should put in an appearance in the family pew under the vaulted wooden beams of the little Episcopal church, whose walls were studded with memorial plaques of the Rogers, the Livingstons and other families we knew as neighbors.

He liked standing up to sing out the Christmas hymns at the top of his voice more than listening to the usual platitudes of the sermon. He used to fancy that he could do better in that line himself, but that was one more ambition he did not realize. He had grown impatient with old-fashioned dogma in religion when he said, a few years later, "The churches today are beginning to go along with the new scientific growth and are opening the way to a simpler faith, a deeper faith, a *happier* faith, than ever our forefathers had." He was in need of happiness that Christmas Day.

We four children—Johnny was too young for churchgoing—burst out of the felt-lined doors, in a hurry to get home for a quick, light lunch before we pulled out our sleds to go speeding down the long hill south of Crumwold, starting on the Rogers' lawn. The other children of working families on the estates, who would make up these coasting parties on other days, were a bit wary when grown-ups showed up, like Father, who belly-whopped with us in flying style, or Granny, who stood watching in her fur coat. Mother preferred to sit at home by a fire.

Back in the house again and thawed out from the cold, we would have time to relight the candles on the tree before the day's finale of feasting, Christmas dinner. Extension leaves had been put in the pedestaled oak table, making it easy for all the family and a dozen guests to sit down together comfortably. On holiday occasions, the Howes were sometimes invited at Father's insistence and over Granny's objections. But they had been with us for Thanksgiving, which was quite enough, in Granny's estimation.

Louis had also been Father's guest last Christmas, which, as an exception, had been spent in Washington. Granny came down, Cousin Alice Longworth and the perennial Blanche Spring joined us, but the centerpiece on the list was Sir Edward Grey, the ex-Foreign Minister of Britain, wearing blue glasses and already going blind; he came out of retirement to serve as a special envoy, attempting to persuade Wilson to compromise with his enemies in the Senate to save the League of Nations. In the middle of the celebrations, Mother learned from the nurse that Jimmy had picked up German measles.

There were no such shocks in store for us at Granny's house this year. The butler, immaculate in tuxedo and white bow tie, emerged to deliver two or three measured taps on the Chinese temple gong at the foot of the front staircase to announce that dinner was served. Granny took her usual place at the head of the table, splendid in jewelry and a lace party gown. Father sat at the opposite end, while Mother, as always, seated herself somewhere midway along one side.

Mary, the cook, outdid herself that evening. From the bowls of steaming soup to the turkey, which Father carved with glowing pride in his paper-thin slicing, from the plum pudding flaming in brandy down to the last walnut, we tucked it all away. For the grown-ups, he poured champagne from Granny's dwindling cellar of fine wines. "As a matter of *principle,* I will not patronize those *people*, Franklin," she insisted in those Prohibition days, but Father, a "wet" by habit and conviction, did not hesitate to call on Walter, who, as one of "those people," ran a bootlegging business in Hyde Park.

After dinner, we settled by the fire at the far end of the library, where fresh logs sent sparks dancing up the chimney. This was the climax of every year's celebration. Father took down from one of the shelves which lined the walls his old, worn copy of Dickens' *A Christmas Carol.* Reading it aloud at this season was a ritual he picked up from his headmaster at Groton school, the Reverend Endicott Peabody; Father kept the faith in a hundred strange ways.

Ever since he had lost a front tooth in his lower jaw at Aunt Kassie's house in Tuxedo four years earlier, he had worn a gold one, fitted in temporarily for public appearance, but for reading like this at home, he unscrewed it and put it in his waistcoat pocket. He invariably occupied his favorite armchair on the left of the fireplace, with his back to his corner desk. Granny installed herself in her matching armchair on the other side of the fire. Mother, with no special chair to call her own, could sit where she pleased.

To the crackle of the fire in the background, the only other sound to be heard in the house, he began, in his clear, calm voice: "Marley was dead to begin with. There is no doubt about that. The register of his burial was signed by the clergyman. . . ." He snarled the words of Scrooge, sent shivers through us when the ghosts stalked the old miser's room, chirruped the lines of Tiny Tim. No actor could do better. He stretched out the performance for two more fireside nights before he came to the last, resounding sentence, "And so, as Tiny Tim observed, God bless us every one."

There were other readings in the years ahead, in the same setting and in the same company. We took them for granted until, one by one, we children finally left the sanctuary of Granny's house. We also took for granted that Christmas the fun we had with Father as we raced around together in the snow. But we could never do that again. It was the last Christmas when he would be able to run with us, or even walk without steel braces gripping both his legs.

2

If someone had asked Father or Mother or Granny whether God had indeed blessed him or her in the course of the twelve months which were about to end, each of them would have answered without hesitation, "Yes." In different ways and for different reasons, they were incorrigible optimists, Father because he believed there was no obstacle that could not ultimately be overcome, Mother because she was gradually attaining confidence in herself as an independent being, Granny because she knew in her bones that God sided with her. Yet in greater or less degree, it had been a demanding year for all three, scarred by doubt and disappointment.

From the August day when Father cleared out his desk and quit the Navy Department, Mother had been waiting for the New Year, when the tenants' lease would expire and we could move back into New York. She was far from being a homebody, but seven years of living in Washington, on rentals from Auntie Bye, had left her anxious to return to East Sixty-fifth Street, with some thoughts in

mind for increasing her future privacy from unannounced calls by
Granny through the interconnecting doors.

Ever since the confrontation over Lucy, Mother had grown
increasingly tense in her treatment of her family. The spartan choice
she made for herself and imposed on Father left them openly irrita-
ble with each other. "I do not think I have ever felt so strangely as in
the past year," she wrote in her private diary a year to the day after
she had seemingly vanquished Lucy. "Perhaps it is that I have never
noticed little things before, but all my self-confidence is gone, and I
am on edge, though I never was better physically, I feel sure."

Because the sexual side of her nature had never been aroused, she
would not have been able to analyze the stark biological reasons for
the tension between them. She was secure from the risk of further
childbearing, and she had imposed a fitting penalty on Father for his
treatment of her. On their journeys in Europe together, when she
sailed with him on the USS *George Washington* soon after his
immediate involvement with Lucy was over, they quarreled bitterly.
The sight of other women more appealing and less restrained than
she outraged her. "Just wait till I get home and tell you what these
respectable people now let their daughters do," she wrote to Granny
from London. "You hair will curl as mine did!"

Paris was worse. "The women here all look exaggerated, you
wonder if any are ladies, though all look smart and some pretty."
The French city was "no place for the boys, especially the younger
ones, and the scandals going on would make many a woman at
home unhappy." She was jealous and simultaneously mystified that
Father could not apparently accept the special kind of asceticism she
demanded of him. He was so taken up with one English lady, she
reported acidly, that she had to drag him away at 11 P.M. "We have
nothing like some of their women or some of their men!"

When they arrived home in Washington, the tension continued.
"Dined alone," said her diary. "Franklin nervous and overwrought
and I very stupid and trying. Result a dreadful fracas." Her mood
drove her to discharging all the household help except our English
nanny. She replaced them with what she called "my darkies," a
butler, a cook, a housemaid and a kitchen maid. Granny, needless to
say, was horrified at the idea of allowing blacks in the house.

Another break with tradition was made by Mother that summer
of 1919. Pleading the need to economize, she took us not to Campobello but to Uncle Fred's summer place in Fairhaven, Mas-

sachusetts. The old clapboard house had been owned by Delanos for
generations. Granny, who came with us when Louis Depew drove us
there, had borrowed it for a few weeks from her brother. Her uncle,
Franklin Hughes Delano, for whom Father was named, lived there
when he married Laura Astor, who in our involved genealogy was
the aunt of Rosy's first wife, Helen.

The house was an easy drive from Plymouth, where the original
founder of Granny's family in America, Philippe de la Noye, who
could trace his ancestry to William the Conqueror, landed in 1621.
"Franklin is a Delano, not a Roosevelt at all," Granny was wont to
say. The little estate, about one block square, stood close to Buzzards
Bay, and it was there that Franklin junior and Johnny were taught
to swim by our chauffeur, Depew. At the end of the pier, he used the
same method employed by Father in his course of instruction for Sis,
Jimmy and myself in the Rogers' pond—dangling us in the water on
a rope attached to a sturdy pole.

We children thoroughly enjoyed our vacation; Mother did not.
Race riots swept Washington when fights broke out between white
and black soldiers returning from the war. She made them her
excuse to keep up a flow of scolding letters to Father. "No word from
you, and I am getting very anxious on account of the riots." Two
days later: "Still no letter or telegram from you, and I am worried to
death. Even if something is wrong, why don't you let me know? I'd
always rather know than worry. I couldn't sleep at all last night
thinking of all the things that might be the matter."

She went hurrying to Western Union to send him a telegram. He
noted calmly that it arrived just as he was going to bed, so it could
not be answered until he got to his office in the morning. When her
sorry vacation was over, she haunted him at the Navy Department
with telephone calls if he was late coming home. Sometimes, nagged
by suspicions, she showed up in person to escort him safely to R
Street.

Was it any wonder that he took off to New Brunswick with Livy
Davis and Lieutenant Commander Richard E. Byrd, who lived in
the next-door apartment to the Louis Howes, to hunt moose, play
poker and sip a little bourbon? But even when he was away, her
letters followed him within hours. On one such occasion, she wrote:
"I'm glad you enjoyed your holiday, dear, and I wish we did not lead
such a hectic life. A little prolonged quiet might bring us all together

and yet it might do just the opposite! I really don't know what I want or think about anymore!"

Such was the climate within the family as 1920 drew to a close. It was not surprising that our parents were looking forward to the move back to New York, where the situation between them could not possibly deteriorate any further.

Mother had made one unexpected visit to Manhattan in response to a telegram from Forbes Morgan, telling her that his wife, Pussie, and two of their children had been killed when their home, a converted stable on Ninth Street, caught fire. "It was one of those horrors I can hardly bear to think of," said Mother, who found the city enveloped in a blizzard and unflinchingly trudged miles through the drifts. Helping with the burial arrangements for the unfortunate, flighty creature who had once been her closest confidante—"You're too plain ever to find *yourself* a beau, poor dear" —made an indelible impression on Mother. From then on, the very thought of funeral parlors filled her with aversion. Pussie and her two little daughters were buried in the Hall vault at Tivoli, sadly falling into decay now, where Grandmother Hall had been lain the summer before.

Remembering the incident, Mother took the opportunity to write another veiled message which, in point of fact, referred to quite a different relationship, that of hers with Father. "It is a curious thing in human experience," she said, "but to live through a period of stress and sorrow with other human beings creates a bond which nothing seems able to break. People can be happy together and look back on their contacts very pleasantly, but such contacts will not make the same kind of bond that sorrow lived through together will create. Happiness will not lead you to feel that your presence is always welcome should an emergency arise, but a period of stress lived through together will give you this assurance."

Ten days after Pussie's death, Mother was in a much less melancholy frame of mind. "Did you know," she asked Granny from Washington, "Lucy Mercer married Mr. Wintie Rutherfurd two days ago?" If for no other reason than that the New York *Times* reported the event, it is certain that Granny did.

When her association with Father and their plans to marry abruptly ended, Lucy needed another job. She had no other income, and there was rent to pay on the apartment which she and her

mother shared. After an interval, Lucy went to work for Winthrop
Rutherfurd, a handsome American aristocrat, descended from the
first governors of New York and Massachusetts, Peter Stuyvesant
and John Winthrop. Her job was much more challenging than
being a social secretary, though it again made her a substitute
hostess. Rutherfurd, at the age of fifty-seven, had been a widower for
nearly three years, with six children, none of them older than teen-
agers, in need of a woman's care.

As a young man, he had won the adoration of lovely Consuelo
Vanderbilt, but her mother broke up that romance and forced her
daughter into marriage with the disagreeable Duke of Marl-
borough, Winston Churchill's grandfather, so that Consuelo might
be a duchess and mistress of the palace at Blenheim. Wintie was a
sportsman, best known as a breeder of champion fox terriers, a good
friend of Rosy Roosevelt's and an acquaintance of my parents. He
had been called "the handsomest bachelor in society" at the time of
his first marriage to Alice Morton, a daughter of Benjamin
Harrison's Vice President, Levi Morton, who had an estate at
Rhinebeck in Dutchess County.

Before Alice died in June, 1917, she was converted to Catholicism,
and her husband followed her example. They spent most of their
lives together at the Rutherfurds' ancestral mansion, called
Tranquillity, on a thousand acres of deer park, mountain streams
and rich farmland in the Allamuchy Mountains of New Jersey.

Little more than a year after Lucy became a foster mother to his
children, Rutherfurd asked her to be his wife. People who knew her
well said that the tall, smiling girl agreed not on account of the
millionaire's money, but because she felt that he and his children
needed her. A few days before the marriage, his eldest son died of
pneumonia, so the ceremony was a quiet one, held in the house of
her sister, Violetta, who was now the wife of Dr. William Marbury.

Lucy, it would seem, had most of the things she had lacked so far:
complete security, a husband of her own faith, and, sixteen months
later, a child of her own, her daughter Barbara. Besides the aptly
named Tranquillity, which was as remote from the hurly-burly
world of politics and pressure as any place could be, Wintie had a
town house in New York and another in Washington. He bought
a second estate in Aiken, South Carolina, the Ridgeley Hall
property, across the road from the Palmetto Golf Club, where he
liked to play. Father's polo-playing friend, the vehement

Republican Congressman "Gussie" Gardner, had owned Ridgeley Hall before he died as an officer in training during the war.

All in all, it looked to Mother as though the attachment between Father and Lucy had come to a tidy, totally satisfactory conclusion. Her question to Granny underlined her empty victory. Mother used to confide to a few of her friends that she had the memory of an elephant, able to forgive but not to forget. As it turned out, Father could not forget Lucy, either.

3

He had survived one of the most difficult and disappointing years in his experience as he reviewed it in his mind at the close of 1920. The expenses of life in Washington had made him chronically hard up. Jimmy had been operated on for appendicitis, and most of us other children had been ill in one way or another. Father had to resort to Granny's generosity to make ends meet. ". . . The doctor can wait," he told her, but "the gas man and the butcher" must be paid "lest the infants starve to death, and your cheque, which is much too much of a birthday present, will do that. It is so dear of you." To an old friend, he was more explicit. "I am honestly a fit candidate for a receiver," he said.

It is not beyond the limits of speculation to wonder whether his hard-pressed financial condition had been worsened because, until she found a new employer, he had been supporting Lucy. No matter what had been demanded of him by Mother and Granny, and irrespective of any promise he made to them, he would not have abandoned her to poverty.

Of course, he was in far better financial shape than Louis, who was bowed down with debts all through his days in the Navy Department. He had managed at last to buy his Horseneck Beach cottage from the landlord, but the Howes' Fall River house on Phila Street had been threatened with foreclosure by the bank that held the mortgage. Mary Howe was a junior at Vassar now, and Hartley in a private school. The Howes ran up big medical bills every year, too.

Once, Father helped hide from Grace Howe the fact that Louis collapsed in a New York hotel room and could be revived by the house physician only after hours of care. On dosages of strychnine,

Louis took extended leave to recuperate at Horseneck Beach. "For a week," he reported to Father, "I was in bad shape, but the pain in my heart left me suddenly just as it did before, and today I can run up the sand pile in front of my house without seeing black, which is my old test for cured. . . . I am honestly O.K. and fit for work."

Father, though sympathetic, tried to ease his conscience over the little man who could never really relax by telling himself that Louis was something of a hypochondriac. Louis denied that. "I have taken it for granted," he warned Father, "that sooner or later I would ignore the danger signals too long and drop out like a snuffed candle."

They were both worried about cutbacks in the department now that the war was over. "Everyone," Louis thought, "is indifferent or hates me, or is afraid of me, or uses me to get what they want." In their endless machinations, they had looked around for months for ways to make money. They hoped they had found one rainbow's end in a new oil refinery to be constructed in Fall River, Grace's hometown, principally with capital lent by the Navy, with the purpose of holding down fuel prices for its ships on the East Coast. Over Daniels' opposition, Father bulldogged the project through Congress. Neither he nor Louis had a direct financial interest in it, but one of their friends, Pat Homer, certainly did, and both of them had shares in his syndicate.

Father paid $5,000 for his, but Louis' stock was apparently a gift. He sent his certificates to Grace, instructing her that, if he died, Father could sell them for at least that amount of money. Then commercial oil prices rapidly fell, the Navy wrote off the Fall River scheme as a mistake, and Father sold out at a loss. According to one friend of his, he "knows nothing about finance, but he doesn't know that he doesn't know."

He disposed of his shares at a time when he had suddenly fallen out of favor with his "dear Chief." Twelve days before the Rutherfurd-Mercer wedding, Father plunged into hot water with a speech in Brooklyn, in which he asserted that Wilson had opposed his efforts to boost Navy strength before 1917. Moreover, Father said, he had risked his career as Assistant Secretary by illegally buying armaments for American warships in that period. Daniels was incensed at the cheekiness of his junior colleague. The word to him from the White House, where the now white-bearded President lay paralyzed from a stroke, was that Father was "persona non grata" with Wilson.

It was time for Father to think about moving out if he wanted to keep moving on. He immediately arranged with two attorneys of roughly his own age, Langdon Marvin, whom he had known at Carter, Ledyard & Milburn, and Grenville Emmet, to go into partnership in the law firm of Emmet, Marvin & Roosevelt. This he regarded as mere job insurance; he was no more fascinated with the legal profession than he had ever been.

He still had to look after Louis, who was frantically casting around for some fresh means of making a living, all too sure that Father's days were numbered in the Navy Department. Once Father had gone, Louis had solid cause to suspect that he would be out, too. In his ceaseless drum beating for Father, he had trampled on too many people's toes. Daniels felt that Louis "would have sidetracked both President Wilson and me to get Franklin in the White House."

Just before Father resigned, he tried to fix a future for his fellow conspirator by blandly informing Daniels that Louis had a bona fide offer of $20,000 a year from private industry. "He believes it," Daniels thought. "I have a great big swallow, but I cannot swallow that." Possibly, Louis had such dreams of a fortune made working for Pat Homer's oil syndicate, but nothing came of them. When Father was chosen as candidate for the Vice Presidency by the party convention meeting in San Francisco, Louis, for once, stayed behind in the Navy Department, with his eye on the job which Father was determined to quit, come what may. He recommended Louis, in fact, as his successor. It was rumored that the nomination went to the White House, but nothing came of that, either.

Both men in their maturing political wisdom calculated the odds against the Democrats as being close to hopeless. In the two years which Father had devoted to being the number two boss of the Navy and to his association with Lucy, he had lost influence with New York State party leaders. He had to suffer the humiliation of a fight for convention delegates in his own Twenty-Sixth District. "It is certainly an awful commentary on our ability to handle the practical end of things," he commented.

Money, not any kind of political acclaim, was both men's immediate goal just then. Father rejected as "stupid" a suggestion that he should run for the Senate. Louis turned down a similar overture from Tom Lynch when, on Father's behalf, he told him coldly, "We thought you had been in the political game long enough to have learned by this time to keep both your feet on the ground."

Father headed by train for San Francisco in a somber mood, while Mother bore us away to the primitive pleasures of sailing and swimming at Campobello. He could sense a swelling reaction in the American people against the idealism of Wilson and the sacrifices entailed by the war. The Republican dark horse, Warren G. Harding, nominated for the Presidency a week or so earlier, looked like a certain winner over anybody the Democrats might select.

Wilson, isolated in the White House by his wife and his watchdog, Colonel Edward House, was toying with the unthinkable idea of running for a third term. Father was a loyal Wilson follower, converted from a kind of Theodore Roosevelt brand of imperialism into a devotee of the League of Nations by Wilson himself when my parents sailed home together with him aboard the USS *George Washington* in February, 1919; that was the trip following the parting with Lucy.

Father made a flashy demonstration of his loyalty by grabbing the New York State banner from its Tammany-dominated guardians to storm down the aisles in the demonstration that erupted in the San Francisco convention hall when a painting of the doomed President was unveiled. But he was in no man's camp. When the name of Al Smith, the cigar-chewing Catholic who was serving his first term as governor of New York, went into nomination, Father made the seconding speech. The forty-fourth ballot chose the city bosses' compromise, Governor James M. Cox of Ohio, as the candidate for the Presidency. Father marched in the winner's parade.

He was unaware that Cox had sent a spokesman to Tammany chief Charles Murphy to ask if Father would be acceptable on the ticket. Cox, a Midwesterner, needed an Easterner for balance. "I don't like Roosevelt," said Murphy. "He is not well known in the country, but this is the first time a Democratic nominee for the Presidency has shown me courtesy. That's why I would vote for the devil himself if Cox wanted me to. Tell him we will nominate Roosevelt on the first ballot."

The play had been started by Father's own friends, Judge Mack, Tom Lynch and Lathrop Brown. In the convention hall, he suddenly heard his name being put into nomination. Murphy had agreed because Father, in Tammany's view, was expendable; their own man, Al Smith, was not and had to be saved for bigger things.

The machine operated with typical Tammany efficiency. Mother had the news again from Josephus Daniels, who also had gone to perform his duty in San Francisco. His telegram to her in Campobello said: "IT WOULD HAVE DONE YOUR HEART GOOD TO HAVE SEEN THE SPONTANEOUS AND ENTHUSIASTIC TRIBUTE PAID WHEN FRANKLIN WAS NOMINATED UNANIMOUSLY FOR VICE-PRESIDENT STOP ACCEPT MY CONGRATULATIONS AND GREETINGS STOP WILL YOU BE GOOD ENOUGH TO SEND MY CONGRATULATIONS AND GREETINGS ALSO TO HIS MOTHER AS I DO NOT KNOW HER ADDRESS."

Mother was not given to rejoicing under any circumstances. Her enthusiasms were guarded and, in a peculiar way, centered on her own achievements, not those of Father or anyone else. "I am sure that I was glad for my husband," she said, "but it never occurred to me to be much excited. . . . While I was always a part of the public aspect of our lives, still I felt detached and objective, as though I were looking at someone else's life." More than four years had passed by then in the cold war between our parents, which started with Johnny's birth.

4

Granny got her first real taste of the democratic process in action one August day when eight thousand people trampled the lawns at Hyde Park and five hundred more crowded into her house. The horde of local admirers and party dignitaries had descended on us for the official ceremonies notifying Father that he would run with Cox. They wandered through her flower beds and buttonholed every member of her family. She was reconciled only momentarily as she sat, with her hair carefully curled and her pearls draped on her generous bosom, in a place of honor next to Father as he delivered his speech from the broad stone porch at the front of the house. Mother, in a plain blue and white dress, sat with others of the crowd on the ornate wooden balustrade, her feet up on a camp stool.

Our imperious grandmother had been delighted with Father's apparent triumph in San Francisco. "I kept wishing for your father," she told her son, "but I believe he knew and was with us." She began to dream of the unfolding of ever greater victories: "If and when you are elected, you will belong to the nation, now you are 'our boy' of Hyde Park and Dutchess. . . . My regards and best wishes to our future President," she wrote.

She made no pretense of liking many of the breed of commoners she met that day, including Al Smith. She soon fell into the habit of sniping at him and most of what he stood for, until Father would burst out, "Ma*ma*, I want to hear no more on the subject." Later, as a dinner guest of the financier John Pierpont Morgan junior, she made excuses for the governor in her own fashion. "I understand it is true," she said in her beautifully precise, clipped voice, "that he does have spittoons in the Executive Mansion, but I am told that when he uses them, he *never* misses."

Meeting *hoi polloi* represented an enormous change from the patterns and standards of previous days for Granny, whose ambition was to leave her whole personal fortune of $1,338,000 inherited from her father to her son so that he might always live and conduct himself as a gentleman. The trodden-down roses in her garden behind the century-old hemlock hedges must have been a sign to her that Father's ties to her kind of people were breaking.

As a patrician in her own right, a Delano, she had known only quiet contentment in her widowhood, lacking nothing, particularly the attention of her son. She thought about him every time she walked along the upstairs hall past the room where she bore him in the great mahogany bed. "I've passed the door many hundreds of times in my long life," she once said, "and, oh! so often I've remembered that there my son first saw the light of day."

Hudson Valley society seemed as secure as her own place in it, one rung down from the top, which was occupied by the Vanderbilts in their Renaissance mansion of fifty-four rooms a little farther north off the Post Road. She loved to put on her best afternoon gown and proceed, in her carriage or her Pierce-Arrow, up the curving driveway over the stone bridge to take tea with Louise Vanderbilt, who was an unimpressive little woman, nowhere near as imposing as Granny.

When Grandfather was alive, he had not approved completely of these inordinately rich newcomers to the village and the way they imported European craftsmen to cut stone and carve wood for the house they built. Granny, at his instruction, sometimes had to turn down invitations from Louise. Now she gloried in taking us children with her into the hideously furnished mansion with its seventeen servants, which struck us as being more of a palace than a home.

The two women were equals to each other. "Perhaps the children might be excused while we have tea, Louise," Granny would say. "Of course, Sara," said the hostess, who appeared to be impressed permanently by what wealth had wrought by way of interior decoration. "Why don't they go upstairs and take a look at the rooms?"

Since we were unawed by anything and free to do pretty much as we pleased in Granny's charge, we scampered out of the echoing oval hall where Louise entertained at teatime, up the forty-odd carpeted stone stairs to the second floor. Peering down on the ladies through a huge opening in the ceiling above their heads, we would shout and swing on the wrought-iron rail which encircled it.

Father followed our grandfather's example and tried to duck out of visiting the Vanderbilts, inventing excuses to avoid being a luncheon or dinner guest—strictly white tie and tails—in the cavernous dining room, which would have made a suitable setting for a Borgia banquet. He found Frederick Vanderbilt, who liked to retire to his overstuffed library, dull and Louise something short of fascinating. He was probably as intrigued as we were by the sight of her tapestried bedroom, one of her proud exhibits, where she slept alone in a canopied bed, surrounded by a very Freudian, imitation-marble balustrade.

Mother, on the other hand, deferred to them. "Yes, Mrs. Vanderbilt" and "Oh, thank you, Mrs. Vanderbilt" studded her conversation when it was her turn to take us to tea, after admonishing us to mind our manners and be sure not to make too much noise. For the company of multimillionaires, Father preferred Vincent Astor, John Jacob's son, who lived farther up the Hudson; his wife, Helen, had succeeded in fulfilling what was only a wartime daydream of Mother's by working in a French canteen.

Granny's calendar was as orderly as her account books. Every Sunday in Hyde Park, she attended St. James', always with an approving glance at the stained-glass memorial which she had installed, "Giving Thanks to God for the Beloved Memory of James Roosevelt, July 16, 1828, December 8, 1900." On each anniversary of their wedding day, she drove up early in the morning to put flowers from the greenhouse on his grave in the churchyard.

Throughout the year, she arranged fresh roses in the Oriental blue bowl on her dining-room table, commemorating the day in May, 1880, when she first called at the house and he asked her to do just that for him.

Most springs, except during the war, she sailed to Europe, as she had with Grandfather when they were man and wife. Her diary recorded the fine details of her trips: pairs of shoes bought for Father from Peel's of London for thirteen pounds fifteen shillings and threepence, two blouses for herself for two guineas. She reminded herself to "pay taxes in New York by May 1 and October 30" and carefully copied down recommended home cures: "Two table-spoons of Calocide Compound dissolved in a basin of water and soak feet in it. Then rub off hard any callous places."

Her artless records told of a "lovely moonlight night, all pic-turesque and comfortable"; of deer hunted in the woods; of thea-tergoing; her lessons in embroidery; guests in the house; the books she read; engagements and weddings in her big but tightly knit family; births and deaths. There were almost daily references, al-ways laudatory, to Father, Mother and us children, whom she treated as if we were hers more than Mother's. She wrote about visits she made to the White House when another Roosevelt and his wife lived there: "Theodore, our President, was as always cordial and interesting and Edith very sweet and nice."

At the other end of the social scale, she sketched in over a four-month period the sorrowful tale of a coachman and her efforts to reform him after he drove her with my parents to the Dutchess County Fair: "September 27: Simms drove the pair badly, I think he has been drinking. . . . September 28: Simms came back from the fair rather *muddled*. . . . November 4: Simms has been drinking again. . . . November 7: I had a talk with Simms and accomplished nothing. . . . January 27: Dismissed Simms, coachman, as he has grown worse and worse."

Sitting next to Father as he delivered his acceptance speech, she surveyed the crowds clustered around the front of the house and applauded when they did. Everyone said he spoke well, including our solemn young neighbor, Henry Morgenthau junior of Fishkill Farms, who was responsible for arranging the whole gathering. Granny kept her doubts, which Father's words aroused, to herself as he declared: "We oppose money in politics, we oppose the private control of national finances, we oppose the treatment of human beings as commodities, we oppose the saloon-bossed city, we oppose starvation wages, we oppose rule by groups or cliques. In the same way we oppose a mere period of coma in our national life."

She frowned when reporters singled out Sis, Jimmy and me for feature-story paragraphs. She refused to talk to them about Father as a politician and flatly declined to kiss him "just one more time," as requested by news photographers who had missed her first embrace of him when he skipped up onto the porch.

Photographs presented a problem for Mother, too. Sorting out the two Mrs. Roosevelts was something of a challenge for strangers when they heard the servants call Granny "Madam" and Mother "Mrs. Franklin." Mother hated having photographs taken; they made her look hideous, she said. When Louis Howe, who was itching by this time to get away from the Navy Department and into this latest fight, urgently wired her asking for publicity pictures, she told him that nothing suitable existed, which was understandable in terms of self-esteem but not entirely true.

To Mother, Louis was still an objectionable little man whose intimacy with Father irked her. She felt that her opinions should weigh more with her husband than Howe's, but it was mainly to Louis that Father listened. She felt sorry for Grace, who could not afford any servant and filled her days with housework, grocery shopping, and walking with young Hartley in Washington parks. Most evenings, Grace, too, went down to the Navy Department to drag Louis away from his desk by seven o'clock. Then the two might snatch a bite to eat at a lunch counter and race across town in his old Overland touring car to catch a movie. Or else Louis would arrive home late and romp with Hartley or read to him before bedtime. Louis hung on to the same automobile until Father became governor of New York. Once, when Howe ordered a junior colleague to chauffeur ex-President Taft in it, the mammoth-sized elder statesman took one look and decided that he much preferred to walk.

Louis handled as much of the press campaign in the race as he could while he stayed desk-bound, but Father had to have other help. As manager of his Vice Presidential headquarters, he persuaded Charles McCarthy to rejoin his staff. That undoubtedly was an idea of Howe's. McCarthy, a Georgetown Law School graduate, had been private secretary to the Assistant Navy Secretary's office since Uncle Ted's time when Father brought in Louis over his head. At first, the seasoned old bureaucrat and the tough little newcomer collided head on. But each of them had tricks to teach the other, and they finished with great mutual respect.

Father proposed to crisscross the country by campaign train in exactly the same way in which a green young politician in a rented red Maxwell had once excited Dutchess County. To take charge of the train, Louis approached Marvin McIntyre, a special assistant to Daniels, responsible for Navy Department public relations. "Mac" agreed. To round out the group, Father found the advance publicity man he wanted for his travels in Steve Early of the Washington bureau of the Associated Press, an old friend of Louis', who took a leave of absence to handle the task.

These men, the nucleus of a personal team that held together through good times and bad for years after Father entered the White House, were of a cut largely unknown to him before 1920. Compared with the products of Groton, Harvard, and Dutchess County society, they were harder, racier, more down to earth. Much less important than the job titles they held in his Presidential terms was their closeness to him as a human being, sharing in his laughter and his secrets. To some degree, in each man's makeup there was a touch of Louis, who handpicked them to contribute to his making of a President.

Indirectly, since he had recommended McCarthy, Louis could be counted as responsible for someone else's presence in the inner circle at whose center Father spent his otherwise essentially lonely life. As a temporary secretary in Washington headquarters, McCarthy hired a bright young girl, antecedents unknown, named Marguerite Alice LeHand, who liked the look of Father from her first sight of him in McCarthy's office.

Two days after the Hyde Park celebration, Father set off barnstorming on a trip to California and back, with speeches to make in twenty major cities and half a dozen trackside chats to deliver every day from the rear platform of the Westboro, the rented campaign coach which was hitched onto any number of different trains. While Louis fretted in Washington, Mother went to Campobello, to remain there until she took twelve-year-old Jimmy to enter Groton in September, the first of our generation to follow faithfully in Father's footsteps to boarding school.

Meantime, our male parent was covering 8,000 miles in twenty states. He won friends with his smile but only limited applause with his crusading speeches for the League of Nations, as he pounded away at Harding's evasiveness on the subject of international cooperation. He sensed from the start that the cause was hopeless, but considerations like that did not deter him. Tom Lynch, who went along as a kind of paymaster of the team, said, "They'll vote for you, but they won't vote for Cox and the League."

Father plugged on. Radio was in its infancy. To persuade the voters, you had to show your face. Among those going to the national polls, there would for the first time be women. He had been speaking in favor of women's suffrage for years, but there was not a sign of any distinctly feminist bloc vote developing. Voters of both sexes yearned for that elusive wonderland called normalcy and the return to the good old days, which Harding promised. The sense of national disillusionment with Wilsonian idealism came through in a favorite chant of the war veterans: "We've paid our debt to Lafayette; who the hell do we owe now?"

Letters from Mother caught up with Father all along the route. "Dearest Honey," she wrote, "Oh! dear I wish I could see you or at least hear from you. I hate politics!" She was "positively hungry for news of you, and it seems a long time since your last telegram and they are meagre enough." She nudged him with reminders to find time to write to relatives: "I hate to add these personal things when you're under such a strain and wish I could do them, but I can't, and they are the kind of things which do mean so much to other people who don't happen to have all the interesting things you have to fill their minds."

Granny's opinion of politics, not much higher than Mother's, was unchanging since she expressed her hope that the San Francisco convention might prove "elevating," but "I fancy that the last epithet is not very likely in a crowd of every sort of politician."

Mother's lack of sympathy for Father's exhausting battle showed itself in a note she sent Granny: "Of course, it is hard to refuse, but I do think he should have cut Monday out and come here directly. However, there is no use in saying anything." This was when he had wound up his first national tour and agreed to fit in an extra speech in Brooklyn.

In a matter of days, he would be off aboard the Westboro again to hit more Western states. He had found his first safari plagued by inept management and skimpy financing, although he had put in $5,000 of his own money and Granny $3,000 of hers. He also paid for many of his personal campaign expenses and passed the hat among his Dutchess County friends to help pay off old Democratic National Committee debts.

It was high time for Louis to dash up from Washington, on a month's leave from the department, to ride with Father when the Westboro rolled out along the tracks again. I believe it was at Louis' urging that Father asked Mother to join the train as its solitary woman passenger. Her constant pinpricking by mail could only irritate Father when he was already under stress, without having to cope with irreconcilable domestic friction. Like a boxing manager handling a man he knows will be a future champion, Louis wanted Mother in his corner and in his training camp. Always hard-nosed and calculating politically, he set out to win her over by giving her a course in what this game was all about.

She must have seemed an unlikely student, unpromising material for what he had in mind, which was to serve as a necessary part of the team, no longer a wife, as he knew, but a supporter of the cause, at least. She found it hard to accept Father's obvious popularity with the crowds, feeling that his "head should be turned if it is ever going to be." The unfailing attention he received from women voters aroused her jealousy as they "crowded around him and exclaimed over his looks and charm."

At the end of each day, she thought he should be settled down in his berth as the train rattled on to the next stop. She was angry with him for sitting down to relax with some of the gang over a drink or two and a few hands of poker. She hid her rage, in a fashion which Father knew too well, by pretending that she was concerned only for the porter of the car, known as Romeo, a would-be black minister who could not take to his bed until his white charges had retired for the night. It is safe to assume that his final tips compensated him for any inconvenience, since one of his willing services was to supply his Bible when Father, who could quote chapter and verse, twitted Louis about the gaps in his theological education.

"We shall run and not be weary, and we shall walk and not faint," Father might say as they discussed the increasingly obvious problems of the contest.

"That's a great line," Louis would answer. "Where the hell does it come from?"

Father could be a trifle patronizing sometimes. "Ask the porter, and if he doesn't know, try Isaiah."

Mother grew impatient, as one week followed another, of hearing him make what was basically the same speech, with variations tailored to the place or audience, over and over again. He delivered more than eight hundred talks, formal or informal, in the course of his campaign. She told Granny, "It is becoming almost impossible to stop F. now when he begins to speak, ten minutes is always twenty, thirty is always forty-five, and the evening speeches are now about two hours . . . when nothing succeeds, I yank at his coat-tails." She was pleased to find, however, that "Franklin had certainly made strides in public speaking." Mother's own experience in that craft amounted to zero. Nervousness caused her wavering voice to rise in an incomprehensible falsetto. Louis knew he would have to work hard on that as part of his curriculum for her.

In general, the whole point of having a candidate's wife along on a grueling whistlestop trip like this was to generate publicity, almost a fetish with Louis. At first, Mother's tightly bound personality made her virtually useless in this respect, and of course she realized that. As the Assistant Navy Secretary's wife, she had tried hard to avoid all personal contact with newspapermen, of whom she lived in mortal fear after the fiasco of the New York *Times'* account of her food-saving efforts. Lucy had acted as Mother's shield, the intermediary through whom reporters' questions were answered, always with the minimum of information.

"A woman's place is not in the public eye," Grandmother Hall had taught Mother, with the result that she thought of newsmen as enemies, not friends to be sought out and flattered with Louis Howe's persistent technique. That highly skilled manipulator of mankind used the reporters who rode the train as accomplices in his immediate plan to remake Mother as a woman and an image. He encouraged them to stand at the back of the crowd making faces at her to see if she would crack a smile as she listened, in carefully concealed boredom, to perhaps the sixth version of the same speech in a day.

Louis, aware of every facet of Father's circumstances, egged on the happy-go-lucky journalists to break down her hostility toward the women admirers who surged around Father at rallies along the route. "Don't they make you jealous?" the reporters would ask her mischievously, dragging a nagging problem into the light. The word was that the Cox campaign train was shrouded in gloom. Louis would have none of that aboard the Westboro. To keep spirits up, he organized bets on the size of the crowds at the next major stop, low man to wear an enormous comic necktie for the rest of the day.

The first tangible sign that Mother's basic scheme of values, drilled into her in her childhood, might be in process of transformation came when the tour was only a few days old. A telegram from Groton reported that Jimmy had been taken to the school infirmary. Mother's code of behavior until then would have compelled her to hurry to his bedside, if possible ahead of Granny, who had also been informed of Jimmy's stomach troubles; the two women vied with each other in this strange kind of contest when members of the family fell ill.

What happened this time gave a foretaste of the cooperation which developed in the years to come between the four adults whose influence directly shaped the lives of all five young Roosevelts. Louis needed Mother for his purposes. Father urged her to stay with the train. She agreed, reluctantly, that there could be more important considerations than the children. Granny took Jimmy to Boston, where his upset was diagnosed as colitis, and after a few days at Hyde Park, she returned him to school.

"I am going gaily on," Mother told her. She did not know when she might be back in Hyde Park, "though I really don't see that I'm of the least use on this trip."

Louis stepped up his program for educating Mother in the addictive power of politics. He took to tapping on her stateroom door to discuss Father's speeches in advance with her. He drew her out on a wide range of subjects, using every skill he knew to break down her shyness and reserve, devoting the time which Father could not, or possibly would not, spare. He taught her the importance of the press in a democratic society and how to be comfortable in the presence of newspapermen, a lesson which she did not forget. Perhaps most significant of all, he sharpened her vision of the size and potential strength of America in the early twenties as they watched scenes brand-new to her roll past her stateroom windows. I am certain, too, that he implanted in her his own perceptions of Father as the man who someday would lead the United States into new dimensions.

Mother was utterly charmed by Louis' attention. She suddenly appreciated the fact that he had sensitivity, a fine mind and, as she said in a telling phrase, "rather extraordinary eyes." She called herself a fool for having judged him only on appearances, his shabby clothes and unwashed collars, his slovenly table manners and his nicotine-stained fingers. She sensed, because she was no fool, that this was a special kind of courtship and admired his cleverness in conducting it. It is more than likely that he was the first suitor she ever had, treating her as the dissatisfied, incomplete woman he knew her to be. She had chosen not to be a man's woman. Louis' sheer physical ugliness, if nothing else, limited his sexual life to marriage with Grace. Louis and Mother made an extraordinarily well-matched couple. Now she became "Eleanor" not "Mrs. Roosevelt," when they talked together. But as a sure indication that he felt less intimacy and more calculation on his side of the friendship than she did, he referred to her privately to Father as "your missus."

And poignantly enough, when the train, on its return to Manhattan, pulled into Buffalo, Mother, like a honeymooning bride, insisted on being taken to see Niagara Falls. Louis stole a day off to go with her, while Father went to campaign in Jamestown. "My first view of Niagara Falls," Mother remembered, "was all that I hoped it would be, a really great sensation. Louis proved to be a very pleasant person with whom to sight-see, silent when I wished to be silent and full of information on many things of which I knew nothing."

In four tumultuous weeks aboard the Westboro, as the car jounced to Colorado, then back across Illinois, Indiana, Michigan and New York, she started to assemble the person she wanted to be. She made great progress in reaching new goals and deeper under-standing. She gained an inkling of what Father learned in the course of the campaign: that people were not so much concerned with political theories as with jobs, their families and security. But jealousy had not died in her yet. Of his day spent in Jamestown, she reported that "certain photographs" were taken "of lovely ladies who served luncheon for my husband and who worshiped at his shrine." The pictures, she said, were "one of the standing jokes of that campaign."

The hundreds of speeches he had made and the thousands of hands he had shaken were not working for him. Father and Louis had to strike harder. "Make Republican campaign ridiculous," Father snapped in a fresh battle order. He was incensed by something Uncle Ted's eldest son, Theodore junior, had said about him, trailing Father in behalf of the GOP: "He is a maverick—he does not have the brand of our family." Father commanded his staff: "Use T.R. Jr's full statement about the Republican Party winning the war. Use the Republican gumshoe campaign in Maine that

Canadian troops are being sent to Poland by the League of Nations. Use, in the proper way, Republican whispering campaign in the backwoods section of Maine that the Democrats have *60,000 useless* clerks in the departments in Washington, and that on March 4 Harding, if elected, will *replace* them with 60,000 tried and true Republicans."

He began to lash out at his opponents' platform as a "hymn of hate." He swung at cool, cunning Coolidge, his opposite number on the GOP ticket, for wanting the Presidency reduced to a mere clerk's job. He denounced Harding as the tool of "Wall Street gamblers and money trust interest." But Wall Street odds favored the Republicans ten to one.

Mother stayed at Hyde Park when Father, still feigning optimism, left on his last swing, taking him through West Virginia, Maryland, New Jersey and Connecticut, to the traditional windup in Madison Square Garden. By now the situation even on his home ground looked desperate. Louis had written to a party leader there, "For Heaven's sake, give me some information about what is being done in New York State.... I can't make head or tail of this madhouse of a campaign." In New York City, things were worse. Boss Murphy's Tammany henchmen were concerned only with winning a second term as governor for Al Smith. They put his picture on gaudy posters next to Cox's, where Father's portrait should normally have appeared. Father continued barnstorming, for an ultimate total of more than a thousand speeches in thirty-two states, not counting informal whistlestop chats with the crowds.

At the final moment, the Republicans added a postscript to their "hymn of hate." They attempted to implant the idea that Father had removed from Navy Department files the records of a seaman convicted of homosexuality. This attack on his personal integrity was an echo of charges, made by GOP Congressmen in the spring, that homosexuals were being sent back to sea duty on release from Portsmouth Naval Prison. The latest smear took the form of a letter, released by the Republican National Committee; from John Rathom, publisher of the Providence *Journal,* who had earlier alleged that, under Father's authority, Navy "fairy chasers," as the antivice patrols were called, had acted as male prostitutes in their search for evidence at the Newport base. Ironically, Louis and Father had once offered to help Rathom clean up vice in Newport. "It will make rich reading if he tells half of what I know to be true," Louis remarked at the time. In the closing days of the campaign, Father sued for libel, but the suit got lost or neglected in the debacle of election day on November 2. To those who knew him at all, the notion of his condoning homosexuality, of all things, was a sick joke.

That morning, he went with Mother and Granny in the rain to vote in Hyde Park village. He held open house for loyal supporters, who crowded in by the hundreds again. He took over the little, disused smoking room to chart the returns as they were fed in by open telegraph wire. But as Joe Tumulty, Wilson's private secretary, observed in the White House, the result was "not a landslide" but "an earthquake." Harding defeated Cox by 7,000,000 votes. In the House of Representatives, the Republicans enjoyed a record majority of 309 seats against the Democrats' 132. In his own state, Father saw years of effort tumble in ruins. Harding outpolled Cox two to one. Not one state office or a single county went to the Democrats. In Albany, Al Smith lost his governorship and then joined a trucking firm as its president.

Father accepted defeat philosophically, with no outward symptoms of depression. "I do not feel the least bit down-hearted," he said. "It seems to me that everything possible was done during the campaign, and no other course would have been either honorable or successful." Mother, after sampling politics from the inside with Louis as her guide, felt much worse about it.

All the Howes basked in the glow of the new friendship. Mother and Grace exchanged affectionate letters. Mother was delighted to stop by at Vassar when Mary was ill, or to help her choose a dress, or have her over for a weekend at Hyde Park. Hartley received a pair of my outgrown socks with a warm note from my parent. There were long evenings ahead when Uncle Franklin, as Hartley called him, Grace and Louis pored over their stamp collections, while Aunt Eleanor sat with her knitting. And no two ways about it, Mother told Granny, we must have the Howes over for Thanksgiving.

Granny cherished the hope that Father, out of public life for the first time in ten years, might at last settle down to the calm routine of being a gentleman farmer with a downtown law practice. He had made a fine fight but lost. Now he could allow himself to sink into gracious obscurity, accepting the usual fate of men like John Kern and Charles Fairbanks. Who remembered *them* as the running mates of Bryan in 1908 and Hughes in 1916?

Father had no such thought. He saw, first of all, his need for

financial security, so he sought out Van-Lear Black, a high-living
Baltimore businessman to whom he had been introduced at the
Democratic convention in that city eight years earlier. Black owned
the Baltimore *Sun* newspaper enterprises and controlled the Fidelity
and Deposit Company of Maryland, the country's third largest
surety bonding house. Moreover, he was, like Father, a yachtsman,
a Democrat and a go-getter. He loved to throw hectic parties, freely
supplied with the best bootleg liquor, aboard his 140-foot yacht,
Sabalo, and on his Maryland estate, Folly Quarter.

In Father he saw just the man he was looking for to head the New
York office of his bonding interests, "an executive," as the Fidelity's
directors had advertised, "with legal training, an alert mind and a
soundness of judgment which has not been warped by specializa-
tion." On top of that, Father had broad contacts in business, labor
and politics, a celebrated name and a salesman's flair for finding
customers. He was appointed to a vice-presidency at a salary of
$25,000 a year, and he could still spend half his time at Emmet,
Marvin & Roosevelt.

Yet Father had other considerations in mind. Neither he nor
Louis dreamed for a moment that Republicans would rule undisturbed for the next dozen years. They fancied that when the
Congressional elections came along two years from now, Father
would have a strong chance for a Senate seat, now that he had
earned a national reputation in the most intensive personal campaigning a candidate had ever undertaken. What had to be done
was rebuild the broken upstate machine. "Thank the Lord," he
wrote Steve Early, "we are both comparatively youthful." He may
well have been thinking, too, about piecing together a life as a
nonpublic person.

He wanted a vacation before he tackled the varieties of challenge
which awaited him in the New Year. With Louis, he left Hyde Park
for Washington straight after the crushing election day. He would
take off from there on a duck-hunting trip with Hall to the marshes
of Louisiana. There were two pieces of business to attend to first in
the capital. On behalf of Louis, who still liked the prospect of an
executive job with Pat Homer, he put in an appearance at the Navy
Department to talk about Homer's New England Oil Corporation.
He received a cold welcome from his successor as Assistant Secretary, Gordon Woodbury.

He also dropped in at his old campaign headquarters in search of a secretary for his New York activities. Something about the looks and the almost permanent smile of Marguerite LeHand must have appealed to him. He sent for her to stay briefly at Hyde Park to tidy up the odds and ends of his campaign. Then he invited her to join him on a permanent basis early in January. She was not sure that she wanted that. "As far as I knew," she once recalled, "he was a lawyer, and if there is one thing I hate more than anything else it is law work. To me, it is dead and dry," said the tall girl with the strong jawline, whom her colleagues identified with a love of laughter.

"I told Mr. Roosevelt that I had made up my mind long ago never to work for a lawyer. He assured me that he had other interests besides the law and that his legal work took up comparatively little of his time." She felt that she was terribly independent—perhaps too independent, when she thought about it—but she would only promise to give him her answer when she had talked it over with "my people," her family, who had moved to the Boston suburb of Somerville soon after her birth in the little town of Potsdam, New York, not far south of the Canadian border.

"Please believe that I deeply appreciate how nice you were to me and that working for you and with you was a *very great* pleasure," she wrote from her parents' home at 101 Orchard Street in West Somerville.

Though there was a long list of other more eager candidates, Father had no one else in mind. He clearly felt that this young woman, twenty-two years old, who had gone straight to work as a typist in a variety of temporary jobs as soon as she graduated from high school, was the right choice for him. He was not disappointed. She was in no hurry to start serving any other boss. Ten days before Christmas, she wrote him, "I hope you will forgive my seeming negligence, but I have been ill for the past week and really did not want someone else to write for me. If you would still like to have me, I will be in New York on January 3."

5

A six-month gap loomed between Father's starting in double harness as a businessman and the expiration of the Lamonts' lease. The solution was a complicated living arrangement, devised by

Mother, which put Franklin junior, Johnny and their nurse into Granny's town house as more or less permanent guests, along with Father. Sis and I, with Miss Sherwood, our latest tutor, stayed with Granny in Hyde Park. Mother spent four days a week, Mondays to Thursdays, in New York and long weekends with Granny.

Returning to a round of social calls, teas and luncheons was a prospect which struck her as an impossible waste of time, now that Louis had stirred her interest in broader horizons in his effort to give her more to think about than her unhappy marriage. She mapped out a schedule for herself to fill her days and all those evenings when Father pleaded pressure of work as his excuse for not coming home to dinner. In her private estimation, she had already become "a good executive, which made housekeeping seem easy."

As a start toward making herself self-dependent in every conceivable fashion, she took lessons in cooking, typewriting and shorthand. She allowed herself to be recruited to the board of the League of Women Voters, as the National Woman Suffrage Association had been renamed now that votes for women were an accomplished fact. Cousin Susie Parish, who had dominated Mother so long with her echoes of Grandmother Hall's admonitions of what was, and was not, proper for a woman to do, was in the throes of a long illness, which put a stop to her interference. Granny remained a mighty force, but Mother increasingly chose to ignore her, limiting the duty time she spent with her to one definite weekly engagement at the Monday Sewing Class, an old love of her mother-in-law's.

Mother moved now in the company of a different species of women from the two she had listened to throughout most of her adult life. These social-minded "she-males," as Father and Louis called them, were as strong-willed as Mother and, in all likelihood, equally disenchanted with men in the role of husbands. Miss Elizabeth Read, a lawyer active in the league, was one of them. Miss Esther Lape, a teacher and publicist, was another. They shared an apartment on East Eleventh Street, where Mother spent many an evening while Father was busy elsewhere.

She thought that Esther had "a brilliant mind and a driving force, a kind of nervous power. Elizabeth seemed calmer, more practical and domestic, but I came to see that hers was a keen and analytical mind and in its way as brilliant as Esther's. . . . Gradually I think they came to feel an affection and a certain respect for me. . . ."

In spite of his campaign attacks on "Wall Street gamblers," respectable bankers and businessmen organized a testimonial dinner at Delmonico's to give Father a solid send-off when he joined their ranks as a Wall Streeter himself. Van-Lear Black got his money's worth from the start. In interviews and articles, his new man in New York, who called himself "one of the younger capitalists," recommended saving and investing as the true path to "real progress," while he boosted Fidelity and Deposit as "a balance wheel in industry."

One side of his highly complex nature laughed at this other, which talked in such honeyed platitudes to the conservative business world. Kidding his new title as soon as he acquired it, with memories of his political frustrations he styled himself at the head of one letter, "Franklin D. Roosevelt, Ex V. P., Canned (erroneously reported dead)." If his own fanciful plunging on the market deserved the description of an investment program, it was designed for quick killings and modest outlays of cash. He checked into possibilities in radio, Louisiana cotton lands and even a staggering scheme for harnessing the mighty tides which he knew so well in Passamaquoddy Bay, due north of Eastport, to generate electricity. He pursued prospects for his law firm, guarding against the exploitation of his recent post in Washington. As he explained later, "There is no legal reason why I should not appear on behalf of clients against the Government, yet I am convinced that for my own self-respect I should prefer not to do so."

Outside of office hours—mornings at Fidelity, afternoons at Emmet, Marvin & Roosevelt—he took on such a load of other activities that Mother was sometimes driven to wonder if he ever again intended to spend an evening at home. Speaking dates crowded his engagement book, kept up to date by Miss LeHand, who willingly kept the same long hours that he did, though she was physically frail from a childhood attack of rheumatic fever.

Dozens of speeches for the Navy kept his name in the headlines. He played politics to the hilt with letters to his old teammates and pressure on the Democratic National Committee to hammer away at Harding. "Reform," which was beginning to fascinate Mother in her preoccupation with the League of Women Voters and her new friends, was no longer a theme to press, as Father and Louis saw it. "The word 'reform,' " said Father, "still brings visions of pink tea artists who dabble in politics one day a week for perhaps two months in the year." There could have been a hidden reference to Mother in his words.

He served as an overseer of Harvard, a director of the Seamen's Church Institute, president of the Navy Club, and a member of the Council of the American Geographic Society and the executive committee of the National Civic Federation. He involved himself in fund raising for the Woodrow Wilson Foundation, the Boy Scouts of America, and Near East Relief Committee and Lighthouses for the Blind. He talked about writing books, and adding the Century Club, with its literary traditions, to his list of club memberships. Mother protested that it was all too much, though, she said snippily, "I know your remarkable faculty for getting through work when you get right down to it."

She relayed some of her frustrations to Grace Howe after she discovered that one week Father had dinner dates for Tuesday, Wednesday and Thursday when he had said that he would be working at Fidelity every night to learn the business. Grace, to be sure, had enough troubles of her own. What was going to happen to the Howes was something of a puzzle. As Father's shadow, his talents recognized by only a handful of intimates, Louis had made no name for himself on a national level. He stayed on in the Navy Department, teaching the ropes to Harding's appointee and joking that he was wanted only as a scapegoat for the Republicans.

He had business offers, like the city editorship of a Manhattan newspaper, but they all lacked the magical promise of power, which was vital for him. Confident that something would turn up, he and Grace took a larger apartment in Washington, then had trouble furnishing it. Mother offered them some of our furniture, which was in storage there. Would Grace at the same time return a rug of ours which they had been using, Mother asked, since it would brighten up Father's office? Would Grace, she requested on another occasion, be kind enough to send up twenty pounds of brown Navy sugar, the kind that Father liked, which was unobtainable in New York?

By March he and Louis had worked out their next step together. Louis would resign in June and join the "Beloved and Revered Future President" at Fidelity in much the same relationship as existed in their Navy Department days. They and their families would spend a summer vacation on Campobello, when the two men would have all the time in the world to lay out their schemes for future conquests. Granny would not be around. She was going to resume her prewar habit of taking a trip to Europe.

Father wrote off happily to Captain Franklin Calder, who had handled our family's boats for years, asking him to get ready the *Vireo*, the little sailboat he bought to replace the *Half Moon* and had delivered to the island on the deck of a destroyer. We all were looking forward to long days of fun together with the parent whom we sorely missed. We knew there would be hikes along the slippery paths of the cliffs and paper chases on the beaches, with Father as the hare fooling us poor hounds into rock-bound corners where we would be sure to get our feet wet in the rising tide. There would be sailing and swimming and picnics, the last of which pleasures were the only ones Mother cared for. "Quite a number of persons really did not enjoy Father's games at all," she remembered, including herself in that group.

Early in July, all of us Roosevelts settled ourselves once more in Campobello. We had our tutor, Jean Sherwood, and her mother in tow, along with a pretty Swiss governess, Mademoiselle Seline Thiel, for Johnny and Franklin junior. The Howes were at Horseneck Beach, waiting to join us in the middle of the month. Father laid in his customary supplies of liquor, locked in a desk drawer. We gathered that Granny, too, who had horrified Father by flying in a cabin plane from London to Paris, was enjoying her wine in a country where Prohibition was mercifully unheard of.

On Wednesday, July 13, Louis received a telegram from a friend in Washington, warning him that Father was the target of Republican muckraking. A Senate subcommittee, two Republicans and one Democrat, under the new administration had launched a major investigation of the trouble in Newport. Its 6,000-page report gave generous space to the testimony of John Rathom, the newspaper publisher who had lent himself to preelection mudslinging. It would severely censure Father, without giving him a hearing. Could Louis reach Father before the report was released?

There was no telephone in the Howes' beach cottage. Louis trudged across the soft dunes to a point where he could send a wire, reporting that he was leaving immediately for Washington to do whatever he could. Father's first instinct was to leave it to Louis. Then he reconsidered and, by telegram, wrested from the committee a promise to let him read the report's fifteen volumes for a few hours before making a statement by eight o'clock the following Monday night.

Unable to intervene in Washington, Louis returned to Horseneck Beach. The two, overwrought and incensed, agreed to meet in Boston that Sunday before Father took the night train alone to face the committee. Meantime, Louis, Grace and Hartley would go ahead to Campobello.

In Washington, the cards were stacked against him. Four hours in advance of the deadline they had set for him, the two Republican Senators gave their unamended report to the newspapers. It charged Father with knowing that Navy "fairy chasers" practiced sodomy to trap homosexuals. It labeled his actions as "a most deplorable, disgraceful and unnatural proceeding." LAY NAVY SCANDAL TO F.D. ROOSEVELT, the next morning's headlines screamed, DETAILS ARE UNPRINTABLE.

As soon as he heard what the two Senators had done, Father sought out Steve Early. They worked far into the night, preparing a statement for the press. "As an American," Father stated, "irrespective of party, one hates to see the United States Navy . . . used as a vehicle for cheap ward politics." His rebuttal and the lone Democrat's dissenting report were overshadowed, but by the time he left Washington for New York the following Wednesday he could sense that the Republicans had overreached themselves and the furor would soon be over. For once, he felt vengeful. He told Charles McCarthy that he hoped the smear merchants "will be duly rewarded for this kind of dirty work after they pass on to the next life."

Like Mother, he could bury his true feelings deep, but where she felt compelled constantly to reexamine the hurts and wrongs she suffered, Father spared no time for brooding, and grudges were soon forgotten. The surface contact between them passed lightly over such matters as hatred or love, other than the routine phrases of letter writing, which came automatically—"Dearest Babs" and "Dearest Honey."

When Mother read the newspaper accounts of his trial by kangaroo court, she advised him, "one should not be ruffled by such things. . . . I liked your answer. You will be starting a week from today," meaning for Campobello. She was mistaken about that, whatever his original plan may have been. He spent two weeks in

New York, broken by a weekend at Hyde Park, where only a skeleton staff stayed on in Granny's absence. Three more weeks, and he would not walk again except as a cripple.

The last picture of him standing unaided was taken in those long July days, when it seemed that summer was endless. He is there in shirt sleeves, arms folded, thin-faced but smiling, skylarking on a Boy Scout outing at Bear Mountain, New York, with a group of civilian supporters similar to himself. One of them, as a joke, took along a hollow cane filled with what the conspirators among them pretended was hard liquor. They passed the cane around until it reached the police commissioner, when they immediately staged a mock trial, charging him with violation of the Volstead Act. Father offered his services as public prosecutor. He took a swig of the evidence, smacked his lips and intoned, "May it please the court, I find that the liquid in this container is nothing more than vanilla extract, and I move that the case be dismissed."

He may have changed his plans and lingered in New York simply because, by doing so, he could avoid a tedious train trip in the blistering heat and hitch a ride aboard Van-Lear Black's yacht. Reaching Campobello by conventional means bored Father. It involved a six-hour journey via the New Haven Railroad from Grand Central to Boston. While we waited for a train connection there, we habitually made our way to the Copley Plaza Hotel, a shabby relic of its former glory, because that was where Grandfather had stayed nearly half a century ago. Occasionally, we took the steamer from Boston to Eastport, but more often than not our parents' choice was the eleven o'clock sleeper to Ayers Junction, Massachusetts. Another change there put us on a little train, pulled by a wood-burning locomotive with smoke puffing from its great stack. The one and only car was lit by oil lamps and heated by a Franklin stove. At one of a dozen stops, Indians from a nearby reservation would board to peddle blankets and baskets. In his youth, Jimmy was always afraid of being scalped. The rest of us were more frightened of being train sick, which some of us invariably would be. Mother would then interrupt her reading to supervise the attentions of one of the servants.

A carriage would take us from Eastport station to the odorous sardine docks, where Calder would be waiting for us with his open motorboat, a dory with an inboard engine, known to us as the "chug-chug." If the tide was high, getting aboard was comparatively easy, except for ladies in long skirts. At low tide, however, you had to negotiate twenty or thirty feet of steep wooden steps, slippery with slime, down to a little bobbing platform, to which the boat would be tied.

The two miles of sea crossing were never anything but rough, windblown and spray-drenched from the swirling tide and the flow of the St. Croix River. Once we had approached our wooden pier after a voyage of half an hour or so, we had to transfer to a rowboat if the tide was low to carry us in. From there, it was a matter of climbing another cliff to the house, while men with wheelbarrows fetched up the hand baggage. At the start and close of every season, the dozens of bigger boxes, crates, trunks and barrels went to and fro by horse-drawn dray to the Welchpool dock. This was the journey Mother organized as an annual ordeal, following the rigid example set by Granny, never questioning these trips, which must have been terribly hard on her. But Mother was a spartan; she suppressed any word of complaint. We children enjoyed every minute as an adventure and concluded that she did, too.

She did not fail to make the crossing to Eastport two or three times a week; she felt that she must go shopping herself, rather than send a housekeeper. The one concession she tried to make for herself was to time her marketing trips to coincide with high tide at Eastport, so that she would not have to clamber up and down those dreaded wooden steps.

Louis had attempted to fill in for Father while he was away. The rambling clapboard house, painted red with green trim, required careful maintenance to keep it in shape in a climate of constant dampness, fog and rain. Electrical wiring was no problem, since there was none; kerosene lamps supplied all our lighting. But that July, Louis acted as overseer of the island's plumber and his mate, who repaired the water pump. There was no oil heat. We relied for heating, a necessity half the time, on burning driftwood in the brick fireplaces, which were none too big for the purpose. Driftwood, gathered from the beaches after storms, also fueled the hot-water boiler, located in the area enclosed with green latticework under the house, which was raised on stilts above the ground. Hot water, let it be said, was mighty scarce in all the bathrooms. We invariably began the day with only cold water in the tubs and hand basins, even when fog hid the Dutch, wood-shingled roof and the drizzle did not let up for days on end. But Mother and Father both professed great enthusiasm for the place, possibly because Granny had, in a sense, forced them into her pattern of living by buying the house for them. We children accepted it as wonderful because we really could not conceive of spending the summer anywhere else.

This year seemed much the same to us as any other, except that we did not have to make the daily call on Granny. She expected that, whenever she was installed next door with the servant or two she brought up from Hyde Park. She was not there to drop in on us, as she did every day usually. Mornings were taken up for two or three hours with tutoring from Mr. Russell, who had been imported for the purpose, or from Miss Sherwood for Jimmy, Sis and me, starting as soon as we had eaten breakfast and picked up our rooms in the off-hand fashion which was our custom. Nobody pushed us very hard in that direction on Campobello or elsewhere. You could call us spoiled.

In the afternoons, if the weather permitted, we would go sailing or fishing or play games, with Louis acting as best he could as Father's understudy. "Dad has slipped on the tennis court and is going through a great performance of having everybody wait on him," Grace wrote to their daughter. "Mr. Howe has endless patience in batting the ball to Elliott and Hartley," Mother wrote to Granny, "and he thinks Elliott will be good, though I can see no signs as yet."

Waiting for Father to step up the pace of our pleasures, we enjoyed a flurry of unexpected high jinks. Mademoiselle Thiel, on whom Jimmy had developed a thirteen-year-old's crush, fell overboard when she was helping to swab the decks of the *Vireo*. A day or so later, she repeated her performance and was hauled out of the icy water of the Bay of Fundy, blue with cold. Mother administered hot lemonade. It could only have been at Louis' suggestion that she added a tot of Father's gin to the glass. "As all good things go by three," Father wrote back when he heard the news, "tell Mlle. to postpone her bath till she can fall off the rocks on our next cliff walk." That was in his first letter home after the Senate subcommittee smear, when he was applying laughter to heal the wounds.

Louis had picked up Father's enthusiasm for making and racing model sailboats, usually with hand-carved balsa wood hulls for lightness and greater speed. "Tell Louis," said the same letter, "I expect those boats to be all rigged and ready when I get up there, and I am very greatly put out not to be there now."

It was dull without Father. Louis and Grace found it hard to stay awake in the evenings, when Mother would stick to her habit of reading aloud to us by the living-room fire, which scented the house with the tang of burning driftwood, and Mademoiselle rubbed her eyes to ward off sleep.

On Friday, August 5, Father joined Van-Lear Black and a party of other people aboard the *Sabalo* in New York to bring his employer to visit Campobello. "I thought he looked tired when he left," Miss LeHand wrote to Mother in a chatty note a few days afterward. Black and his vice-president had a high regard for each other, dating from their first encounter, when the Baltimore financier thought Father was the "most attractive man I have ever met."

Toward the end of their three-day cruise, as they passed along the coast of Maine, bad weather set in. The *Sabalo*'s captain was a stranger to the treacherous tides and rocks of the Bay of Fundy, so Father, for the last time, took the helm. In dense fog, he navigated for hours, easing the yacht through treacherous waters he had known since childhood, repeating the demonstration of a pilot's skill as he had done aboard the destroyers. By Monday the *Sabalo* was safely anchored in Welchpool Harbor.

Father was bone-weary, but Black, forever restless, planned to spend only one night at Campobello, and Father was eager for us to see the wonders of the big yacht. All the family went aboard that afternoon. After Black's stewards had served cocktails on the huge fantail, we youngsters went home, while our parents stayed for dinner.

The next day, the weather cleared, and Father showed the party the techniques of cod fishing. He said later, "I baited hooks, alternating between the fore and aft cockpits of the motor tender, crossing beside the hot engine on a three-inch varnished plank. I slipped overboard. I'd never felt anything so cold as that water! I hardly went under, hardly wet my head, because I still had hold of the tender, but the water was so cold it seemed paralyzing. This must have been the icy shock in comparison to the heat of the August sun and the tender's engine."

He ignored the chill which seemed to cling to him, making it a joke that an old salt like himself could be so fumble-footed in taking an unexpected dip. With our visitors gone, we went sailing the following afternoon on the *Vireo*. He spotted the smoke of a forest fire on a nearby island, so we went ashore to help fight it. He cut evergreen boughs for us all, and we spent hours thrashing at the creeping flames.

Around teatime, he docked the *Vireo*, leaving the fire under control at last. "Our eyes were bleary with smoke," he remembered; "we were begrimed, smarting with spark-burns, exhausted." The solution, he thought, was a swim in landlocked Lake Glen Severn on the other side of Campobello. He led us on a two-mile dogtrot in our bathing suits. We swam across the lake to the far side, then scrambled out and over the beach for a quick plunge into the chilling waves of Herring Cove, before we trotted home.

We children were still shivering a little, so we bustled off to change into warm clothes, but Father was too occupied for that. Calder's motorboat had brought the day's mail and yesterday's newspapers from Eastport. Father could scarcely wait for that event of the day. "I sat reading for a while, too tired even to dress," he said. "I'd never felt quite that way before."

Close to an hour later, a chill ran through him. "I think I shall do without supper tonight," he said. "I'll go to bed and get warmed up. I mustn't catch cold and spoil the fun."

He had been counting on taking all us children, with the exception of young Franklin and Johnny, and any grown-ups who cared to come along on a three-day camping trip up the St. Croix River. He wondered whether it would have to be postponed if what he felt coming on turned out to be an attack of lumbago, which he had suffered before.

The next day was Thursday, August 11. "When I swung out of bed, my left leg lagged," he said afterward, "but I managed to move about and shave. I tried to persuade myself that the trouble with my leg was muscular, that it would disappear as I used it. But presently it refused to work, and then the other." Nevertheless, when Sis carried up his breakfast on a tray, she received a smile and a joke for her trouble. His temperature was climbing; the thermometer registered 102. Stabbing pains came and went. Mother decided early that morning to send Captain Calder to fetch Dr. Bennett from Lubec.

Even today, more than fifty years later, after the spending of uncounted millions of dollars on medical research, poliomyelitis persists as a deadly enigma, difficult to diagnose, preventable by vaccination in the overwhelming majority of cases, but still incurable. Polio is an unconquered enemy, held at bay only by the vaccines of Sabin and Salk.

Dr. Bennett knew no more than the average country doctor of his day. The thought of polio did not enter his mind. That was a disease of children, as its common name of infantile paralysis indicated. The reference works on his library shelf probably said, as others did, "The infection is caused by a special microbe, the nature of which is not fully understood."

In its early stages, polio mimics the symptoms of a dozen other diseases: headache, fever and sore throat. Bennett, "our faithful friend" in the words of Mother, who never found it in her heart to blame him, decided that Father had nothing more serious than a common cold and left for Lubec. Mother and Louis were not entirely reassured. To keep the house quiet for the invalid in his big bedroom on the second floor, they thought it best for our camping trip to proceed as planned, since the food and the tents were already packed. Miss Sherwood's mother and Grace Howe were put in charge, and our expedition got under way.

Before that excursion was cut short and we hurried home, each of us children had some of the same symptoms as Father but in much milder form. We had runny noses, slight temperatures, and, a tell-tale sign, an odd feeling of stiffness in the neck. These comparatively minor aches and pains got overlooked in the developing crisis which gripped us all. But according to medical opinion later, in adult life, there is very little doubt that all of us children had contracted polio, with nobody recognizing it. The symptoms slowly disappeared.

By Friday, Father could not stand. The pain in his back and legs began to turn into numbness as the day wore on, yet his sensitivity to the touch mysteriously increased, until he could not bear even the pressure of a sheet. As darkness fell, paralysis began to set in from the chest down, accompanied by such weakness in his upper body that he could not hold a pencil.

Dr. Bennett was recalled. He was at a loss to explain why an ordinary cold should take this course, though Father's wracked body was signaling every warning in the current medical books. "Early symptoms are fever (not usually higher than 103), vomiting, bowel disturbances and headache. Accompanying these there may be symptoms associated with other diseases, such as sore throat and infected tonsils, discharges from nose and eyes, and a distressing cough. Specially characteristic of infantile paralysis, however, are the pains that occur in the legs and feet, stiffness of the neck and sensitiveness of the spine. Complete paralysis of the limbs is liable to result within twelve hours."

Louis and Mother concluded that they must have a second

opinion immediately. In the normal course of events, anyone in need of anything more than everyday medical care on Campobello went to the mainland. Since Father's deteriorating condition put that out of the question, somehow another doctor had to be brought over to the island, the first seemingly qualified man they could find.

Louis volunteered to go with Dr. Bennett to search for the help they needed. Up until this time, Louis had been helping Mother with the round-the-clock task of nursing, snatching catnaps in his little downstairs room, while she moved a couch in beside Father. With the doctor, he crossed to Eastport, where they checked around by telephone to see who could be located. In Bar Harbor, Maine, close to a hundred miles down the coast, they found an old Philadelphia surgeon, Dr. William W. Keen, on vacation. He must have struck Louis' cynical eyes as pompous and opinionated, but the important thing was that he agreed to go back with them and stay overnight on the island.

Dr. Keen examined Father as soon as he arrived that evening, then repeated the excruciating process in the morning. Father now was completely paralyzed, even his face. The aging physician had no doubt of the cause: A sudden congestion of the blood had resulted in the formation of a clot, he said, which had settled in the lower spinal cord, producing temporary loss of movement. The condition would right itself in the course of time. Father should be able to return to work in New York by mid-September. Meantime, massage was essential, but until a masseuse could be obtained from the city, Mother and Louis could continue their nursing. He wrote a prescription and left instructions on how Father's tormented legs should be rubbed at regular intervals throughout the day.

Mother sat down to report all this to Rosy as soon as Dr. Keen departed to resume his interrupted vacation. "I hope you will think I am doing right and have done all I could," she said pathetically. "I do not want particulars to get into the papers, so I am writing the family that he is ill from the effects of a chill. . . ." She also asked Rosy to meet Granny at the pier on her return from Europe in two weeks' time, since neither she nor Father could be there to carry out that task, which had previously been one of the family rituals. Mother left Rosy to explain why, though, in fact, he did not go to greet Granny; Uncle Fred took over from him.

The only news Mother gave Father, whose fever refused to fade, was that the doctor was sure he could leave for New York when the

weather grew cooler and then, perhaps, in a wheelchair. Dr. Keen
was pleased to cooperate in her desire to keep the tragedy a secret.
"Do not say a word about Mr. Roosevelt," he warned the telegraph
girls at Bar Harbor as messages rattled to and fro. He happily
reported that a third physician brought in for consultation at
Mother's request, a certain Dr. Jameson, "did not know where he
was going or who the patient was until I took him into the auto."

On this second visit, Keen changed his mind about what was
wrong. Father, he concluded, must have a "lesion" in the spinal
cord, but the massages should be continued. In his heart, as he
confessed later, Father felt that God had abandoned him. He kept
his despair to himself. A man did not whine about trouble under
Father's code. "Now I don't want any sob-stuff in the relation of my
experience," he told a newspaperman afterward. "Of course, it was
a great shock to be stricken down at a time when, except for natural
exhaustion after a hard campaign, I felt myself to be in the pink of
condition. And it was rather humiliating to contract a disease of
which seventy-five per cent of the victims are children. But I am
thankful that my children were spared."

Hour after hour, Mother and Louis spelled each other in massaging Father's contorted legs and feet, a torturing treatment which
deepened the dark depression enveloping him for the first time in his
life. Yet when we children were allowed a glimpse of him through
the doorway, he grinned and struggled to gasp out a word or two in
answer to our weepy "hellos." He wanted to ease our fears, no matter
what his own were.

It is impossible to assess his courage or the emotions of Mother as
she compelled herself to perform the necessary physical tasks on the
body of the man whose intimate touch was only a memory. He had
to be bathed and rubbed to guard against bedsores. With Louis
panting from the effort of helping her, he needed to be lifted and
turned. All his bodily functions were paralyzed now. Catheters and
enemas had to be used to do the work of powerless muscles.

His condition grew worse, not better as Keen had forecast. On the
day following the first examination, Louis, darkly suspicious of him,
wrote a detailed letter to Uncle Fred, the calm, wise head of the
Delanos. That was the true turning point in Father's treatment,
resulting in an end to the kneading which brought him to the point
of screams.

Louis' explicit report sent Frederic Delano hastening to Boston, to consult Peter Bent Brigham Hospital about the best men to bring into the case. The letter "gave me the data I required to present the matter to the doctors," said Uncle Fred. The first specialist he saw, on August 20, read Louis' letter and another written by Mother. Dr. Samuel A. Levine, found by Uncle Fred, straightway diagnosed the illness of the patient he had not seen: polio, for a certainty. Uncle Fred passed on to Mother the expert's advice. "He said you should stop the manipulations and massage as unwise so early in the game. His argument is that the disease attacks the nervous system, and you must give the patient rest to rebuild etc. . . . You are aware, too, that the practice as to massage has changed, and the doctor says it is bad to begin it too soon. Let the patient have as much rest as possible for four to eight weeks."

He rated Dr. Keen as "a fine old chap, but he is a surgeon and not a connoisseur of this malady. I think it would be very unwise to trust to his diagnosis when the infantile paralysis can be determined by test of the spinal fluid. . . . As to possible other cases, Howe spoke of other symptoms felt by some of you. Don't let these be treated lightly. The disease is too serious to be trifled with."

A spinal tap was more than a test for polio. When the science of virology was young, it had not been discovered that polio is caused by viruses dstroying a portion of the brain or cells of the spinal cord which control the muscles; how much paralysis will be produced depends on the amount of nerve damage. But experiments had shown that the most helpful known remedy was to inject into the spinal column a dosage of blood serum taken from someone cured of the disease. Father was flattered, later on, to donate such serum because, he said, it made him feel like a hero without having to be one. "How many cocktails does one need," he joked to his doctor, "after a blood-letting to restore the circulation?"

On the arrival of Uncle Fred's urgent letter, the massaging ended. Mother, against the stubborn opinion of Dr. Keen, brought in a Boston specialist in polio, Dr. Robert Lovett, who immediately confirmed Levine's diagnosis. It was useless to try to determine the source of the disease, but the overexertion and chilling of ten days earlier had intensified the force of its onslaught. The massage prescribed by the surgeon in his tragically wrong analysis had increased the damage to muscle tissue. Recovery would be that much harder. Other than that, he said, Mother and Louis had done a fine nursing job; no professionals could have done better. He prescribed the soothing comfort of hot baths to replace the terrible pounding of legs.

Dr. Lovett, making a report to a colleague, thought that Father had "some facial involvement, apparently no respiratory, but a weakness in the arms.... There was a scattered weakness in the legs." He was optimistic about the outcome. "It seems to me that it was a mild case within the range of possible complete recovery. I told them very frankly that no one could tell where they stood, that the case was evidently not of the severest type, that complete recovery or partial recovery to any point was possible, that disability was not to be feared...."

Dr. Keen, off the case now and relaxing at the Seaside Inn in Seal Harbor, saw no reason for self-reproach. He wrote Mother a rambling, four-page letter, the greater part of which was devoted to his reminiscences of teaching surgery for forty-one years. He continued: "I wrote yesterday to Dr. Bennett, especially stressing the need for a second nurse. You have been a rare wife and have borne your heavy burden most bravely. You will surely break down if you do not have immediate relief. Even then, when the catheter has to be used, your sleep must be broken probably at least once in the night. I hope that he may be able, by having his urine drawn the last thing at night, to wait until the morning." One is tempted to wonder if the old doctor was sure which one of my parents was the patient.

He went on: "I was very happy that I succeeded in getting Dr. Lovett. On the way back, he told me that that evening (Wednesday) he and Mrs. Lovett had a large and important dinner party at Newport, and you know that Newport is very exacting in its social functions. It is one of the glories of our profession in my mind that, come what will, 'duty' always stands first. I have seen the time when for thirteen nights in succession I have not had a half or a quarter of my usual needed rest."

There was a hint of defensiveness. "On the way back also Dr. Lovett said to me, 'I do not recall any more puzzling or obscure case especially in its early manifestations than Mr. Roosevelt's.' I feel supremely happy in the definite result of our consultation and that the prospect is so bright for Mr. Roosevelt's restoration I think to complete (or at the worst almost complete) health and activity."

He added a final line or two: "As to the financial side, will you kindly send me at your entire convenience a thousand dollars."

When she learned the real nature of Father's illness from Dr.

Lovett, Mother fell into a momentary panic. Most health authorities rated polio as an infectious disease. Quarantine rules were generally strict, calling for victims and contacts to be isolated in their homes or in hospitals. Dr. Lovett calmed her. "No one knows exactly how poliomyelitis is communicated," he said. "I change my clothes when I go near my grandchildren after visiting a case, but I regard that as being entirely useless."

By now, members of the family and the three Howes constituted the total resident population of our house, the other guests having left one by one. Carrying the massive, inert patient into the nearest bathroom and making sure of the hot water supply doubled the load on Mother and Louis. He kept up his share of the work until a trained nurse, Miss Rockey, could be brought up from New York, then went down himself at the end of the month to pick up the threads of business affairs at the law firm and the bonding house in his new role as personal aide, companion and comforter to a helpless cripple.

The guilt he felt over the interminable hours of damaging massage he had given the man he was devoted to can only be guessed at. If the bond between them had needed final sealing, that was done now. He agreed completely with Mother that the outside world should not be told yet that Father was bedridden. Though the word had spread, he found, at the Wall Street offices of Emmet, Marvin & Roosevelt, at least no one was aware of the real reason. Louis kept the facts to himself. Under quarantine regulations, he should not have left Campobello. He stuck to the story that Father should be back by the middle of next month.

One of the people he impressed enormously was Father's secretary. "It really was awfully good to see him," she wrote to Father. "I like him so much." Marguerite LeHand was a perceptive girl, whose shining gray eyes could probe surface appearances. In the six months she had worked for Father, she had been drawn to him. They had rapidly built an exuberant, laughing relationship, full of jokes and gossip, not at all the conventional boss and secretary.

Back at her desk after a vacation, she had written to Father, knowing nothing of his illness, asking for a salary increase. In the middle of nursing him, Mother took time to reply, her strong handwriting showing no sign of pressure: "Your letter has been so long unanswered because Mr. Roosevelt had a severe chill last Wednesday, which resulted in fever and much congestion, and I fear his return will be delayed. He has asked me to write you that his impression is that you are now getting $30 a week, and he fears neither the F&D nor EM&R would be willing to jump to $40, but he feels sure he can get you $35 and hopes that will be satisfactory for the present."

Over the following weeks, a strange, three-cornered correspondence developed. The secretary, unaware that Father was incapable of opening an envelope, much less of writing a letter, kept up a steady flow of cheerful notes to him, while she faithfully replied immediately to any instructions which Mother sent.

To Father, she reported from his law office, "The mouse came out and has made me very unhappy, otherwise things are deadly dull." She felt badly about her raise: "I never would have bothered you about the question of salary if I had known you were ill. I am awfully sorry you are feeling so wretched." A week later: "I am making such marvelous strides in the law work that I feel sure you can soon turn over all your cases to me!"

On September 1, she said, and you could almost see her grin, "I have moved my desk and typewriter into your office, right beside the telephone. Do you object?" A day or so after that: "It is just getting ready to pour broomsticks, and *you know* how dark this office gets when that happens, so if I slip an occasional letter, please forgive it." Always lighthearted gossip, the weather and the hint of two minds meeting. "September 8: It is hot! There is nothing more interesting than that, I think. . . . I wasted a perfectly good evening seeing George White's 'Scandals' last night, and it is terrible. I never heard such perfectly awful voices from chorus girls." There was a postscript: "A letter came to me this morning addressed to *me*, 'Esq.' I love it!"

"I love it!" was always one of Father's favorite phrases.

Her correspondence to Mother might have been composed by someone else entirely: "I have made an attempt at not letting people know that Mr. Roosevelt is ill, but it apparently is known." And in a fascinating glimpse of the fact that Father somehow sensed that bathing in bubbling spring waters might be the answer to his pain, she wrote, "I wonder if Mr. Roosevelt still intends going to White Sulphur." That was White Sulphur Springs in West Virginia. The date of that letter was August 25, before polio had been finally diagnosed and Dr. Lovett had ordered hot baths for his patient.

In New York, Louis took on the same task as Miss LeHand in

restoring Father's spirits. "Everything in connection with your affairs is in the best possible shape," he said reassuringly, as impressed by this model young woman as she was with him. "I took breakfast with 'Uncle Fred' before your mama arrived and filled him full of cheery thoughts and fried eggs. That night, being so exhausted with his day's labors, he decided to take dinner with me, and we went together to the movies."

Mother's advance warning to Granny said only that "Franklin has been quite ill. . . . The island is really at its loveliest. . . . We are both so sorry he cannot meet you." Uncle Fred revealed the full facts to Granny when she landed on August 31. The next day, she was in Campobello, concealing her anguish as Father did, falling in line with his resolution to be cheerful at all costs. He had no problems with speaking now.

As soon as we had exchanged kisses with her, she went up to his room. "Well, I'm glad you are back, Mama," he said, "and I got up this party for you."

We children still had not been told that he had polio. "Your father has an infectious fever, and you must not go into his room," Mother told us. He remained completely paralyzed from the chest down, but he knew from Dr. Lovett the identity of the illness he was suffering; Mother had dreaded telling him.

Louis, trading on his reputation for square dealing with the press, had fed the Eastport correspondent for the Amalgamated Press a crumb of information that Father had been ill, but "he is now improving." Lovett's belief that the attack was mild encouraged everyone in that respect. Dr. Bennett, too, on his calls at the house insisted, "This boy is going to get all right." At that point, Father had implicit faith in what his doctors told him.

Louis held the options open for him to continue an active career in politics or in business, should that remain possible. Twelve days after the onset of the disease, Father authorized the use of his name in a fund-raising drive for Vassar, Mary Howe's alma mater. Though Louis had to sign for him since Father could not hold a pen, he agreed on September 12 to join the Executive Committee of the New York State Democrats. Even earlier, he dictated a letter to his law partner, Langdon Marvin, to let him know, "The doctors say, of course, that I can keep up with everything, and I expect to do this through Mr. Howe." Infantile paralysis, he jested, is a "cheerful thing for one with my gray hairs to get."

In that period of false hope, preparations got under way for Father to be returned to New York. Mother, struggling to think of everything, wanted to present a watch to Captain Calder in gratitude for his help. A "Dear Boss" letter from Louis, which he knew she must read, pinpointed his way of working with people, with tact, sly humor—and firm persuasion. Mother telegraphed him to buy the watch from Tiffany's, he said, "without mentioning whether it was to be a $1,200 Jorgerson or a Waterbury Radiolite; also to have it inscribed without mentioning what to inscribe on it! Lord knows, I have acted as your alter ego on many weird commissions, but I must positively and firmly refuse to risk my judgment on neckties, watches or pajamas."

As a man of total resourcefulness, Louis bought the watch and told the Tiffany salesman that he would stop by later with the inscription. "Don't send a night letter," he twitted Father and Mother, "as Eleanor's last night letter to me arrived at 1:45 in the morning on the day after she sent it, somewhat disturbing my slumbers."

Buying the watch proved to be a little premature. Father, buoyed by the expectation of recovery, spent hours every day trying to wiggle a big toe, knowing that muscles had to be worked or else they would atrophy. But two more weeks went by before he was anywhere near ready for the journey home. While he waited, he heard from Uncle Fred, who has been mostly forgotten by some historians as a key factor in Father's battle to get well. Uncle Fred offered some fatherly advice.

"To my mind," he said, "philosophy means in substance 'making the best of the situation,' or in other words taking things as they are, analyzing the facts, above all not *fooling* yourself, and, by intelligent reasoning, determining the right course to pursue. I never worry, I accept things as they are, I look forward and not back. I realize that you are up against a hard problem and hard, cruel facts, and yet I feel the utmost confidence that you will emerge a better and stronger man."

It was Uncle Fred, a highly successful railroad operator who had served as vice-governor of the Federal Reserve Board, who solved the problem of getting Father to New York with the minimum of jolting; he supplied a private railroad car, which waited on an Eastport dock siding. The task remained of carrying the patient to the car.

Louis was in charge of the arduous exercise in transporting an invalid, who could not so much as raise his head, out of the house, down the steep path, out onto our little pier, into Calder's bobbing "chug-chug" for the two-mile sea crossing, then up the hazardous wooden steps to the sardine dock for the final stage of the journey to the train. "This is my job—helping Franklin," he explained.

He had Calder nail together a homemade stretcher and engage island men to carry it. Father had his favorite fedora placed firmly on his head and our Scottie dog, Duffy, cradled in his arms. Someone lit a cigarette for him in the plastic holder Louis had given him. He stuck out his chin, flashed a big grin for us children as we mumbled, "So long, Pa," and he was lowered down the front steps in a canvas sling onto Calder's stretcher, headfirst, his legs tilted higher than his head.

He was determined not to display his weakness to any strangers, which included the crowd of well-wishers and reporters who waited for his arrival in Eastport. Louis passed the word around that Father would be landing at a distant dock, to draw the spectators there. Then he signaled Calder to bring the stretcher in at a nearer place. They loaded the stretcher onto a steel-tired luggage cart and bumped over the cobbles to the train. They passed the stretcher through an open window of his compartment, and Father was off to New York, where Granny was waiting. We all rode with him in the car, which went right on through to Grand Central.

He had been settled in, and the sweat on his face wiped dry, before the crowd found him. A reporter who saw him in the car told his New York *World* readers, "Mr. Roosevelt was enjoying his cigarette and said he had a good appetite. Although unable to sit up, he says he is feeling more comfortable."

His immediate destination was Presbyterian Hospital, which I would soon pass twice a day on my way to school. The specialist in charge of the case was an associate of Dr. Lovett's, Dr. George Draper, whom Father had known at Harvard. The records said he had acute anterior poliomyelitis. He still showed "definite signs of CNS (central nervous system) prostration. This is very marked."

But for the time being, Draper shared his colleague's optimism. When Louis at last broke the story to the newspapers two days later, he quoted Dr. Draper: "He will not be crippled. No one need have any fear of permanent injury from this attack."

F. D. ROOSEVELT ILL OF POLIOMYELITIS, said the New York *Times* front-page headlines, RECOVERING, DOCTOR SAYS. That day, Father dictated a note to Adolph Ochs, the *Times* publisher, to joke that as a result of seeing the statement in that august newspaper, "I feel immensely relieved because I know of course it must be so. I am ¨eling in the very best of spirits and have already been allowed to take up part of my somewhat varied interests."

The false dawn still painted the sky a promising pink. If Father was deceived, Louis appeared not to be. When Herbert Pell, of the Democratic Executive Committee, invited Father to attend an early meeting, Louis commented, "Mr. Pell had better wake up and hear the birdies."

Marguerite LeHand was not yet sharing the secrets. "Everyone is much excited about your coming back and much pleased," she wrote from the office. "By the way—I wish I could say, 'Your Majesty.'"

The Larooco

1924

1

FATHER dearly loved a bargain, and the haggling he had done over the price only increased his pleasure in the weird-looking boat which had just been bought as part of his program to teach himself to walk again. Compared with the trim lines of the *Half Moon* or the speedy little *Vireo*, this one was a barge, more like a floating summer cabin than a yacht, with no sails but two crotchety thirty-five-horsepower inboard engines, which had a tendency to balk during crucial moments of navigation. But it rode low enough in the water to enable Father to be lowered in a canvas sling to go swimming or into a skiff to do some fishing.

The previous owner of the houseboat had it on the market for a year. He was up against it financially, so Father could drive down the asking price from $8,000 to a successful bid of $3,750. Our strained finances, stretched to cover the upkeep of two homes, enormous medical bills and the education of us children, could never have managed the original figure.

"It's a pretty fair bargain," Father said when he took his first look at the seventy-one foot acquisition and concluded that she needed only recaulking. The price covered all the furnishings, including the brass double bed in the main cabin halfway below the waterline with the other sleeping quarters. He slept there at night and for his afternoon naps, unless the weather was insufferably hot, the mosquitoes were not hungry and the swarms of black flies that came out of the mangrove swamps were taking a holiday. In that case, he sometimes bedded down under the canopy on the railed deck above the main stateroom-cum-wheelhouse, which occupied the space over the little cabins.

He paid only half the purchase price, which was split fifty-fifty with John Lawrence, a Boston banker who was in Harvard's class of 1901, three years ahead of Father. Lawrence, too, was crippled in the legs. The arrangement between them was simple. All out-of-season and repair costs would be shared, with a joint account kept in Father's office. To his friend's approval, Father suggested, "Whichever one of us uses her assumes all maintenance expenses, including wages."

Wages ran to $100 a month for Captain Robert Morris and another $75 for his wife, Dora, who cooked and served good plain food from the galley, which lay forward. Two other men completed the crew, but finding them presented a problem; the captain was something of a martinet, and the turnover rate was high.

The *Roamer,* as she was called at the time of purchase, clearly had to be renamed by the former Assistant Navy Secretary, whose pride in seagoing matters had prompted him to design his own pennant when he held that office. He rather fancied *Larose* or perhaps *Rosela,* each hinting at the joint ownership, but he and Lawrence settled on an amalgam of the first two letters of "Lawrence," the first three of "Roosevelt" and the first two of "company." *Larooco* she became, pronounced to rhyme with "cocoa," when she was commissioned, under Father's New York Yacht Club flag and his own private blue signal, at Jacksonville, Florida, in February, 1924.

The search for a suitable boat began the previous spring, when Father, who had taken to prescribing his own methods for restoring power to his leg muscles, chartered a similar vessel, the *Weona II,* for a fishing cruise along the Florida coast with Lawrence and Louis. He had no hesitation about discussing his crippled condition. "What I am looking for," he said, "is a boat that is fairly low in the water so that I can easily drop overboard and crawl back on deck. Also, if possible, a boat whose cabin is not down a ladder."

He felt absolutely no embarrassment about the inevitable consequences of being unable to walk. At home with us, he would discuss the importance, muscle by muscle, of finding the best exercises for himself so that he might one day be able to stand without braces. He would ask whichever of his two older sons happened to be around to lend an arm to help him to the bathroom and stay to lift him. He felt no false modesty over the sight of his wasted limbs, which could support only a fraction of his increasing weight.

Together, he and Louis set the style of fun to be had aboard the lumbering old vessel with a spicy, daily record entitled "The Log of the Houseboat Larooco, Being a More or Less Truthful Account of What Happened, Expurgated for the Very Young." It was dedicated to Ananias and Sapphira, patron saints of lying fishermen, and lavishly adorned by Louis with line-and-wash drawings, like a medieval Book of Hours. Louis also drew up the rules, typed out by the girl everyone now called Missy LeHand, whereas the day's entries were handwritten, usually by Father. Sometimes a guest who really caught the spirit of the whole thing was invited to contribute. The rules said:

1. This Logbook must be entirely accurate and truthful. In putting down weights and numbers of fish, however, the following tables may be used:
2 oz. make 1 logbook pound
5 logbook pounds make "a large fish"
2 "large fish" make "a record day's catch"
2 inches make 1 logbook foot
2 logbook feet make "big as a whale"
anything above "whale" size may be described as an "icthyosaurus"
(Note—in describing fish that got away all these measures may be doubled. It is also permitted, when over 30 seconds are required to pull in a fish, to say, "After half an hour's hard fighting—.")

2. The poetically inclined are warned that *Larooco* does not rhyme with Morocco. Also the combinations "knows I felt" to rhyme with Roosevelt and "saw hence" to rhyme with Lawrence are not permitted.

3. Verbatim reports of the private conversations of the chief engineer with his carburetor must be represented only thus: "x ! ! x ! − ? ? ? x ! - - - ."

4. All references to "community life" must be written in code.

5. The leaves of this log are made to be easily removed. All frank opinions as to the character, habits and general personality of one's

shipmates written after a 3 days' nor'wester and no fish will be so
removed.

On their dawdling days of cruising, Louis demonstrated that his
deftness with a rhyme had not disappeared under the pressure of
serving as Father's legs, ears and eyes in business, politics and every
place else that he went as the alter ego. He scribbled:

> *Colder, colder grew the night, we really suffered pain,*
> *We'd sat and sat with rod and reel and fished and fished in vain,*
> *And that, we thought, was reason fair to take to rum again.*

This was more than enough to spur Father to try his hand at
versifying in a saga of his own, "Community Life." One extract will
serve to depict its tone:

> *You can slack off peak halyards and eat with your knife,*
> *You can dine in your shirtsleeves, and so can your wife.*
> *These are some of the joys of Community Life. . . .*
> *When they first come aboard, they think it's so nice.*

The captain was kept in a state of high nervous tension half the
time by Father, who would constantly urge him to lay off mangrove
islands or coral reefs where the navigation charts could not really be
trusted. "Well, let's go in anyway," Father would say, "and we'll
throw the lead-line to see what we're coming up toward." Morris
had to look for spots in sheltered waterways or off open beaches to
anchor overnight where the mosquitoes were not biting too hard so
that sleepers on the upper deck would not have to douse themselves
with citronella and where hordes of vicious black flies would not
darken the screens of the cabin windows. Who slept where on the top
deck was a matter of some debate, having to do with the question of
whose snoring might disturb the others.

Each day began soon after first light, when the song of a hundred
different kinds of water birds sounded across the water. Some male
guests, after sleeping alfresco above, would seize the opportunity to
dive overboard *au naturel* in lieu of washing in the minute hand
basins. Livy Davis was one of the visitors who came and went during
the three months of the *Larooco*'s first winter cruise, and he turned

out to be a back-to-nature lover, to the point where Father's sense of propriety was upset. The log related the event:

> *Sunday, March 16.* Livingston Davis arrived at 1 P.M. weighted down with sundry wet and dry goods—he looks like a sick child and is recuperating from shingles, boils, bunions and cold in the head. A blowy day, and we stayed in Tavernier Creek, L. D. unpacking fishing gear and I making boats.
>
> *Monday, March 17.* Water too cold to swim and wind too high to go to reef. L. D. went to the R. R. bridge to fish and came back minus trousers—to the disgust of the two ladies. Earlier he had exercised on the top deck à la nature. Why do people who *must* take off their clothes go anywhere where the other sex is present? Captain Morris remarked that some men get shot for less.

The two ladies about whom Father felt so protective were Mrs. Morris and Missy, who had come down with him from New York in February. Missy's pleasures that season had been dimmed temporarily by the death of her father, Daniel, employed in the real-estate business in Somerville. The telegram reached her when the *Larooco* anchored off Daytona Beach. Father used his influence to get her an immediate train berth to Boston, then welcomed her back little more than a week later on a Saturday when she poured tea as hostess at a party for Governor Cox, his old running mate in the 1920 debacle.

Louis was the tireless go-between who made certain that Father's political career was in no way finished, even if so far it had proved impossible to get the boss back on his feet again. The cruises of the houseboat served a multitude of purposes in their planning and plotting. Father could enjoy himself, far away from home and his two offices, which was important for his morale, but Louis kept him in close contact with the outside world, filtering out inconsequential or irritating affairs, focusing on priorities only.

Discussions with Cox were one such priority. Father still maintained that, given enough time, he would walk once more without braces or crutches or hands to help him. He was ready to get back into politicking, but as a featured player, not a star. He must concentrate, to the exclusion of everything else if necessary, on making himself entirely whole again. He and Louis had already sized up the year as another bad one for the Democrats. That put them in a

minority among party leaders, who whooped with glee over the
Teapot Dome oil scandals following Harding's sudden death, which
put Coolidge in the White House and branded Interior Secretary
Albert Fall as a crook for accepting bribes.

"There is no question," said Father, with his customary tolerance,
"that poor old Harding was perfectly honest himself, but was not
the kind of man who could ever tell the difference between a real
friend and a crooked one, and he allowed himself to be surrounded
by a pretty rotten crowd."

But American industry was booming, as he knew at the Fidelity
and Deposit Company, where he continued as a $25,000-a-year
vice-president in a "Van" and "Frank" relationship with Black.
New highways were being built, automobiles were streaming out of
Detroit, radios and washing machines were changing domestic living. "I cannot help feeling," he said, "that Harding's unfortunate
taking off has helped rather than hurt the Republican Party."

Nevertheless, Al Smith, a Catholic, a dandy, and an open enemy
of Prohibition, was rearing to take a crack at being elected President.
As early as January, Father had pledged himself to support his
candidacy on the basis of his reputation as a progressive and effective governor of New York. Though cocktails were routinely served
at the evening "happy hour" on the top deck before dinner in the
Larooco, Father's public statements qualified him as a "moderate
Dry," in the terminology of the times. He and Louis shared some
doubts about Al.

"In one way, at least, Smith is much drier than he used to be,"
Louis commented. "How long he has sworn off for this time, God
knows. Let us trust until after the national convention."

Father was more tactful in replying to a question from the
president of Vassar's wife, Mrs. Henry MacCracken, about Smith's
drinking habits. "I can only tell you that he used to drink beer in the
old days, that after 'prohibition' came in, he tried drinking whiskey
and found that it was poison to his system. Since last autumn, it
happens to be a fact that he has been entirely on the water wagon,
and you need have no fear that he has ever been or would ever be a
drunkard."

The main purpose of Governor Cox on his visit to the *Larooco* was
to sound out Father on whether he might be available if the need
arose to manage Al Smith's campaign for the nomination before the
Democrats' convention in Madison Square Garden late in June.

Father permitted Maunsell Crosby, Harvard class of 1908, a Rhinebeck neighbor and a regular cruising companion, to mix the cocktails that evening, while Missy took care of the tea.

She spent virtually every hour of the day with Father, her fair skin lobster red from the beating sunlight no matter what oils and lotions she applied and with even more mosquito bites than the rest of us. They were partners in work, when she wrote his letters and took care of the mail, and in play, too. She joined him in the fishing parties that chugged off in one of the sea skiffs, which were an essential item of *Larooco* equipment. With his wrestler's shoulders, built up by constant exercise, he could land any fish he hooked. The following year, on a similar cruise, he was thrown to the deck in a rain squall that blew up after he had a thirty-five-pound barracuda on his twelve-thread line. In darkness and blinding rain, they found the *Larooco* pounding heavily at anchor. Missy clambered safely aboard, but Father, following her, was thrown to the deck of the skiff, with one uncontrolled leg twisted under him and possibly broken. They were somewhere close to Tavernier, a village named for a buccaneer, on the Florida Bay, with Miami and the nearest doctor more than a long day's run away.

After a night of more heavy weather, the *Larooco* crept northeastward up the Intercoastal Waterway into Biscayne Bay. Everyone on her kept his ears cocked, wondering if her ancient engines would hold out. She chugged along without complaint all day, until nightfall compelled them to anchor again. Early the next morning, they were off on the last lap. Missy went ashore at Miami to find a doctor for Father's swollen and discolored leg. The diagnosis brought them profound relief. A fracture in a paralyzed limb can be so slow to heal that gangrene is a danger, but Father had nothing more serious than torn knee ligaments. Nobody thought to bother Mother with the news.

The *Larooco* was turned about for the run back to the keys, this time to Duck Key, about halfway along to the tip of the peninsula at Key West. Four days of Missy's nursing got Father on his feet again and out on deck with a stiff brace on his slowly healing leg. Tom Lynch, his old Poughkeepsie comrade, came aboard in time to celebrate what Father, with his incorrigible dedication to atrocious punning, called "Birthington's Washday" on February 22. "After lunch all off to Duck Key and swam in shallow water among the sponges," he noted in the log. "Business of washing each other's backs with sea soap. After grog, Missy and Frances rowed over to 'Whileaway.' . . . Service on deck in eve. . . .' "

Frances was Mrs. Henry de Rham, the shingle-haired Catholic beauty who had been one of Father's idols before his marriage and hers. "Grog," said his next day's entry, "in midst of glorious sunset which was almost as poetic in coloring" as the nightgowns of Frances and Missy. Frances was one of perhaps a half dozen women whom Father was delighted to welcome aboard "the old *Laroo*," along with about the same number of men who enjoyed those lazy days of fishing for game fish and always for the galley, too, so fresh-made chowder and every delicious variety of seafood appeared at most evening meals. Cynthia Mosley, wife of Sir Oswald, who at the time was a respectable Member of Parliament and not the British Fascists' leader of the 1930's, was another lovely-looking woman high on Father's preferred list. He thought so well of her that she was accorded the rare honor of keeping the logbook for a day.

To certain kinds of people, he sparked like a dynamo. Resourcefulness and good humor weighed heavily with him in a man. In a woman, he looked for warmth of spirit and physical attractiveness. Artificiality he could not stand. His comments on Palm Beach when the *Larooco* put in there showed that: "I found the growth of mushroom millionaires' houses luxuriant. The women we saw went well with the place—and we desired to meet them no more than we wished to remain in the harbor, even an hour more than necessary."

Guests came aboard for a weekend, a week or longer and were immediately caught up in the whirl of things, if they were Father's kind. Swimsuits were the order of the day until cocktail time, when men changed into slacks and shirts and women into summer dresses. Anyone who did not want to fish could help with odd jobs of painting ("Painted three-quarters of a chair—booful blue," Father reported in the log) or dip into what he called the "library of the World's Worst Literature." After dinner, there were bridge or poker games for penny stakes ("The Admiral won all of 41½ cents," Louis noted on one of Father's winning nights) and marathon Parcheesi tournaments, in which Missy usually came out ahead ("Ma and Pa Cheesy," in Father's words).

Sis, a quite dazzling blonde by now with her thoughts turning to marriage, came down at the end of one of the cruises, which Father relished for four consecutive winters. Jimmy and I both joined in on a number of separate occasions during vacations from Groton,

The pictures on these pages, with few exceptions, come from
   my personal collection. They evoke the people and
the events that determined my parents' lives, beginning
   many years before this morning when young
Franklin Roosevelt and the girl he married stood
   waiting between trains at Eastport, Maine, on their

A May morning at Hyde Park, 1912. Father took this picture of Sis and Jimmy on the swing, where he latter exercised his crippled legs. He caught them again, both a little shy (below left), then with Mother on the steps of Granny's house before the new wing were added (below right). I was twenty months old (bottom left). Mother swings Sis (bottom right).

Granny dressed up for an afternoon call, perhaps to take tea with the Vanderbilts.

She took Father off cruising in the Caribbean in the forlorn hope that he would find someone other than Mother to be his wife.

Golf was a favorite game of Father's before disaster struck at Campobello.

He could also be exceedingly formal in an English suit and his Harvard pince-nez as a young New York state senator.

With Hall Roosevelt (center)
and Maunsell Crosby,
duck hunting in Louisiana,
December, 1920.

(Bottom Left)
Louis Howe, who made a
President of the United States.

(Bottom Right)
Laura Delano, "Aunt Polly"
to all of us, who made sure
that Lucy Mercer remained
more than a memory.

Anna Roosevelt (above), who feared that her daughter, Eleanor, would be an ugly duckling. (Left) The solemn little girl is Mother, in the distant embrace of the grandmother none of us children ever knew. (Bottom Left) Elliott Roosevelt, my grandfather, a misjudged man. (Below) Mother had a fancy for sailor suits for her children, myself included.

Missy LeHand, who dedicated herself to Father.

Lucy Mercer, a love that lasted to the final day.

Mother on her wedding day.

Mother and Father in a new birch bark
canoe set out to race two Indians and their
passengers clean around Campobello Island.

A summer day on Campobello when
the world was young and my parents still
shared life together.

where I was following, most reluctantly, in my parent's footsteps. Mother had backed me in my wish to go to public school in Hyde Park, but "Father knows best," said the head of our family, in a rare intervention in his children's affairs.

Going fishing with him made all necessary amends where I was concerned. It was a new challenge, a new world opening up for me. Sometimes, we fished in the bayous of the Ten Thousand Islands, which are not true islands at all, but a maze of mangrove roots twisting out of the water, with fish teeming among them. He loved to demonstrate the various different kinds of fishing to be done, from using six-ounce fly rods to the heavy equipment needed for tarpon. He taught me the tricks of keeping your catch out of the mangroves. They would head for those roots once they were hooked, and once they got in there, your line could snap before you knew it.

One glorious day in March, when I was a chunky fifteen-year-old, his logbook entry said: "Last night we caught the record fish of all time! Elliott had put out a shark hook baited with half a ladyfish and about eight o'clock we noticed the line was out in the middle of the Creek. It seemed caught on a rock and we got the rowboat and cleared it. It ran then under *Larooco*, and with E. and Roy and John and the Captain pulling on it, we finally brought a perfectly enormous jewfish alongside. We could just get his mouth out of water and put in two other hooks and a gaff. Then Roy shot him about eight times through the head with my revolver. As he seemed to be fairly dead, we hoisted him on the davit, which threatened to snap off at any moment. He was over seven feet long, over five feet around, and his jaw opened eighteen inches. We put him on the hand scale this morning, which registers up to four hundred pounds. He weighed more than this, as he was only two-thirds out of water, so we figure his weight at between four-hundred-fifty and five-hundred pounds. . . ."

The co-owner, John Lawrence, showed up no more than once to go cruising with us. Though he sensed, as he once said, that "Franklin had very few real friends," he liked a less boisterous life than the *Larooco* offered every day from the time we gathered in Father's cabin, where Mrs. Morris served him breakfast in bed and plans were laid out for the next twenty-four hours. There was usually a brief chat, too, about what was happening in the country and the world, as reported in the newspapers, which were picked up every time we docked.

Lawrence, year after year, pleaded pressure of business as the excuse for his nonappearance. "You need to change your doctor," Father told him, "and again come under the administrations of old Dr. Roosevelt. . . . The business will survive during your absence. It is one of the horrible comments on the indispensableness of each of us that the foregoing is true in every indispensable businessman's business that we know of. . . . If you will cut yourself off from home, business and all worries completely for two months, I will guarantee to have you back to good health on the *Larooco*."

The main problem caused by his friend's persistent absence was, frankly, money. Under the terms of their arrangement, Father carried the full load of expenses when only he used the boat. The ship chandlers' bills ran high, when there could be as many as thirty guests at a time if Father wanted to entertain someone such as William Green and a delegation from the American Federation of Labor. "Grog" from the bootleggers was expensive, too, but in Father's case a cocktail or so was Dr. Roosevelt's own prescription. It helped to soften the twinges and warm his legs when the chills set in, making him sit and gently rub them.

Father was apt to ignore financial problems; he was chronically slow in paying bills. Mother's acceptance of the hair shirt as a permanent costume made her almost pleased to have a desperate shortage of cash added to all her other worries. At the time of the boat's first commissioning under Roosevelt colors, Jimmy was urging her to "please write Father that he still owes me $202. I don't know his address, so I can't."

Simultaneously, she was writing to Florida, "I find after paying all the household bills up to date and cash for food . . . I have $151.16, which I can put in my account and deduct from your Xmas check to me. . . . You still owe on Xmas, weddings etc. . . . $398.54. . . . Please send me what you can . . . but in any case be sure to send me the house $1,000 so I will *get* it on the 1st. . . ."

During his second month away, when Missy had just returned to the boat after attending her father's funeral and Livy had disgraced himself by removing his pants, Father lopped $300 off the family budget on the ground that his absence cut the food bills and called for one less household servant, a saving of $80 a month. There *were* two fewer to feed in New York, Mother acknowledged, "but you hardly eat $220 worth of food and the regular expenses go on the same as ever. . . . I just pray I will have enough with your $700 and my $300 this month." The inescapable inference was that, under

Cousin Henry Parish's cautious management, Mother's trust fund had begun to shrink alarmingly, in spite of the general boom on Wall Street.

At one point in that period, our family cash situation got so critical that Father had to surrender some of his prized naval prints and ship models to an auction house, New York's Anderson Galleries, to raise $4,537. He was increasingly reluctant to go begging to Granny, who would have been more than happy to tighten the control over him which her money inevitably exercised. He was all too aware that she disapproved completely of the course he had chosen for himself, just as she perpetually frowned on Louis and, of course, on Missy.

Granny was beginning to be bothered with arthritis, which put her temporarily on crutches and ultimately had her walking with a cane; she did not once set foot on the *Larooco*. Mother, all reports to the contrary notwithstanding, did not go aboard until the old boat's days were almost over in 1925. As a special favor to his most notable legal client, Julian Goldman, president of multiple chains of stores, Father encouraged him to write up the log that Sunday, March 8. His account combined a touch of irony with a telling picture of Mother:

"Could we commence the Sabbath in any better way than to proceed to the station to greet the heavenly Mrs. Roosevelt? . . . Mrs. Roosevelt upon her arrival at the *Larooco* vindicated my high opinion of her by seizing the heavenly deck for her sleeping quarters. Mosquitoes, flies, etc. mean nothing to her so long as the citronella holds out. The lunch was delightful. Bowing to the latest arrival from the civilized world . . . we listened with much interest to charming stories about the Roosevelt children. . . ."

That afternoon, Father caught a fish. Mother stayed aboard knitting and reading. After dinner, she joined the captain in evening services, "which were concluded by all singing 'Onward Christian Soldiers.' A rubber of bridge, a hasty retreat by FDR, who with his big boyish smile found it was time to retire as he was about to lose, concluded a perfect day."

Mother had less felicitous recollections of her first trip South in winter. She tried her hand at fishing, but caught nothing. The nights which the *Larooco* spent anchored in some moonlit backwater seemed strange and menacing to her. Miami struck her as a positive nightmare when she went ashore to buy provisions. "I had never considered holidays in winter or escape from cold an essential part of living," she said primly, "and I looked upon it now as a necessity and not a pleasure."

2

The most necessary business that occupied Father on every possible day on the *Larooco* was the exercise of his body. Every morning, unless the weather was too cold for it, he put on his black swimsuit, the tank type with legs reaching halfway down his thin thighs. His two heavy steel braces stayed in his locker; he detested wearing them. They chafed his flesh painfully. More than that, they were a symbol to him of the disability he had set his heart on conquering.

He would swim in virtually any water, even if sharks were known to be around. For preference, he chose the shallow sea, shelving up to a nearby beach. He swung himself with his massive arms to the ship's stern, to ease himself down on a rope into one of the fishing skiffs. Missy watched and helped, as smiling and relaxed as he was.

"Missy," he might say, "if you get any more sun today, we can use you tonight as a port running light and save some oil."

Her strong face would break into a broader smile, showing teeth that were slightly overlapped. No one would have called her exceptionally good-looking, but, five feet seven inches tall and straight-backed in a swimsuit, she had considerable sexual attraction. One of us, a guest or a crewman, would tug the starting rope of the outboard or pick up the oars to row, and we would be off for another session in "old Dr. Roosevelt's" recovery program.

"The water," he said, "put me where I am, and the water has to bring me back."

Lowering himself unaided over the side of the skiff, he could swim like a seal, his massive shoulders pulling him through the water. He was a real champion at water polo. In the shallows, he could take on two of us at a time in wrestling. More important to him, in shallow water, he could stand upright like the man he once had been. He had come a long way since his discharge from Presbyterian Hospital more than two years ago when, after six weeks in bed there, the bleak medical record stated, "Not improving."

Two fears had haunted Dr. Draper. Would bladder infection set in? And, as he wrote to Dr. Lovett, suppose that "when we attempt to sit him up he will be faced with the frightfully depressing knowledge that he cannot hold himself erect." But the danger of infection had passed, and catheters were no longer necessary. Father, by pulling up on the strap over his head, was strengthening his arms and helping to turn himself in bed.

Dr. Draper believed that "the psychological factor in his management is paramount. He has such courage, such ambition, and yet at the same time such an extraordinarily sensitive emotional mechanism that it will take all the skill which we can muster to lead him successfully to a recognition of what he really faces without crushing him."

In Father's judgment, the doctor had to be considered a pessimist, in spite of his professional eminence. When Josephus Daniels, one of a flock of visitors, came to call on the patient who lay flat in bed, Father beckoned him over and sent him staggering with a friendly punch. "You thought you were coming to see an invalid," he said, chuckling, "but I can knock you out in any bout."

Granny's commanding instinct was to take him straight from the hospital to Hyde Park, to shelter him there, with possessive love and unstinted money, from further hurt. She was far from being alone in thinking of him as a life-term invalid whose dream of becoming President like Uncle Ted had been abruptly ended. Mother had similar thoughts to Granny's. In her stoic's view, he should accept his fate and make the most of whatever ability was left to him. Only Father and Louis had the unimaginable gall to think that the game was not over and the dream could still be realized.

Father refused point-blank to take sanctuary in Hyde Park. To continue in politics and business, he must be in New York. He was taken by ambulance back to East Sixty-fifth Street, where a wheelchair was bought for him. Within a day or so, he could partially swing himself into it by means of a strap and ring hung from the ceiling of his quiet third-floor bedroom at the back of the house. He suffered a serious relapse within three weeks, when his temperature shot up to 101 again and sudden pain in his eyes raised the question in Draper's mind whether Father's sight might be affected. Granny, in her house next door, seized the opportunity to press her relentless crusade to take her son home.

She dreaded the day when the crutches and braces prescribed by Dr. Draper would arrive. She was so wrapped up in anxiety about him that she hated to see him make the least physical effort. She could not understand that his gut drive for independence was more powerful than her own. The connecting doors between the two houses were constantly opening as Granny came and went, until Mother in self-defense had a big breakfront moved against the entrance which linked the twin dining rooms. Granny's resentment of her daughter-in-law's newfound determination flared up over that. She saw it only as insulting ingratitude, coming from someone who had unfailingly needed and begged for her help in the past.

"In many ways," Mother remembered, "this was the most trying winter of my entire life." Discussions with Granny about Father were "somewhat acrimonious on occasion," she said mildly. There were, in reality, bitter, running arguments which left Mother fluttering with rage and Granny with her jaw outthrust in indignation. "She always thought that she understood what was best, particularly where her child was concerned, regardless of what any doctor might say," Mother recalled.

The fact that Louis had moved in with us added high-octane fuel to Granny's righteous anger. To put him as close as possible to Father, he was given the big bedroom with its private bath on the third-floor front. He had a habit of burning incense there in the evenings, in the belief that it eased his asthma. The sickly fumes filled the house and filtered through to Granny's patrician nostrils, a constant reminder of the ill-mannered intruder—"that ugly, dirty little man," as she called him—who represented everything she wanted her son to give up.

During the daytime, when Louis worked downtown at Father's two offices, his room doubled as a place to sit for Miss Rockey, the nurse. Sis, who was fifteen, had the choice of using the room, too, or having a little bedroom completely to herself on the fourth-floor rear. She chose that for the privacy it gave her, on the same floor as Franklin junior, Johnny and their nanny. With nowhere else to go in the house, by now more overcrowded even than No. 1733 N Street, Mother slept on a bed in Johnny's room and dressed in Father's bathroom one floor down.

She made a crucial error, as she admitted later, in not taking Sis, Jimmy and me into her confidence and telling us what Father was going through. The wisdom of doing that was beyond her power of understanding at the time. There was no intimacy between us and Mother. To her, we remained children, too young and callous to be talked to seriously. Sis was chaperoned until she passed eighteen, and Mother still bought the suits of Jimmy and myself.

Sis was bewildered, like the rest of us children, by the transformation of feelings toward each other which we saw with painful clarity in the grown-ups. We had no basis of knowledge to enable us to comprehend in any way the workings of human emotion. Father, understandably, shied away from any discussion of sex. Instruction was left exclusively to Mother, who got no further in her embarrassed talks with us than the birds and the bees. Her method was to encourage us to observe the reproductive habits of the horses, dogs and rabbits which were kept at Hyde Park. Sis and I, at least, got to know how animals mate, but our education stopped there. I became a precocious expert on the breeding patterns of goldfish, which I carried religiously back and forth on the train between New York and Hyde Park until I was sent off to Groton and, in a sad farewell, dumped them in the ice pond in the woods below the house. Their descendants still thrive there, as big as carp.

Granny played maliciously on the situation that developed in the twin houses. Loathing Louis Howe, she needled her perplexed, adolescent granddaughter with the thought that she was being discriminated against by being "banished," as she said, to a dark cubicle while he luxuriated in the main bedroom. "It is inexcusable," said Granny.

Sis, who had recently been enrolled in Miss Chapin's starchy school a few blocks away and hated it, was encouraged by Granny to believe that they both were being shunted aside by Mother in her mysterious new fondness for Louis. At mealtimes, she would irritate Father so much that he would say, "Anna, I will hear no more from you. You may leave the table whenever you choose." She would rush sobbing to her despised little room.

Finally, she was provoked enough by Granny to go to Mother and demand that she must move into the third-floor front and Louis must move out. "You don't care about me anymore," she wept. "You never consider my feelings." Mother would have none of that. She showed no sympathy with her daughter's outburst. The room arrangements were not to be changed.

"It never occurred to me," Mother said, "that the time comes, particularly with a girl, when it is important to make her your confidante. If I had realized this, I might have saved Anna and myself several years of real unhappiness." She reached that conclusion in 1937, at the start of Father's second term as President. She added fondly: "Today no one could ask for a better friend than I have in Anna, or she has in me. . . . No one can tell either of us anything about the other; and though we might not always think alike or act alike, we always respect each other's motives, and there is a type of sympathetic understanding between us which would make a real misunderstanding quite impossible."

In the course of his next four years in the White House, events showed that she had been mistaken about the confidence she had suddenly placed in Sis. We all turned out to have long memories. It was impossible to discount the coldness with which Mother treated us when we were young or to be immune to the animosity we observed between the adults in our family.

Meantime, straight out of the hospital, Father forced himself into some of the most grueling exercises that a man ever devised for himself, confident that he would make himself walk by sheer effort of will. If not next month, then possibly the month following. If not this season, then in the one after. If not this year, then surely twelve months later.

His old fear of fire spurred him on. "If I ever get caught," he said, "I might be able to save myself by crawling." He began by dragging himself hour by hour around his bedroom floor like a child, his legs dragging behind him. Once his arms and shoulders were strong enough, he tackled the stairs of our house, although we had an elevator. Step by step he would climb, hauling his weight until sweat trickled down his face. He liked to have close friends or some of the family standing by for him to talk to and joke with. If he had to crawl to make himself independent, then he was going to prove there was nothing much to it.

He got down on the floor of his room to Indian-wrestle with all his sons, including Jimmy when he came home for Christmas vacation. "You think you can take the old man?" he would say. "Well, just get down here and try." He won, of course, every time. He had his bed moved so that, through a gap in the buildings, he could watch me roller-skate around the corner to school on East Seventy-third Street that first winter when he was housebound. He turned his mind to experimenting with lazy tongs to pick up books beyond his reach and with a park keeper's spiked stick to retrieve papers off the rug. Occasionally he would carry a book between his teeth as he crawled. More often, he clenched the cigarette holder Louis gave him and dipped the ashes in the swivel tray fitted under the seat of his wheelchair, designed by himself, which was built without arms so that it would fit our narrow hallways and the tiny elevator.

He was not yet ready to wear braces, and he was never reconciled to being carried anywhere, which he felt to be demeaning. Besides, Louis laid down the law over that: "We are not going to have the public see that you're crippled like that."

Soon after Christmas, the tendons behind his right knee tightened, pulling the leg up under him like a jackknife. Dr. Draper's remedy was to put both legs in plaster casts and, every day for two weeks, tap wedges deeper and deeper into each cast to stretch the muscles and straighten the legs. No pain had matched this. But by February, Father was ready for braces to be fitted.

The steel in each of them weighed seven pounds, and they stretched from his hips to his shoes. He could not put them on or remove them without help from Miss Rockey, Mother, Louis or one of us children. He learned to get up from a chair by lifting one leg with both hands, then locking that brace at the knee. After the process was repeated on the other leg, making them both as stiff as pokers, he would push himself up by his arms from a chair, hold himself erect and tilt forward, reaching for his crutches before he tipped forward into a fall.

Without feeling or power in his legs, he could only move like a stilt walker, swinging each leg from the hip. Yet that was enough for him to call in Louis and comb through the long tally of his business and civic activities to decide which he should concentrate on to keep him in the public eye, prepared to make his mark again when the time was ripe. Louis' pencil crossed off one name after another until they came to the Boy Scouts. "Let's leave them on the list," Father said. "I have a job to finish there."

With memories of the day at Bear Mountain when he stood bareheaded in the summer sun—only eight months ago, but in a different world—he wanted to help with a reorganization project. Through Louis, he issued a call for war veterans to volunteer as scoutmasters to raise the number of New York City boys enrolled from 20,000 to 100,000. He also took the opportunity to answer an anti-Semitic letter from an American in Paris, who argued that only "Nordic" and "old American" youth should be allowed to join.

"If you were familiar with the Boy Scouts," said his angry reply, "you would realize that thousands of Scouts are of Jewish origin. . . .

I want to suggest that you come back home and spend the next few years in getting to know your own country."

At last, he was ready to move somewhat toward appeasing Granny by revisiting Hyde Park for the first time since his illness. She was waiting for him, to press her pleas that he remain there as a country squire for the remainder of his days. Her chauffeur, Louis Depew, drove him to the calm, roomy house, a sharp contrast to the tensions which had erased all tranquillity on East Sixty-fifth Street.

At that time I came home from Buckley School one afternoon and found Mother sobbing uncontrollably in the sitting room, more pitifully than at the height of the crisis over Lucy. She had been trying to read to Franklin junior and Johnny but could not go on through her tears. My efforts to comfort her failed completely, and I left to look for Louis.

"Come on, now," said the little, gentlehearted man when he saw her. "Keep your chin up. Things will work out." For a long time he tried to console her, but it was useless. She still sat weeping on the sofa when their nanny led my two young brothers off to bed. The thought that she had somehow to make an appearance at dinner drove her to take refuge in Granny's empty house. She slipped through one of the connecting doors, from the turmoil at home into peaceful silence. She ran into an upstairs bathroom and turned the key. In an effort to control herself, she began dabbing at her flushed, lumpy cheeks with a towel soaked in cold water. She had never been fond of the face she saw in the mirror. "Ugly duckling" was an unhealed wound. Now the red-brown hair, which was all that everyone praised, hung unkempt, and her eyes were swollen with tears. Her fortieth birthday waited none too far ahead. In her heart, she felt that she was a failure.

She had failed as a wife and mother, failed to find pleasure in life, failed to make any mark as an independent being. Polio, she imagined, spelled frustration and failure for Father, too. The ambitions he had set for himself, which she had just started to share, could never be realized. The career she wanted in order to justify herself was impossible if she remained tied to an almost helpless cripple. She was constrained in a marriage between two hopelessly incompatible people, unloved and largely unwanted. Nothing could ever work out for them, it seemed, at that moment. It was assuredly the nadir of her existence.

But Mother's reserves of a special kind of self-centered strength were close to limitless. Despair was no stranger, but she refused to make it her companion. She fought down her tears. Reality must be stared in the face and its cruelty accepted. I believe that in her appraisal in those hours of anguish she erased whatever pity she might have felt for my father. She would go it alone, regardless of him.

In a guarded way, she hinted at that when she wrote nearly thirty years later, "People have often asked me how I myself felt about his illness. To tell the truth, I do not think I ever stopped to analyze my feelings. There was so much to do to manage the household and the children and to try to keep things running smoothly that I never had any time to think of my own reactions. I simply lived from day to day and got through the best I could." She also embarked on a career of her qwn, hesitantly at first, then with ever-increasing determination.

By the time she reentered our house to sit down to dinner with us she was her usual calm, composed self. "I eventually pulled myself together," she said afterward, "for it requires an audience, as a rule, to keep on these emotional jags. That is the one and only time I ever remember in my entire life having gone to pieces in this particular manner." It was, of course, the second time, but she tried to obliterate the memory of Lucy.

Granny's hopes of corralling Father once she got him under her roof again were quelled by the elaborate preparations he made for his exercises. He had a set of bars installed outside the house, ten feet long, with one pair of parallel rails at hip level, another pair high enough for him to swing from. He worked his way back and forth on these as part of his daily training. At his order, a metal-frame contraption was suspended over his bed, its purpose being to lift and lower his legs a counted number of times at every session. He had an exercise board, a traction frame and a device of his own design for hoisting himself out of the bed and into a wheelchair. He spent a minimum of two and sometimes three hours a day with these various pieces of equipment, then rounded out the morning by setting off on his crutches down the graveled road leading from the turnaround in front of the house between a double row of maple trees to the brownstone gateposts more than a quarter of a mile away. He should try this, Dr. Draper advised, until he could finally reach the entrance. Because he refused to quit until he was literally incapable of taking another step, the strain on the muscles of his legs and probably on his heart was enormous. Hindsight told him later that he may have done permanent damage to both.

Getting as far as the highway was usually too much for him. Once, in the middle of his exercises, he slipped and sprained some leg ligaments, which made it necessary to take time out from his recovery program. But he persevered, always with a friend, a guest or one of us to keep him company, so that he could chat and grin while he dragged his useless legs along.

Horrified by his struggles, Granny sent away to Europe for a battery-propelled electric tricycle, blind to the fact that he had imposed this iron discipline on himself not merely because he disliked being carried or pushed in a chair, but because he must *walk*. He tried the gadget out of politeness, just once, then never sat in it again. But Granny found it useful to help her arthritis.

Sis went up to Hyde Park that spring to recover from an attack of measles, which was followed immediately afterward by a case of mumps. In June, when Father and his nurse went to Boston to confer with Dr. Lovett, Mother followed her. She walked into the library one day and found Sis writing a letter to one of our cousins and looking very sheepish about it. Mother's view about any letters her family wrote or received was that she had the automatic right to see them. Her demand this time prompted Sis to burst out crying. She had been setting down her opinions of Louis, leaving no doubt that she could not tolerate him. When Mother read what Sis had written, the familiar icy look appeared on her face. "I shall have to make sure that you have no further contact with Mr. Howe when you go back to school," she said.

According to my sister's version of the incident, Mother wept again in the course of their conversation and, before it was over, promised to "make things easier for me with regard to Louis." That did not entirely jibe with Mother's claim that, after her "emotional jag" which neither Louis nor I could cope with, she was never again bothered by nerves and uncontrollable tears. But in the fall, in a kind of general post, Sis was given the big room on the third-floor front, Louis moved into my old room, and I was quartered in a front bedroom in Granny's house. The terms of the arrangement made with Granny called for its cleaning to be done by one of Mother's maids, not one of hers.

There were changes to be made in the house at Hyde Park, too. The little elevator, hand-operated by pulling on a rope, which was installed in what had been closets on the ground and bedroom levels, was put to constant use by Father, who found it difficult to crawl up the angled main staircase. Ramps were made to fit on the carpeted stairs leading down to the library and on another set of shallow steps in the upstairs hall. The little servants' sitting room at the far end of the front terrace, where we children had once been given lessons by various tutors, was converted into a study, with a Dutch door opening onto the porch. Father could sit and work there, glancing up at the huge pines and maples of the front lawn, which he had climbed as a child. A gravel path was put down to skirt the lawn so that the wheelchair could be pushed more easily, usually by Robert McGaughey, Granny's houseman, over to see Rosy.

Swimming was an essential feature of "Dr. Roosevelt's" self-prescribed treatment. As soon as the weather promised to be warm enough, he was carried to the ice pond, where he had dangled his first rod and line in boyhood. Lifted onto the stone dam, he would lower himself into the water, in which we had learned to swim. Depew or one of us stood by to help him out. But the temperature was often too low, and his legs would feel chilled. He was happy to be given the use of Vincent Astor's heated indoor pool at Rhinebeck. In warm water, he could convince himself that, no matter how long it took, the day would come when he would put aside the crutches and leave off the braces for good.

3

Granny reluctantly condoned the presence of Louis only during the hours he spent working with or entertaining Father. She refused to allow him houseroom otherwise. He had to resort to a cheap, rented apartment in Poughkeepsie, cheap because his Fidelity pay was his sole source of income and his finances were stretched more tightly than ours.

His job demanded all his time and very often more strength than he could command of his pathetic body. A home of his own in New York was out of the question. Living anywhere close to East Sixty-fifth Street meant paying more rent than he could afford, and Grace knew that she would seldom see him. Poughkeepsie was the answer, where she would be close to Mary at Vassar, and Louis, in theory, could relax on weekends.

As a Friday night commuter, he arrived home so exhausted that he wanted to sleep the clock around on weekends. And with Father spending the summer just a few miles up the Post Road, he spent much of Saturdays and Sundays at the house where Granny froze at the sight of him. If Grace was upset by his continual absence, she complained only to him, never to my parents.

Louis had placed loyalty to Father above any other allegiance, including his own family. He fretted over Hartley, whom he saw growing up with the same lack of closeness from which the Roosevelt children suffered. Louis, in his heart, lacked the same full measure of supreme self-confidence which Father enjoyed. Black moods of doubt in his ability to pursue their dream to its conclusion swept him now and again.

"It will not be such a very long time," he confided once. "All the doctors have told me that my terrible struggle had burned up my life and that between fifty and sixty some little thing—a cold or something like that—would take me away." He was now fifty-two, chain-smoking Sweet Caporals more heavily than ever, relying on sticks of incense, burned in a saucer, and dozens of varieties of patent medicines to keep his chronic ailments in check.

Before very long, he was compelled to live through the week on his own personal resources. As soon as Mary graduated, Grace went back to Fall River to make a more certain life for herself and Hartley and wait for those weekends when Louis could get away. She and Mother continued to exchange letters, two women with bonds between them which their husbands, in many ways, had been responsible for forging.

One of Louis' contributions toward his closest friend's recovery was to rekindle his interest in making and racing model boats. They sat for hours of the day together on the porch outside the Hyde Park study, Louis concentrating on new hull designs and Father on the carving and rigging. "A man diligent in his business shall stand before kings," Father might say, chuckling, as they made ready for their next race.

"Now who in hell said that?" Louis would grunt, bent over his sketch pad.

"Try Proverbs Twenty-two, you unbeliever."

A rare gift of appreciation to Louis was a handsome new Bible.

On the flyleaf, Father inscribed: "For Louis McH. Howe's Soul and Delectation and English, from One Who Has Read It."

Between them, they made twenty-seven models during the next few years. *Horse's Neck* was Louis' standard label for his, but Father passed up such irreverence for the more stately *Crum Elbow* as his favorite choice, the original historic name of the Hyde Park property. The departure point for the races was usually a boathouse. With one of us boys at the oars, Father and Louis set out in separate rowboats. The latest *Crum Elbow* and *Horse's Neck* were launched from the stern, with sails set to speed them across the Hudson, while the rowboats pulled along behind. In the spring, they competed for the Roosevelt Cup, in the fall for a similar gimcrack trophy, the Hyde Park Cup. A *Horse's Neck* had a habit of winning, but a model of mine once covered a mile in just under fifteen minutes. And timed by stopwatch, a balsa wood *Crum Elbow*, thirty-eight inches long, with six feet of aluminum mast, made an all-time record crossing to the far bank in ten minutes fifteen seconds.

Rivalry with Father, who was intensely competitive about new forms of rigging and fresh ways of paring weight, was a vital part of Louis' devious schemes for getting him into fighting trim for a future first in business and then for the goal on which both of them kept their sights fixed. Laughter also figured in the training program. Father's annual birthday parties with members of the Cuff Links Club were made to order for Louis.

On the first Christmas after the Cox-Roosevelt rout by Harding, Father remembered the team who had ridden with him aboard the Westboro campaign train by presenting each of them with cuff links engraved with his initials and those of the recipient. They held a reunion for each birthday, a dinner in our New York house, where Louis struggled perpetually to brighten up the state of gloom.

"We try to have stunts of some kind," he explained in a plot with the telephone company, "and this year we want to set up on the dining-room table what looks like a radio outfit with a loud-speaking horn, but which is really hitched in some way to a telephone set in another room, so someone can go in the other room and telephone fake radio broadcasts."

The necessary installation was made, and that night Louis fell happily back on his brief career as an actor. His humor, as usual, had an edge to it, but this was a stag party, so nobody, especially the host, gave a damn. Louis' rich voice sounded from the loudspeaker with a recollection of Father's day with the ladies in Jamestown when Mother stood enthralled by Niagara Falls:

"This is Station B-U-N-K, Skodunk, Maine. Before introducing our next speaker, I desire to broadcast this message. 'Chief Sweeney of the Jamestown, New York, police force requests all radio fans to assist in the search for two married women who left that town in the latter part of October, 1920. They were last seen on a railroad siding, talking to a handsome man about six feet tall, wearing glasses, a dark suit, a soft fedora hat and brown shoes. This tall gentleman was accompanied by a shorter man, about five feet two inches, also dressed in a dark suit, which wasn't pressed. He needed a haircut, leading to the belief that he was a one-time newspaperman. Any information concerning these ladies or men will be deeply appreciated by Chief Sweeney.' "

With help from the old gang, coached in advance by Louis, the birthday party then swung into gear with an uproarious interview with "Professor Irving Fishcake of Yale University" on the subject of political economy—Irving Fisher had been an adviser to Father on League of Nations topics. Louis' script supplied both questions and answers:

Q. What is a political platform?

A. It is a promissory note to the American electorate that is never paid.

Q. What has the income tax done for the U.S.A.?

A. It has made us a nation of liars.

Q. What are the duties of the Vice President?

A. To attend formal dinner parties and run the largest hot-air plant in the United States.

Q. What is the salary of a Cabinet officer?

A. $12,000 and leasing privileges.

Hard liquor was one of Louis' favorite themes, though he was careful about his own intake. At Father's poker games, Louis would be in charge of keeping bourbon in the players' glasses while he took steady sips for the sake of conviviality. Later, in his incredibly cluttered room in the White House, when the years had turned his face to the color of clay, he kept a litter of bottles of medicine, brandy, whiskey and wine on top of his safe, but he was in no way an alcoholic.

On his runs down to Washington on Father's behalf, he might drop a note to Charles McCarthy, urging him to "get the gang together and let me know the date for the big drunk," promising that "my brand has no wood alcohol in it, and I have my doubts of the batch you furnished last year."

As Father's go-between with their boss at Fidelity, Louis would report to his companion in plotting and partying, "Black insisted on giving me ten quart bottles of rye. I positively and firmly declined to let you consume that quantity between the time of my arrival and the 14th, so I am leaving ten of them with Mrs. Ramsey, the Hibernian housekeeper at your mother's residence, trusting there will be a half-pint or so left by the time you return."

His chameleon nature made it simple for Louis to adopt a different approach in his dealings with Mother. To her, he showed courtesy, patience and a deep understanding of both kinds of problems, those created for her by circumstance and those she relentlessly made for herself. She had to be converted from a nervous introvert into an outgoing political being for her to serve his master plan for Father. She had to be taught and toughened, yet find enough personal satisfaction in the process to ensure her loyalty to the man she no longer loved.

Training her to make speeches was one of the early steps. Louis' tutoring consisted of private lessons, in which he had her follow phrase by phrase the sounds of his own rich voice, which emerged like a kind of miracle from his hollow chest. "Have something to say, then say it and sit down," he told her.

When she was booked to deliver a speech, he would sit in the back row of the hall and conduct an inquest afterward on the mistakes he found in her performance. "Why did you laugh in the middle of it? What was the point of that?"

"Why, I really didn't know that I did."

"There wasn't a reason in the world for laughing just then."

"I know there wasn't, Louis," Mother would say meekly.

"So why did you give that silly giggle? Next time, let's cut out the laughs, and keep your voice down." Louis believed in firmness in handling everybody.

Speechmaking was the most painful thing Mother was driven to doing, the crucial dividing line between a private and a public personality. Louis realized that once she had conquered this problem, the rest would be comparatively easy. He worked on her without letup. Unless she could learn to be useful to Father in this way, she would get diminishing respect from her tutor.

He pushed her into the women's division of the Democratic Committee of New York State not, in Mother's opinion, because he "cared so much about my activities, but because he felt that they would make it possible for me to bring into the house people who would keep Franklin interested in State politics." She had no illusions about the motive underlying Louis' attentive courtship, but she was happy to be a chess piece in his game. She did what he demanded of her for her own sake, not for Father's. She was starting to enjoy herself in what is politely called public service, which is more accurately identified as the obtaining and exercise of power.

Her zest for it grew by leaps and bounds from the day she presided over a fund-raising luncheon for the women's division. Granny sat in the audience, nodding approval, while Mother trembled like an aspen leaf. But the job held a double attraction for the recruit. She counted herself extremely capable in matters of money. And money spelled power, as she knew from life with Granny. "When the women's division has its own money," the chairwoman said later when the days of her apprenticeship were over, "it can make its own plans and carry them through." If her own income had not melted away in Cousin Henry's charge, her drive for personal independence would have gone rapidly into high gear. As it was, the desire was slowly growing in Mother to find some fresh way of increasing the amount of cash available to her.

The dollars she raised as a result of the luncheon convinced her that she was ready now for bigger things. With help from Mrs. Thomas Lamont, our previous tenant on East Sixty-fifth Street, she set about drumming up $35,000 for the Women's Trade Union League. Louis showed her how to make up a magazine dummy, copyedit, and proofread to qualify her for editing a little monthly, *Women's Democratic News*. He found that she was hopeless at writing headlines, but, she said, "I became quite proficient in planning, pasting and so on." He wrote speeches for her and made her memorize them line by line like an actress with a script until she was letter-perfect. He repeated the instruction course he had once given Father in how a newspaperman can skim through a newspaper and not miss a word. "You're not a pro until you can read the New York *Times* in half an hour," he insisted.

Independence for Mother always meant the ability to drive a car. Freedom of movement was essential in her way of thinking. But handling an automobile presented a challenge rivaling public

speaking, and Louis had no time to help her. That summer, while
Granny took Sis and Jimmy to Europe, Mother had Depew give her
a brushup course. The pretext was that she wished to chauffeur
Father three times a week to swim in Vincent Astor's pool. The
result came close to a catastrophe.

She took Granny's Buick at such a clip down the driveway that, as
she attempted to turn into the Post Road, she swiped one of the
stone gateposts. "Your running into our gatepost was all right,"
Granny said, "so long as you were not hurt." But acid references to
Mother's lack of driving skill were added to Granny's store of ammunition, for future use against her.

A subsequent accident threatened serious injury to us all. She was
taking us through the woods in the Chevrolet station wagon to a
picnic. When the narrow road turned sharply uphill, Mother lost
control of a gear change. As the car rolled backward faster and
faster, she fumbled the braking. We went careening off among the
trees, promising to overturn until the rear bumper crumpled up
against a sturdy maple.

"From then on, I seemed through sheer determination to gain
self-confidence, and I have had no further accidents, though I knock
on wood whenever I say it," Mother wrote as First Lady in the late
thirties. That was before knocking on wood failed her, and she ran
into more trouble on the Taconic State Parkway. The crash, which
could easily have killed her, knocked out all her front teeth. Within
the family, we heartlessly considered that the replacements which
her dentist provided made her much better-looking.

As she slowly emerged as a political personality in her own right,
though still much in Father's shadow, she was a curiously
unprepossessing figure in public. Her shyness was disappearing, but
her physical awkwardness remained. She had an air of carrying the
burdens of the world on her rounded shoulders. In her sensible
tweed skirts and her hand-knitted sweaters, she seemed prematurely
middle-aged. She had never had the glow of sexuality which Father
still exuded, in spite of his lame legs. Now she appeared to be
completely asexual, as if any passions had been so long dampened
that they had died.

She mixed in a world of women, with only a handful of men
besides Louis whom she counted as friends. In that era when the
spirit of the suffragettes was a powerful force among organized
women, there was no shortage of man-haters in Mother's circle. She

had a sort of compulsion to associate with fellow sufferers in frustration, women like herself who had found it impossible to get along with the opposite sex.

Her understanding of the psychic forces which drove her was naïve. Her sensibilities were not tuned to sexual attraction of any kind, whether it existed between a man and a woman or between members of the same sex. On the strength of their appearance and knowledge of their living patterns, I suspected that some of the women, all dead now, who flattered my unwitting mother with their attentions were active Lesbians.

Her activities brought her into contact with a variety of women, married and single, dedicated amateurs and hard-bitten professionals in union or welfare work, idealists and self-seekers. With Granny's grudging approval ("Eleanor's work among the women will, I trust, bear fruit," she said to Father), she made Hyde Park a gathering place for the "she-males" whom Louis studiously tried to avoid, unless some pressing question of politics figured on the agenda.

There was Elinor Morgenthau from Fishkill Farm, the wife of Henry junior, "an awfully nice fellow," in Father's judgment, "and one who will be a tremendous asset to us in the county." Granny approved of her upper-class background and the Morgenthaus' unfailing contributions to party funds, but Father and Louis, in their unsentimental assessment of everybody's character, privately marked Henry a good-natured lightweight then and later.

There was Nancy Cook, the crop-haired, cigar-smoking organizer in the women's division, whose hobbies ranged from silversmithing to cabinetmaking. She had been a suffragette and a wartime volunteer in a British hospital, like her schoolteacher friend Marion Dickerman, with whom she now shared an apartment in Greenwich Village. Mother was immediately impressed by both of them, and she persuaded Miss Dickerman to try tutoring me. When I kicked at that and insulted her, Mother demanded once more that I must be dealt with by Father.

I sat beside his desk in the little study, where he could reach almost anything he wanted by stretching out for it with his lazy tongs. We talked about everything under the sun except my solemn-faced, temporary tutor. After something more than half an hour, Mother walked in. "Is everything settled?"

Father put an arm around my shoulder. "Everything is settled," he said. Out of loyalty to him, I submitted again to the scholastic instruction of Mother's new friend. She saw less and less of her old ones. Since she and Father never went out together, she thought it best to drop out of what many of her present companions sneered at as "society." She decided that she wanted nothing more to do with polite tea parties with her social peers, afternoon calls and sewing circles. She had done her duty in that respect for Father's sake in the past. That phase was over. It had brought her more anxiety than satisfaction. It was a poor substitute for being a true wife. Malleable to her new friends' influence, she turned her back on the empty rituals of receiving and being received. She had to find more rewarding ways to spend her time.

She won her first set of political spurs in the campaign, largely masterminded by Father and Louis, to make Al Smith the Democrats' choice for governor of New York again at the 1922 state convention, to be held in Syracuse the coming September. In spite of Al's perennial problem with liquor, Father maneuvered successfully to persuade him to quit the United States Trucking Corporation, which Smith joined as chairman at $50,000 a year forty-eight hours after his previous two-year term as governor ended, and try once more for his old office, which paid only $10,000. It represented a considerable sacrifice for a man with a big, growing family, but Al was itching to oust Governor Nathan Miller, the quiet homebody who had defeated him in the 1920 Republican sweep.

Al was the only candidate strong enough to beat down William Randolph Hearst, who was in an office-seeking mood again, with his eye on being governor as a step toward the White House. The king of yellow journalism had Tammany under his thumb and money to burn in buying votes. Father loathed everything he stood for and felt certain that nominating Hearst would spell suicide for the Democrats. Just how fantastically successful Louis had been in keeping the Roosevelt name alive was revealed when Father, counted as the best-known Democrat in the state after Smith, had to ward off a move to make him the nominee for the Executive Mansion in Albany.

In July, less than twelve months after being crippled, he had such confidence about reentering politics as soon as he could walk again that he wrote, "Though I am very much better and improving every day, I am still forced to get about on crutches and could not possibly run a campaign this fall. There is no possibility of my running for the governorship this year." He had to tell Al Smith much the same thing when he wanted Father on his ticket as candidate for the United States Senate.

Mother and Louis organized a mammoth picnic for Al at Hyde Park on the eve of the convention in Syracuse. Father and Louis by this time had sewn up the Dutchess County delegation for him. The party faithful milling around on Granny's lawns had the chance to meet Smith—and Father, wearing the Roosevelt grin as he was wheeled through the crowd, shaking hands.

Louis went off with Mother and Henry Morgenthau junior, who were both convention delegates. His telegram from Syracuse told the story in his best reportorial style: "AL NOMINATED WITH GREAT ENTHUSIASM, MORGENTHAU AND YOUR MISSUS LED THE DUTCHESS COUNTY DELEGATION WITH THE BANNER THREE TIMES AROUND THE HALL." As for Hearst, his name was "chogged in" once, Louis said, but it brought "not over five handclaps and at least fifty loud hisses." Dr. Royal Copeland, he said, had been named for the United States Senate race "in the hope that he could keep the cooties out of Congress."

Back at Hyde Park, Father and his heavy-eyed lieutenant took a hard look at the national situation and predicted that this would be a Democratic year. Unemployment was up under Republican rule; "normalcy" had proved to be a will-o'-the-wisp. Yet when Dr. Copeland came to dinner, he was gloomy about his prospects because most newspapers were ranged against him.

"Is it worthwhile even to try to make a real fight?" he wondered.

Father heard him out, then injected a dose of his own philosophy. "No fight is lost in advance if it is entered into with all one's mind and heart."

He was happy when a letter arrived from Al, with his account of events in Syracuse. "Everything went along first rate. I had quite a session with our lady politicians, as Mrs. Roosevelt no doubt told you. I was delighted to see her taking an active part, and I am really sorry that you could not be here, but take care of yourself—there is another day coming."

Mother took over the Buick on election day to drive voters, including Father, to Hyde Park town hall, where he had voted since he was twenty-one. His instincts were right. Al Smith won by the biggest plurality a governor had ever achieved in New York State.

The entire Democratic ticket, not overlooking the pessimistic Dr. Copeland, was carried to victory.

4

Myths sprang up around Father like weeds and grew like mushrooms. He played little part in creating them, but he let them flourish if they suited his purposes. Among all his political and business contacts, Louis cultivated the impression that the boss' total recovery was only a matter of time; it was simply taking longer than the doctors had originally anticipated. Another legend, which persists to this day, had it that a devoted wife, with virtually no outside help, nursed her spiritless husband through the ravaging disease. That suited the long-term interests of Father and Louis well enough. The public would be better off not seeing him carried like a helpless child and not knowing the truth about his domestic life.

Of all the concocted tales about him, perhaps the most fanciful was that in some mysterious fashion, polio completely changed his nature. He was pictured as a restless, flighty young man who learned to concentrate only when he lost the use of his legs, thereby acquiring fresh stability of mind and compassion through suffering. The playboy, it was alleged, was transformed into the statesman because he could not jump up from his desk.

People close to him, who should have known better, contributed almost eagerly to fostering this fancy. Frances Perkins, the inquisitive, sad-eyed woman who became his Secretary of Labor when he went into the White House, met him steadily from 1912 on. Seeing him at Hyde Park, she imagined that he "underwent spiritual transformation" as a result of poliomyelitis. Her perceptiveness as a reporter was questioned by some of us after reading, in her memoirs, of the "unforgettable picture" she allegedly saw "many times in summer" when "the family was on the lawn":

"Mrs. Sara Roosevelt in a soft, light summery dress with ruffles, her hair charmingly curled, sitting in a wicker chair and reading; Mrs. Roosevelt, in a white dress and white tennis shoes with a velvet band around her head to keep the hair from blowing, sitting with her long-legged, graceful posture in a low chair and knitting, always

knitting; Roosevelt looking off down the river at the view he admired, with a book, often unopened, in one hand, and a walking
stick in the other; dogs playing nearby, and children romping a little
farther down the lawn. The scene was like a Currier and Ives print of
Life along the Hudson."

That glowing, fantastically misleading description, incidentally,
continues to be reprinted by the Department of the Interior in its
folder on Hyde Park, which now, of course, is a national historic site.

Mother herself did more than her share in spreading the illusion
that Father was somehow transformed. His illness, she said, "proved
a blessing in disguise; for it gave him strength and courage he had
not had before. He had to think out the fundamentals of living and
learn the greatest of all lessons—infinite patience and never-ending
persistence." It was small wonder that the great majority of historians accepted those platitudes, at the cost of accuracy in depicting Father as what he truly was, a man who grew steadily in stature,
resourcefulness and zest for power from the time his school days
ended. Throughout his adult life, his was the same, consistent personality, the mixture, as perhaps his most observant biographer
noted, of lion and fox. There was just one, purely physical
difference: After 1921 he could not walk.

Men around Hyde Park who had known him since the day he
rode his first pony, Debby, on his seventh birthday detected not a
particle of change in him when he first returned as a cripple. He had
more time to spend with his friends now, that was all. He used his
eyes and ears to clarify his thinking and teach himself as he went
along, his habitual method of absorbing facts to fuel his brain. He
tried horseback riding again some afternoons, with someone leading
on foot and holding the halter. It was a tricky way to travel, since he
had no grip on the saddle with his legs, but he got around the dirt
roads and forest paths by the best means possible, to gossip with the
neighbors and tenant farmers about their fields and crops, about
fences that needed mending both literally and politically.

Moses Smith saw a lot of him as Father picked up the threads of
managing the property. Moses was the forthright tenant farmer on
property Father owned to the east of the Hyde Park house, a dyed-
in-the-wool Democrat who punctuated his salty opinions about
Republicans with squirts of tobacco juice. When it came to writing
speeches, Father kept him in mind. "The language must be clear
enough to go over with Moses Smith," he would tell us.

One afternoon Father rode past the old Wilkes farmhouse on Quaker Lane at the northern edge of town, where two old men and their even older sister scratched out a living raising chickens and selling milk. Nothing appeared to have changed there for half a century. After a winter spent in the warm South, Father heard the next chapter in the Wilkes' story from Moses. The snow had been deep and the weather bitter. One brother had been found frozen to death between the house and the barn, where he had been milking their cows. The older brother was in the Hyde Park poorhouse. The eighty-two-year-old sister had been committed to the insane asylum.

"Moses," said Father, "this kind of thing cannot go on. I am going to find some way or somehow to put over an old-age security program so that the poorhouse will be done away with."

When fall came, thirteen months after the disaster at Campobello, he made one more visit to Boston, to be fitted with new braces and a surgical corset by Dr. Lovett. As usual, Nurse Rockey, who had been caring for him all along, rode up in the car with him. It was the last trip of its kind. Determined neither to be thought of nor to be treated as an invalid, he dispensed with her services soon afterward. He hired no more professional nurses but a black man-servant to help him dress and to push the wheelchair.

His concern for fellow victims of polio prompted him to recommend the doctor to other paralytics, though he was not satisfied that Lovett was being imaginative enough in his treatment. The new braces had to be returned, since they dug into his calf. "The corset I am getting on fine with so far as walking goes," he told the specialist, after a month or so of trial. "It almost cuts me in two when I sit down. I am more glad than ever that I do not belong to the other sex."

He started experimenting with the methods of an assortment of practitioners, some of whom his doctors frankly looked upon as quacks. The equipment they sold or recommended arrived regularly at East Sixty-fifth Street when we moved back there. He was intrigued with a Kansas City doctor's aerotherapeutic methods, which involved use of an oxygen tank. One acquaintance recommended "Abraham's Treatment," a form of osteopathy, but Father rejected that. "It is merely a question of time before I am able to get about again without the use of crutches as at present."

He wanted to buy a rowing machine, but Lovett said he was not ready for that yet. His impatient charge tried out an old-fashioned children's swing. "I sit on one seat, put my feet on the other seat and push down and pull up with my legs, thereby making the swing go forward and backward. It seems to develop the knee muscles in a splendid way," Father thought.

Someone suggested an electric cart to ferry him around Hyde Park. He turned that down because the roads were too rough. "I have been able to sit on a horse and be led around the place. Of course, I would fall off if the horse reared. What I need . . . is a horse which is constitutionally unable to trot and which is also guaranteed against any sidewise motions."

As the months added up to years, he was ready to try anything. He studied the methods of practically every doctor in the country. He could talk knowledgeably about the approaches of Lovett, Goldthwaite, Hibbs and the possible benefits of Professor Emile Coué, the French advocate of autosuggestion: "Every day in every way, I am getting better and better." Mother privately considered all this to be mostly a waste of time.

He bought a deep-therapy quartz lamp and gave himself an artificial sunbath for one hour every morning. That was on the recommendation of one of the osteopaths whom he finally consulted in spite of his physicians. Father wanted their visits kept a secret. "Frankly I can see no harm in doing this," he said, talking about his new lamp. "If I do not get my sunbath, the legs freeze up from about five p.m. on. . . . I have impressed on Starr (an osteopath) the ab-solute necessity of saying nothing to anybody about the fact that I am taking any treatment from him."

That fall, he set up a daily routine which afforded roughly equal time to his treatments, to work at the office and at home, and to politics, including in the last category participation in public affairs to keep his name impressed on voters' memory. After Father had finished breakfast in bed and thumbed through the newspapers, Louis came in for a bedroom conference, to map out their schedules in a thickening cloud of cigarette smoke. Exercises and the sun lamp took up another hour or so, until it was time to be chauffeured down to the offices of the Fidelity and Deposit Company at 120 Broadway. With an effort, he could swing himself into and out of the car now and, on his crutches, navigate the single front step leading into the polished marble of the lobby floor. One morning the crutches slipped, and he toppled to the floor. Within a second, he pushed himself up into a sitting position. The smile flashed as passersby crowded around him. "Do you mind giving a hand to help me up?" he asked, as if it was almost as funny as a slapstick movie.

The offices of Emmet, Marvin & Roosevelt he had to regard as out of bounds. At 52 Wall Street, the front steps were too high for him to manage alone. He refused to be carried up them. So Missy waited for him at Fidelity and Deposit, unless it was a day when they worked together at our home.

He ate lunch, served by Missy, at his desk, usually with a business associate or client. She knew his mind well enough to be able to write his letters once he had scribbled a "yes" or "no" on most of the incoming correspondence. She had expanded the job of being personal secretary to become his shield, nurse and outspoken friend. Louis Howe could not have been any happier about the relationship. Missy filled exactly his prescription for the kind of woman Father's needs demanded at this point.

In the afternoons, the boss, his secretary and Louis would work on Fidelity business, mixed occasionally with cases the law firm was handling. Father was falling out of love with his legal practice. He found it as dull as Missy had anticipated it might be, and he disliked having his name at the tail end of the partnership's.

Invitations flowed in for him to take on new directorships, to join new charities in fund raising, to preside as chairman of a dozen and one organizations. It was hard for him to refuse, though Louis of necessity had to tackle the hard work involved. The two of them, with Missy's assistance, functioned as an overseer at Harvard, a trustee of Vassar, a board member of the Flower-Fifth Avenue Hospital, the president of the Navy Club, chairman of a drive for the American Legion. Louis stayed out of sight, like the rear half of a two-man circus horse.

They congratulated themselves when the Woodrow Wilson Foundation, which was one of the fund-raising assignments they had undertaken, could announce the following spring that it had $700,000 in the bank. They schemed endlessly to drum up financial backing for their old companion of Washington days, Dick Byrd, to carry out his seemingly far-fetched plans to fly over the South Pole. When that dream finally came true for him, Byrd was a rear admiral and Father was governor of New York. All he asked of his explorer friend was "a scrap of something which you took over the South Pole flight—even if it is a scrap of your sock." Byrd, in fact, had carried an American flag for him as a memento.

Father's original promise to Missy that "legal work takes up comparatively little of my time" was working out precisely as he had said. Authorship intrigued him, and he talked a lot about it. Perhaps he might spend his summers at Hyde Park writing a life of John Paul Jones, or a history of the United States, or a book or so about the Navy? Louis, who did most of the writing of the political articles which appeared under Father's name, knew better, as did Missy. Father's readiness to jump into almost anything that might prove interesting was a standing joke between the three of them.

"I am always in the delightful frame of mind of wanting to say 'yes' to anything in the way of writing," Father confessed to one would-be collaborator, "be it a magazine article or a twelve-volume history of the Navy—always provided that the writing is to be done next week, or the week after. (Miss LeHand, who is taking this, is nodding her head and saying, 'Too true—too true!')"

She had begun to make her life his. At his desk, in a chair or lying in bed, he could fend for himself, but he had to be helped from one place to another. He could not be left alone for long. She lived in an apartment on 200th Street in the Bronx, which she shared with a cousin and his wife. Its one bedroom made it necessary for her to sleep on a couch in the living room. She gave up accepting invitations if that meant leaving Father to fend for himself. She had never admired a man more.

"He doesn't need to ask to be waited on—in fact, he never asks," she once said. "I know without being told."

At four o'clock, she usually drove back with him to East Sixty-fifth Street and remained for the evening, taking dictation and instructions, joining increasingly in discussions with the stream of callers that Louis and, to a lesser degree, Mother brought trampling into the house, to the disdain of Granny, who had not counted on this kind of traffic passing through the single entry door when she had the Siamese-twin establishments built.

Throughout these months, Father listened to any suggestion about a possible cure, never really kidding himself that any of the highly touted miracles would be effective. An electric belt? He thought not. A magical medicine advocated by an English friend of his? He dictated a note to Dr. Draper: "It may be monkey glands or perhaps it is made out of the dried eyes of the extinct three-toed rhinoceros. You doctors have sure got imaginations! Have any of your people thought of distilling the remains of King Tut-ankhamen? The serum might put new life into some of our mutual friends. In the meantime, I am going to Florida to let nature take its course—nothing like Old Mother Nature, anyway!"

He had arranged by then to charter the *Weona II* for six weeks to go on his first Florida cruise. "What I want," said Father, who was henceforth addressed as the Admiral by Louis, "is nothing fancy. An old schooner with a kicker on her will do." The vessel he rented was a little dressier than that, with a captain and four uniformed crewmen. Father haggled with the Pine Street brokers who set up the deal to reduce the crew to three to save money, but it nevertheless cost him $1,500, which was more than he could afford.

From his point of view, the expense was worth every penny. The sense of returning strength that he felt in his legs from swimming in Vincent Astor's heated pool convinced him that, if he kept up the process in warm seawater and soaked up some winter sunshine in place of his quartz-lamp sunbaths, his recovery would be speeded. Salt water would provide added buoyancy, and he intended to swim for hours on end.

Almost simultaneously, Mother found time to take swimming lessons. She did not discuss her motives. I do not believe that, at this late date, she had any thought of affecting a reconciliation by learning to share in a pastime which to him was a potential means of achieving his immediate goal of restoring himself to full manhood. More likely, she wanted to demonstrate that she was capable of doing almost anything that he could.

She previously had been no more proficient as a swimmer than at golf or tennis or on the dance floor. She had tried often enough, but necessary determination had been lacking. This time, it was not. In all probability she would have been welcomed during the summer at the Astors'. She chose instead to go to the YWCA with Nancy Cook and Marion Dickerman. She felt that when the classes ended, she fared better in the tiled pool than did Miss Cook, who tended to lose her nerve if the water rose above her waist, but not so capably as Miss Dickerman. Mother was quite content to paddle a few strokes at a time. "By spring," she recalled proudly, "I felt prepared to start in teaching the boys." In point of fact, all four of us could already conduct ourselves in the water with verve equaling Miss Dickerman's, thanks to being dangled from a pole by Father or Depew.

Mother took along Esther Lape, her League of Women Voters friend, when she followed Father to spend a week or so aboard the

Weona II. Louis and Missy had gone on ahead with him, to be joined by John Lawrence, Frances and Henry de Rham and others, all having "great fun . . . in this somewhat negligée existence," according to Father. "All wander round in pyjamas, nighties and bathing suits," he said in a teasing letter to Granny, who was off to Bermuda for a spring vacation, too.

Nothing about shipboard life appealed to Mother, from the mosquitoes to the gaiety of Frances de Rham. Her only pleasure was in enduring it for ten days until it was time to take the train back to New York. But Father, bronzed by the sun and feeling a tingle in his toes for the first time since August, 1921, had enjoyed every minute. Some more of his "Community Life" verses testified to that:

> *When they first come on board they think it's so nice—*
> *With staterooms and bathtubs and comforts sans price—*
> *Till they suddenly realize that every partition*
> *Sounds intimate echoes of each guest's condition*
> *Of mind and of body—for whispers of details*
> *The wall in its wisdom with great gusto retails. . . .*
> *No secrets or thoughts between husband and wife*
> *Can safely be had in Community Life. . . .*

He was so pleased with the improvement in his condition that he decided to buy his own houseboat, in partnership with Lawrence. The outcome was the purchase of the old *Larooco*, which Lawrence privately derided as "a floating tenement."

"Except for the braces," Father reported happily when he was back at his New York office, "I have never been in better health in my life."

There was an additional reason, besides the return of sensation in his legs, for his mood of exhilaration. One of the innumerable medical reports on his general well-being stated explicitly: "No symptoms of *impotentia coeundi*." The Latin translates as "the inability of the male to perform the sexual act." The report held true when he started campaigning for the Presidency ten years later at the age of fifty.

5

Granny moved with unflagging firmness to fill the gap as it widened between our parents. To her mind, her motives were unquestionable, like everything else she did. Her son was physically incapable of devoting all the time and attention that growing children need. Her daughter-in-law was obviously bent on building a career for herself at their expense. So the old lady must take the guiding reins more tightly into her own hands.

She scorned the thought that possibly she took unfair advantage of the fact that she held the purse strings as well as the reins. She would never acknowledge that she continued to use her grandchildren as a weapon against Mother, whose performance as a housewife Granny regarded as inferior. Where she had responded sympathetically in the past, she now chose to ignore her daughter-in-law's protests that we were being sadly spoiled.

Her opinions about women in politics coincided exactly with her stepson's. "Once they mount the soapbox," Rosy told Father when Mother made her first hesitant appearances in public, "mark my words, they never get off."

In Granny's imperious view, working people of the kind that Mother consorted with these days had their place, but it was located several steps down the social ladder. A gentleman might properly attend to necessary labor on his own land, as she personally tended her rose garden, but otherwise he should remain aloof from common toil. When Jimmy once mentioned to her that his hands were dirty, she reproved him. "A gentleman's hands may be *soiled*, James, but they are never *dirty*."

Sis was brought up along much the same lines by Granny. "No *lady* ever crosses her limbs when seated. A lady sits with her limbs straight in front of her and her knees together."

She spotted a tiny tattoo on one of my arms when I, a brash fifteen-year-old, came back from a summer trip out West. "Franklin!" Granny exclaimed. "Look what this boy has done to himself!" She refused to tolerate Father's laughter over that. "It is no laughing matter, Franklin. No gentleman would submit to such a *mutilation*."

Father knew how to silence her. "Well," he said, "one of your favorite British cousins is Charlie Gordon, and he's an officer in the Royal Navy. Doesn't he have tattoos all over both arms?"

For all her airs and graces, we loved her dearly, as we had cause to, and she showered us with marks of her appreciation in return. She gave us money, watches, horses—virtually anything we asked for or she fancied we might enjoy. Discipline was nothing she cared to discuss. Father was almost equally lenient. Mother fumed in silence unless she felt compelled to protest—not to Granny, but to Father, who seldom listened.

When, for once, my parents concluded that Franklin junior and Johnny must be punished for an especially wanton breach of rules by having their pony taken away, Granny thwarted their efforts by buying each grandson his own horse. "Now what am I going to do?" asked Father.

Granny heard nothing that she did not want to be told. Her defenses were impenetrable. "I had not realized that you would object, Eleanor," she would say if Mother ventured to disapprove of some extravagant new present she had given one of us. As a result, we could wheedle out of Granny whatever our greedy young hearts desired. There was no question about it: We recognized the hostilities existing among the three grown-ups, and we exploited the cold war to the hilt.

Granny literally removed Sis and Jimmy from Mother's hands by taking them off to Europe during their school vacations after the cruise of the *Weona II* was over. Mother, with distant memories of the happiness she found briefly there as a schoolgirl and then as a young bride, had wanted herself to show them the sights and scenes she had known. But the household budget would not cover travel on that scale. She mournfully decided that she would, at least, give Franklin junior and Johnny a less expensive trip by taking them camping with Miss Cook and Miss Dickerman. Father would stay in Hyde Park, with Missy looking after him there and Louis commuting to New York.

Mother wanted more to do with bringing up her children than in the past, when Granny and a succession of nursemaids made hers a comparatively minor role. She felt that she had not personally done enough with Sis, Jimmy and me. Consequently, we were too close to Granny and not close enough to her. She was determined that things would be different with Franklin junior and Johnny. The camping trip was designed to be the start of a much greater measure of togetherness.

As companions for my young brothers, she invited Dr. Draper's son, George, and Hall's boy, Henry, to join the party. She assembled two tents, a stove on which Miss Cook was to demonstrate another of her skills, some pots and pans, and a Red Cross medicine kit. The three women, four boys and the paraphernalia were loaded into the family Buick, with Mother at the wheel, to set off on what turned out to be a disastrous excursion.

The young Roosevelts, cramped day after day in the car, were a continuous headache to Mother's spinster friends, who had no understanding of ebullient schoolboys. They became irritated by my rowdy brothers and proceeded to show it. Franklin and Johnny evened the score by playing every kind of trick on them.

The first stop was in a farmer's field by the Ausable River in upper New York State, where Mother aimed to show her young charges Ausable Chasm and Fort Ticonderoga. She was relieved to find another family camping there, so that when the boys dashed in for a swim, there would be someone to lug them out if they got out of their depth. Her faith in her own swimming powers had faded fast.

At another camping spot, the farmer was less cooperative. "Where are your husbands?" he demanded.

"Mine is not with me, and the others do not have husbands," Mother replied.

"I don't want women of that kind," snapped the farmer. The Buick drove on.

Montreal may have appeared to be too sinful a city for an overnight stay, since Mother paused there just long enough to pick up groceries. The first real trouble came on a French farm halfway to Quebec. There, Franklin persisted in trying to cut down a tree, missed his swing, and slashed his foot with the ax.

Out came the first-aid box. Mother fancied that the cut did not need stitches, so she bandaged the wound without resorting to a doctor, "which proved in the long run a great mistake," she confessed afterward, "as it took weeks to heal."

In Quebec City, a degree of panic set in among the adults when Johnny and little George wandered out of the hotel, and it was feared that they were lost, unable to utter a word of French. Before anyone called the police, they strolled back and did nothing to disarm Mother's anger by telling her that they had been sight-seeing. She did not count the experience as fruitless, however, since she felt very fond of Quebec and "the boys discovered that there was some point in knowing how to speak the French language." That was something else on which Mother prided herself.

A burro ride was the most memorable attraction of two days spent in the White Mountains as they headed eastward across Maine. Mother reported that everybody had great fun, except Nancy Cook, whose animal lay down every few yards and tried to roll her out of the saddle.

Farther along on their journey, the Buick skidded off the road, and they had to wait to be hauled out of a ditch. Just as they approached Lubec, Mother ran into a dray, dumping its load of lumber and the boy who was driving it. Ten dollars paid for the damage done.

Their destination was Campobello. None of us had been there during the four unended years of Father's battle for recovery. Mother felt no sentimentality about returning there without him. Any such squeamishness had no part in her makeup. To go back alone, as the only parent able to do so, may have been a deep satisfaction to her in her new independence of spirit. The place, she found, "was still serene, beautiful and enjoyable."

Father often spoke of his homesickness for the island. But he did not see it again until he had completed the hundred days and nights of toil and talk that launched the New Deal in the summer of 1933. Then he went through the arduous journey which he had last undertaken strapped to a stretcher and told the crowd of islanders who had gathered to greet him, "I was figuring this morning on the passage of time, and I remembered that I was brought here because I was teething forty-nine years ago. I have been coming for many months almost every year until twelve years ago, when there . . . (was) a gap. . . ."

No one in Mother's travel-weary group could face the ride back from Campobello by Buick. Miss Dickerman's sister came up with another party. They drove the car to New York, camping out along the way. Mother came home completely worn out and upset. Franklin was still in bandages, but it was nine-year-old Johnny who showed the greatest antagonism and made the most cutting remarks about Miss Dickerman and Miss Cook.

Those years settled down into a repetitious pattern, in which most of us lived on parallel lines that seldom converged. Jimmy and I plodded on at Groton. Sis was reconciled to finishing her schooling at Miss Chapin's but had no enthusiasm for making her formal debut into society, as Granny insisted, this time with Mother's support. Franklin and Johnny followed me at Buckley.

Mother's year-round schedule of keeping busy meant that she had limited time for her family, and she had been disillusioned about togetherness with her children after the horrendous camping trip; it was the first and last of its kind. Father spent much of the summers at Hyde Park and went off to the *Larooco* for two or three months from February on, always with Missy at his side. Louis worked the rounds between New York, Hyde Park and the Florida Keys with the dependability of a mailman.

He catered to all the interests of the boss, from making a quick million or two on the stock market to racing ever-faster model boats. "I have designed and tried out an eighteen-inch model ice boat that goes like the devil. Will send you drawings etc. . . . It would be rather nice some winter to race them across the Hudson on the ice. As near as I can judge, upon a firm, long pond you can get very nearly twenty-five miles out of them. . . ."

He occasionally served as the only channel of communication between Father and Mother when the distance which separated them, in miles and in attitudes, temporarily stretched to the point where their regular, ostensibly fond correspondence ceased. From "My-am-eye," Father wired him, for example, "PLEASE ASK ELEANOR TO BUY 'PINK WHISKERS' BOOK. I WILL REPAY HER. . . . MISSY AND I BOTH SEND OUR LOVE. . . ."

Louis would pass along Mother's messages without comment: "YOUR MISSUS THINKS YOU OUGHT TO BE KEPT IN TOUCH WITH AND THAT YOU SHOULD WRITE." . . . Or he would take on yet another job, that of keeping Father posted on the day-to-day trivia of the family, which was the only one that Louis knew as an uprooted husband. "Little Franklin," he related faithfully, "came home from dancing class all puffed up with pride at having won a gold medal and the prize for being the best tango dancer. Johnny's nose is out of joint, and he professes a great contempt for the terpsichorean art generally."

An early spring heat wave in New York prompted him to report laconically, "It has been so hot that the furnaces have been let out in the house, and in consequence a cold wave has swept in from the West and taken an unfair advantage of us. I expect to spend the balance of the springtime sitting around 49 East Sixty-fifth Street in my overcoat with a quilt over my shoulders, for I rashly suggested to your Missus that one hot day did not make a summer, and in consequence, as you can easily guess, 20 below zero would not let her admit she was wrong by having the furnaces started up again."

Aboard the *Larooco*, one season merged almost indistinguishably into another, as the senile old houseboat meandered through the mangrove swamps and sandy bays between Miami and Key West. Father could have been talking about any day of the week when he wrote Granny, "Today, Maunsell and I took the motorboat to an inlet, fished, got out on the sandy beach, picnicked and swam and lay in the sun for hours. I know it is doing the legs good, and though I have worn the braces hardly at all, I get lots of exercise crawling around, and I know the muscles are better than ever before."

The ship's log read like a litany: guests arriving and departing, the engines breaking down and being repaired, Maunsell Crosby going off bird watching, Missy picking up mail and the laundry. On the top deck, under the awning, Father spared a little time from working on his stamp collection to tackle his long-postponed writing projects. He sketched out the John Paul Jones biography and finished fourteen yellow pages of his history of the United States, but that was as far as either manuscript went.

"Down there," he said, "I average ten hours sleep every night —you simply can't keep awake after nine or nine-thirty p.m."

Sometime after the end of the 1924 cruise, Father could stand unaided in water up to chest height. "Dr. Roosevelt" felt confident that, if he persisted, water would work a total cure. Toward the close of the year, Dora Morris, the much harassed ship's cook, wrote to Missy about tidying up an outstanding bill or two. "Our kindest regards to Mr. Roosevelt and you, Miss LeHand," said her letter. "We think of you and Mr. R. Take care of yourself, little lady."

She could not fail, of course, to be alert to something that was treated as a simple fact of life aboard the *Larooco*. Everyone in the closely knit inner circle of Father's friends accepted it as a matter of course. I remember being only mildly stirred to see him with Missy on his lap as he sat in a wicker chair in the main stateroom, holding her in his sun-browned arms, whose clasp we children knew so well. When Sis and Jimmy on occasion witnessed much the same scene, they had a similar reaction, as I learned when we spoke afterward. It was not in Father to be secretive or devious in his dealings with us. He made no attempt to conceal his feelings about Missy.

Because we had first sensed and then seen the state of unveiled hostility which had corroded any love between our parents, it was no great shock to discover that Missy shared a familial life in all its aspects with Father. What did surprise us was the later knowledge that Mother knew, too, and accepted the situation as a fact of life like the rest of us.

Warm Springs
1928

1

"Home" was much too grand a word for the dilapidated antebellum cottage with its paint peeled away by the hot Georgia sun and its walls so warped that daylight filtered in through the chinks, but it was the first place where Father could live with the minimum of interruption with those he felt close to.

It stood forlorn, surrounded by weeds and remote from the world outside, in 12,000 acres of Meriwether County hillside, 70 miles from Atlanta, the nearest big city. Much of the time he and Missy were alone there, except for daily cleaning help. Later, when he built a cottage of his own, he had the services of Irvin McDuffie, known variously as Mac or Duffie, who had been a barber in Atlanta before Father hired him. As a valet, McDuffie had one weakness: He was a hard-drinking man, but he was faithful and discreet.

Warm Springs had been a flourishing vacation center when nineteenth-century Georgians flocked there to bathe. The only souvenirs left of its heydays as a winter resort were a ramshackle hotel, some tumbledown cottages and a deserted auditorium. As Father remembered his first sight of the territory, "Everything was closed and almost everything was falling to pieces. Most of the roofs leaked. . . . It was in awful condition." In his unending, unsatisfied search for health, he was ready to put up with anything, and, therefore, so was Missy.

201

What mattered to them were not the rickety ruins but the marvelous Pine Mountain spring water which flowed, heedless of change in fads and fashion, into a natural pool, 1,800 gallons every minute, heated in the depths of the rock to a constant temperature of 88 degrees. Its mineral salts made it as buoyant as the ocean, yet for some odd reason bathers could stay in for two hours on end without the fatigue which would normally follow such a length of time spent in water so warm as this.

Father heard about Warm Springs in the early summer of 1924 from George Foster Peabody, the philanthropist and banker who had supported him in his Vice Presidential campaign. With his letter, he enclosed a testimonial from a young New Yorker, Louis Joseph, who, after a polio attack, had gone down there completely crippled except for the use of his arms. Now, three years later, he could walk with the aid of two canes. Peabody had been sufficiently impressed by what he called "the miracle of warm water" to buy a half interest in the resort, or the remains of it. Another part owner was Tom Loyless, a former editor of the Atlanta *Constitution*, who came to New York, painted a glowing word picture of the spring's effectiveness, and arranged for Father to talk with Louis Joseph. Father's interest was captured immediately. The young man's case history bore out what Dr. Lovett had told him in Boston, where he had new braces fitted a few weeks earlier.

Lovett urged all his polio patients to swim as much as possible. He found that those who went into the cold Atlantic off the North Shore or the coast of Maine, and could stay in for only a few minutes, improved much less than those who resorted to warmer waters. If Father wished to exercise regularly by swimming, instead of submitting to pounding daily oil massages, as he did unless he was in Florida, a pool had to be built at Hyde Park, something easier for him to get into and out of and less chilling than the ice pond in the woods.

With his contractor friend, Tiny Brown, who had added the wings to Granny's house, he made provisional plans for a pool to be put in close by in one of the lawns. Mother talked him out of that. She wanted a cottage built for Nancy Cook and Marion Dickerman so that the three of them could be close neighbors. Why not have the pool where they could enjoy it? Father, who avoided arguments whenever he could, agreed and gave Mother a piece of land about a mile and a half east of the house, known as Val-Kill, meaning "Valley Stream" in Dutch.

Father notified Tiny: "My missus and some of her female political friends want to build a shack on a stream in the back woods and want, instead of a beautiful marble bath, to have the stream dug out so as to form an old-fashioned swimmin' hole. Apparently the girls think that this will get them more closely back to nature, and I foresee that I shall have to put a substantial board fence around the swimmin' hole to keep interested neighbors from seeing how close they can get back to nature when they take the morning plunge. I know your Missus would love it, too—aren't these wives of ours funny things?"

Now that, to appease Mother, he had given up the idea of a pool at Granny's doorstep, he let the thought of Warm Springs lie fallow for a while. He was not certain that there was any practical alternative to driving between Hyde Park and Val-Kill every time he wanted a swim. Besides, he had promised to lead Al Smith's drive to win the Democratic nomination for the Presidency against the governor's chief rival in the party, old William McAdoo, Wilson's Secretary of the Treasury and son-in-law.

The promise did not come easily. The hard slogging that Louis put in had made Father a power again in New York State, probably capable of delivering the vote of the whole state delegation at the forthcoming national convention at Madison Square Garden in June. He was so doubtful about both principal candidates that he said pointedly, "If I did not still have these crutches, I should throw my own hat in the ring." That was a gambit worked out with Louis, who throughout the campaign played at the business of arranging a complimentary convention vote or two to make sure that the boss was not forgotten.

McAdoo was a Dry, a key consideration when the country as a whole still favored Prohibition, though the big cities detested it. He counted on support from the unions and the farmers. But he had one black mark against him, in Father's judgment—and possibly two. He carried the taint of Teapot Dome oil money; he had accepted a $25,000-a-year retainer as legal counsel to Edward Doheny. That California tycoon had been a major beneficiary of the crooked dealings of Albert Fall, Harding's hatchet-faced Secretary of the Interior. And Attorney McAdoo, who married his third wife after he was seventy, had taken it on himself to advise Father, "I cannot help but feel that you would be benefited by the gland treatment." Glandular transplants from monkeys were a popular rejuvenation procedure of the day. Father despised them.

Smith, on the other hand, an unregenerate Wet, had ignored Father's warnings to him as governor and gone ahead to repeal the state's Prohibition laws, making wine and beer legal drinking. He was not yet widely known outside the boundaries of New York, except for the fact that he was a Catholic. This made him a sitting duck for the gunfire of the Ku Klux Klan, a force to be reckoned with in the South and Midwest. Father's prejudices in that respect were more pro than anti. Missy, like Lucy, happened to be a quietly devout Catholic.

Through February and March, Father bided his time aboard the *Larooco*, pretending to be out of touch with events because he picked up only an occasional newspaper, while bulletins from Louis told him that support within the party for McAdoo was shrinking. Louis begged him to ask Boss Jim Curley of Boston down for a cruise, to persuade him that Father was worth backing in a show of strength if the appropriate moment could be engineered in Madison Square Garden. No invitation was forthcoming. Louis was getting ahead of himself. Both he and Father sized up 1924 as another black year for Democrats, anyway.

Mother, meanwhile, went about supporting Smith in her own fashion. For weeks past, she had been roving around upstate New York, with either Nancy Cook or Marion Dickerman in tow, to canvass various women's organizations. The cause was to guarantee a voice for their sex in the predominantly male business of politics. In April, at the state convention of the Democrats in Albany, when Father was on the final leg of the season's cruising, Mother tangled with Charles Francis Murphy. The longtime boss of Tammany insisted, with his usual silky politeness, that male party leaders should choose women delegates to the national convention. "I have wanted you home the last few days," she wrote to Father, "to advise me on the fight I am putting up. . . ."

She headed up a committee of women rebels, who succeeded in convincing Smith of their right to pick their own delegates. At Albany's Hotel Ten Eyck, she told an all-female dinner meeting, "To many women, and I am one of them, it is extraordinarily difficult to care about anything enough to cause disagreement or unpleasant feelings, but I have come to the conclusion that this must be done for a time until we can prove our strength and demand respect for our wishes." As she was increasingly prone to do, she was already employing her special brand of concealed references to spell out something of her own life story, now that she wrote her own speeches as a graduate of Louis' teaching. No one in the audience knew enough of the circumstances to appreciate that.

In return for his favor in the matter of women delegates, she was committed wholeheartedly to Smith ahead of Father. As an apprentice in politics, she often consulted with him. As a seasoned, circumspect professional, he turned not to her but to Louis in his deliberations at this stage. It was not Father's choice to manage the governor's preconvention campaign, but Smith's asking prompted him to take on the job. Boss Murphy, who had been leading Smith's battalions, died shortly before the opening day in Madison Square Garden. Smith calculated that Father, a kid-glove politician unstained by Tammany connections, was just the man to replace him. He was, in Al's ingenuous opinion, a useful, sympathy-evoking showpiece who would appeal equally to Protestants, the Drys and the rural vote.

Neither Louis nor Father saw it quite that way. A month before Father agreed to fill a dead man's shoes, Louis came up with an amazingly exact prediction of what would happen in the Garden: "The leading candidates will be trotted out one after another for enough ballots to make it evident that they cannot secure the nomination . . . after that they will hold a conference in a back room amongst the leaders of the largest blocks of votes, at which some unguessable and perhaps unknown John Smith will be picked on as the man whom every Democrat has been really yearning to see as the standard bearer of his party."

In the expert opinion of the firm of Roosevelt and Howe, Smith had no chance of being nominated. But they must apply their trusted principle of putting their minds and hearts into his fight. Then, if Al lost, his campaign manager would nevertheless have built his own standing within the party by the sheer doggedness and devotion of his services. A certain hard-nosed cynicism was a vital element in the Roosevelt-Howe approach, plus an irrepressible sense of humor.

Josephus Daniels was a McAdoo backer. At the start of his battles for Smith, Father wrote him a long reply to a joking proposal his old chief had made for a Daniels-Roosevelt ticket: "There is still, of course, a chance in this year of grace—if things come to the pass of keeping us all in New York until the 255th ballot on July 31, you and I can end the deadlock dramatically and effectively by putting your candidate and mine into a room together armed with a complete Navy outfit ranging from bean soup to sixteen-inch guns with orders that only one man can come out alive. Probably neither will come out alive, and a grateful convention will give us the nomination by acclamation."

In the same letter, he picked up another point which Daniels had made—how the New York *World* ran a picture of Mother alongside its story that Father was taking over leadership for Smith: "You are right about the squaws! Like you, I have fought for years to keep my name on the front page and to relegate the wife's to the advertising section. My new plan, however, seems admirable—hereafter for three years my name will not appear at all, but each fourth year (Presidential ones) I am to have all the limelight. . . ."

In New York, Louis took over Smith's headquarters in the Prudential Building on Madison Avenue as though it were Father's. He roughed out the stock letter which Father sent to delegates: "Governor Smith is the most wonderful vote getter that I have ever seen. . . ." He set up a prodigious mass-production line for a mail campaign and methodically analyzed all incoming correspondence, including the letters of hate: "You are being criticized by your old friends in your class for bring [*sic*] Smith out, a Romanist. . . . It is belittling a good Roosevelt name." And then: "Keep the Pope out of the U.S. He is bad enough where he is. Yours, KKK."

Mother was firm for Smith, but hostile to Tammany, his principal source of support, and did not hesitate to say so in public. That could be interpreted as either political naïvety or the courage of conviction, depending on how it was looked at, but it was an embarrassment for Father and Louis. Their strategy was to conduct a Simon-pure campaign with no name-calling and implore their opponents to follow suit. Smith, the "knight of the brown derby and the cocked cigar," as he was labeled, was too vulnerable a target. His manager demanded that the party must hold together, come what may, and not be split apart by the explosive questions of Protestant or Catholic, farm or factory, Wet or Dry.

Father dodged taking any stand that would alienate one side against another. The New York *Post* decided that "Franklin D.

Roosevelt at the Manager's desk looks like a magnificent St. George who is just throwing off his mail coat after side-stepping the distilled dragon. Why fight dragons when they can be side-stepped?"

But Smith was Irish among the Irish, and double-talk about Prohibition was not good enough for him. He blew a lot of Father's conciliatory work sky-high by declaring flatly, "There is no committee or any other power . . . that will . . . prevent me from giving full expression to just what I think about any public question." Something about that line of talk appealed to Grace Howe, at home in Fall River. She plunged into the campaign for him just like Mother and started earning a role for herself in Massachusetts politics with no particular help from Louis. Her reward came when Father, in the White House, appointed her postmaster of Fall River, giving her the first financial security she had known since the day she and Louis were married.

As the battle for delegates neared its climax, Smith's dissatisfaction with the manager whom the governor's friends and relatives categorized as an "awful stuffed shirt" reached the point where he pushed Father aside. His policy of fighting without leaving scars did not satisfy Al. He got ready for a test of strength with a resolution which he wanted in the party platform condemning the Ku Klux Klan by name, scorning Father's suggestion for denouncing secret organizations in general.

Yet Father's luck held; it involved another death. If Bourke Cockran, the Tammany spellbinder, had lived, he would have been the man to nominate Smith, as he had done four years earlier in Baltimore. To fill the gap, Al tried out several speakers before he turned to Father. "I shall be glad to nominate him," said Father privately, "provided I do not have to audition." His real liking for this particular man of the streets was not much stronger than Al's regard for Father.

At Hyde Park one sunny afternoon, Moses Smith, working in the rows of a field of ripening corn along the Val-Kill road, came across Father and Missy stretched out on a blanket with a scratch pad between them. "Moses, what do you think I'm doing?" he called when he knew they had been spotted. "I am writing a speech to nominate Al Smith for President."

If he was, then a number of other hands certainly worked over his draft. He was none too easy about the catchphrase "happy warrior," which one of Smith's advisers borrowed from a poem written by

William Wordsworth in 1806; wasn't it perhaps a bit too poetic? Smith had a different worry on his mind. Could Father, for all his self-confidence, really make it into Madison Square Garden with braces and crutches and still deliver a speech?

Both men had no cause to fear. Louis' preparations were faultless. Father practiced for days the awkward business of getting from the entrance of the auditorium to the microphones of the speaker's stand, using a crutch under his right arm and gripping Jimmy's right arm with his left hand. He taught my sixteen-year-old brother to match his step to his own and copy his calm smile.

He spurned the thought of making any entrance in a wheelchair. He would arrive early before the crowds on the floor thickened. By the crutch-and-arm technique, he would be seated, with Jimmy taking the crutch from him once that had been accomplished. He would sit on the center aisle among the throng of New York State delegates and take his chance of being accidentally roughed up when the wild demonstration parades began. Jimmy would stand by to run errands, deliver messages, and lend his arm when it was needed.

Mother found Louis "much excited." She said, "I fear I did not understand the importance of many things as he did." In the middle of a June heat wave, she opened up our house, which rapidly filled with chattering women delegates, creating inevitable turmoil. Four weeks later, as the sweltering, shattered convention drew to its close, they were still there. "At least, we were in our own home," Mother protested afterward.

She was taken up with her own job as chairman of a group designated to present some social welfare planks, demanding that more attention be paid to women, to the resolutions committee. The treatment she received disillusioned her. Women, she discovered, could only stand and wait outside the door when important meetings were in session. How much consideration her resolutions got remained a mystery to her. National conventions, so far as she was concerned, were largely a waste of her time from then on.

Tammany had loaded the galleries and armed its claque with klaxon horns, though McAdoo men dominated the convention machinery behind the scenes. After gawking a few times at the sweating, smiling cripple who could only nod his head in greeting as he swung in and out of the hall on Jimmy's arm, the gallery mob took to applauding his comings and goings. The first time he was recognized by the chair, he could not make himself heard for some minutes. He had only a few matter-of-fact words to say: "It is now nearly two o'clock of the morning of the Sabbath Day." He moved adjournment. The McAdoo-Smith contest had already reached such a pitch, with nobody nominated yet, that some delegates immediately opposed the motion, but the chairman's gavel ruled it carried.

For his nominating speech on Thursday, June 26, Father had set his heart on walking alone onto the rostrum. On Jimmy's arm, he made his way up the aisle to the rear of the platform. "Go up and shake it, will you?" he asked a delegate standing near. He got only a puzzled look in response. "Shake it," he said almost fiercely, his head wet with perspiration. "I must know if the speaker's stand will bear my weight."

He let go of my brother's arm, grasped his second crutch from Jimmy, and swung himself forward until he could grip the edges of the stand. The crowd roared its approval. He dared not let go a hand to acknowledge the cheers; a broad smile had to serve the purpose. Jimmy felt close to tears, but weeping was a privilege reserved for women in the Groton code.

The speech was a personal triumph in a disastrously divided convention. Out from the loudspeakers rolled the ringing actor's voice that later raised the spirits and hopes of America in an era of torment. It was as distinctive as his signature, not organ-stop oratory like William Jennings Bryan's or the lisping rhetoric of Winston Churchill, but intimate, simple and, above all, confident and inspiring confidence. In the next thirty-four minutes, applause often interrupted him, though not always for the passages he had personally written.

"You equally who come from the great cities of the East and from the hills and plains of the West, from the slopes of the Pacific and from the homes and fields of the Southland, I ask you in all sincerity, in balloting on that platform tomorrow, to keep first in your hearts and minds the words of Abraham Lincoln: 'With malice toward none, with charity to all.' " Those were not a ghost-writer's words, but Father's.

So he came to the closing paragraph. "He has a power to strike at error and wrongdoing that makes his adversaries quail before him.

He has a personality that carries to every bearer not only the sincerity but the righteousness of what he says. He is the 'Happy Warrior' of the political battlefield.''

The klaxons shrieked and the rattles whirled. Every aisle filled with dancing, yelling delegates and Smith supporters, with heavy support from the Tammany claque. The band, which had made four false starts before Father finished, let go with "The Sidewalks of New York," "Sweet Rosie O'Grady,'' and, inevitably, "The Bowery,'' but its blare went unheard in the din. More than an hour later, the pandemonium continued. Louis' planning, two men's deaths, and the combination of courage and craft that was distinctively my parent's had brought about a result way beyond Father's immediate expectation: He was the most popular figure in Madison Square Garden, far more so than his candidate.

Smith needed 731 votes to clinch the nomination. He started with 241, McAdoo with 431½. Father and Louis spent most of their time at their man's headquarters, trying to scheme ways to shift votes for him from favorite sons or dark horses. The days rolled by, the balloting ground on, but neither of the leading candidates could pull far enough ahead of the other.

After twelve days of deadlock in the sweat-scented Garden, the ninety-third ballot gave Smith 355½ votes to McAdoo's 314. Father addressed the crowd again, promising the withdrawal of the governor's name if his rival would do the same. McAdoo refused, obsessed now with crusading against liquor, Popery and the Tammany Tiger. Father's mounting fatigue had already dented his temper. "It is incredible," he snapped at the old attorney, "that you would be willing to ruin your party by . . . dog-in-the-manger tactics."

On the hundred and third vote—a dismal record which still stands today—the bankrupt convention made its hopeless compromise choice on July 31. John W. Davis, a lawyer from Locust Valley, Long Island, was as conservative as his starched stand-up collars. His professional ties with J. P. Morgan & Company put the brand of Wall Street on him, which made his name poison in the West and South. His running mate was William Jennings Bryan's cloddish brother, Charles. Louis' predictions had come true to the last letter.

The Democratic pair had not a chance in the world of beating the Republicans. At Cleveland in June, on the first ballot, the GOP had chosen Coolidge, already in the White House following Harding's death the previous August, and Charles Dawes as his running mate.

Father said loftily that Davis' "little speeches ... are always charming and beautifully expressed, but during the campaign he will have to be more dramatic. To rise superior to Coolidge will be a hard thing, as Coolidge is inarticulate to the extent of being thought a mystery. To stick a knife into ghosts is always hard."

Mother washed her hands of the whole Madison Square Garden mess. The brightest spot in the convention, she reflected, was the chance it gave her to meet an old friend, Isabella Ferguson Greenaway, who arrived as the wife of a delegate from Arizona and took Sis back for a vacation on their ranch there before the final ballots were counted.

Louis interpreted Mother's sudden disenchantment with politics as a potential danger to Father's career. Somehow, he had to keep her hitched to the team. A way had to be invented to contain and control her. The obvious answer was to get her campaigning for the Davis ticket, in particular for Al Smith. He had decided to run as governor for a precedent-shattering third term. The Republicans' choice for the Executive Mansion in Albany was Uncle Ted's eldest son, another Roosevelt with his sights set on being President of the United States. Young Ted, at thirty-seven, was trying to follow his father's route step by step, just like our own parent. The white hope of the Oyster Bay end of our family had been Harding's Assistant Secretary of the Navy. The next chapter called for him to be elected governor of New York.

Though the voters in general gave every sign of wanting to "Keep cool with Coolidge," Louis calculated that the best way to win in New York State was to splash some Teapot Dome oil over Ted. Louis had no love for Oyster Bay Roosevelts and their acid tongues. One of the clan, Congressman Nicholas Longworth, whose wife was Cousin Alice, had publicly sneered at Father. Mother made sure that he heard about it by writing to him in Florida, "Mama is wild over Nick L. having called you 'a denatured Roosevelt.' " Father must have smiled. It was an odd choice of words to come from a man who remained childless after sixteen years of marriage.

Louis soon overcame the objections which Mother halfheartedly raised about the ethics of smearing Ted, who assuredly had no active involvement in the Harding scandals. She loved to win, so she jumped at the idea which Louis came up with of having her and fellow "she-male" Democrats tail her cousin around the state in a motorcade. On top of the lead car, a framework of his design was built to resemble a huge teapot, spouting steam to remind every audience of corruption under GOP rule.

She protested halfheartedly that the whole thing was vindictive. That did not stop her from sniping in her speeches at her blameless relative as "a personally nice young man whose public service record shows him willing to do the bidding of his friends." She was deep into politics again with what she acknowledged later to be "a rough stunt."

Father doubted whether the country would put a Democrat into the White House until Republican administrations had brought about "a serious period of depression and unemployment," as he said at the year's end. "Every war," he wrote prophetically, "brings after it a period of materialism and conservatism; people tire quickly of ideals, and we are now but repeating history."

He limited his own campaigning for a lost cause by making a radio speech for Davis. Talking into a microphone was a technique he had not perfected yet. He was still on the air when we heard him ask the announcer, "How did it sound?" He liked to learn from an expert.

The first priority he had that summer was to rest and catch up on his exercising after the wear and tear of managing Al Smith's fight. Like Louis, he was close to exhaustion. With the task of tailgating young Ted with the motorcade lined up to keep Mother busy, the two men went to Howe's weather-beaten house at Horseneck Bend to relax and mull over the implications and consequences of their bittersweet victory at the convention. Everything else in the world was pushed a long way off. There was no telephone and no road, except the path a mile and a half long down the beach and over the dunes to Westport Point. Telegrams went no farther than the village store, waiting to be collected the next time Louis stopped by. Wagons delivering milk or groceries were the only scheduled link with the outside world.

Two other distant houses like Louis' were the only intrusions on absolute privacy. Once Father had been carried from the car over the soft, shifting sand into Louis' place, he could drag himself from the front porch into the rolling surf. Roughing it in this style appealed to him. "As you know," he wrote to Livy, "Louis' cottage is wee, and there is really no room, and we live in a distinctly informal way with only two of our colored servants to do everything."

He can only have spent the following weeks there for two reasons.

Hyde Park lacked any facility for swimming and sunning himself without the chance of callers dropping in. And aside from a probable visit by Missy, nobody disturbed the deliberations at Horseneck Beach.

He had something else, quite apart from politics, to think over following the Madison Square Garden fiasco. Major John Cohen, publisher of the Atlanta *Journal*, a McAdoo supporter, had been introduced to Father and urged him, in the course of conversation, to visit Warm Springs as his guest to test the qualities of the water.

Some of Father's biographers have it that as soon as he heard about the promise that Warm Springs offered, he dropped everything in pursuit of the special dream of walking alone again. He was never that impulsive. Months elapsed between his receiving George Foster Peabody's letter and his decision to go and see for himself. It was October before he arrived there. Missy was with him, and so was Mother.

The following morning, he was carried to the water's edge. The pool in its original state looked like nothing any doctor in his right mind would recommend. Native Indians long before the white man came attributed magic powers of healing to this ever-moving water. In tribal wars, fighting stopped short of Warm Springs, which was sacred ground, where the braves could come and go in peace to bathe their wounds. Indians still visited there, uninvited guests padding around the piazza of the Meriwether Inn, as the decaying hotel was called. Gypsies showed up, too, along with other ailing wanderers in search of free miracles. Some suffered from twisted limbs, others from skin afflictions and open, running sores. Father did not hesitate to join them in the pool.

Mother had close family ties with the South, yet ironically they served only to add to her instant disenchantment with Warm Springs. The little village itself down by the railroad depot had been known until recently as Bullochville; her father's mother, born Martha Bulloch, was a belle of Savannah in the 1850's. Mother never knew her, but Martha's sister Anna, later Mrs. James King Gracie, made a home for Mother and Hall toward the close of their father's broken life. Aunt Gracie was an unregenerate Southerner like her brothers, Irvine and James, both Confederate blockade-runners who had to exile themselves in Liverpool, England, when the Civil War ended. Father loved to tease Mother about her "pirate uncles."

✓ Living in New York during that war, Aunt Gracie once helped break out a Confederate flag to celebrate a victory over the damned Yankees. She filled her niece's ten-year-old head with tales of those days, picturing a Southland that was all Brer Rabbit, moonlight and magnolias.

Though a cousin of hers, Minnie Bulloch, still ran the Warm Springs dry-goods store, featuring parasols, sunbonnets and high-button shoes, Mother's first taste of Southern living came as a cruel shock to her thinly concealed romanticism. She had anticipated that everything would be gracious and easy. "It was a disappointment to me," she confessed, "to find that for many, many people life in the South was hard and poor and ugly, just as it is in parts of the North." She never liked Warm Springs. She was content to leave keeping house there to Missy.

The two of them drove one morning soon after their arrival to the little town of Manchester, five miles away, to buy what Father described as "chickens on the hoof," to be cooked by Mary, the daily maid. He had already been helped down to the pool by Roy, who, like the maid, came as part of the rent and doubled as chauffeur and butler. The hard-drinking valet, McDuffie, had not yet appeared on the scene. Mother's experience of going to market Southern style spoiled her appetite for flesh or fowl. She was horrified to learn that the "chickens on the hoof" had to be taken home alive. They escaped and ran around the yard until Mary caught them and wrung their necks.

"At Hyde Park, there were chickens in the farm yard," Mother said, "but that was a mile away from the house, and I didn't hear them being killed."

The kindness of their neighbors impressed her, notably that of Mr. and Mrs. Tom Loyless, who lived in a similar cottage next door. Scarcely a day went by without a gift of wood to burn in the fireplace as the nights grew cool or flowers already arranged in a silver bowl or china vase that had survived the ravages of Sherman's armies. Mother had long since given up fretting over Father. "I would worry," she said, "until the flowers faded and the container was returned to the owner."

She grew restless to get back to New York and her Teapot Dome motorcade. She was glad to cut short her stay and leave Father in Missy's care. He gloried in the improvement he felt in his legs from swimming in what he called "the most wonderful pool in the

world." He worked out his own exercises and at last felt life returning to his toes. "This is really a discovery of a place," he told Mother,
"and there is no doubt that I've got to do it some more."

The days slipped by, their pattern developing along lines not
unlike those aboard the houseboat. It never seemed to rain. Every
morning, Father and sometimes Missy swam in the spring water,
where he believed something near to a miracle was happening to
him—"I walk around in water four feet deep without braces or
crutches almost as well as if I had nothing the matter with my legs."

Most afternoons, Loyless took them driving through hillsides
covered with peach orchards, with Father seated beside him and his
wife gossiping to Missy in the back. "I hear an occasional yes or no
from Missy to prove she is not sleeping," Father reported to Mother
as a matter of course. There was no hesitation on either side in
discussing Missy. Where Mother had noted only that the cottage
walls let daylight through, he found the place "delightful and very
comfortable."

Conversations between Father and Tom centered as much on
business as on health. Father was anything but single-minded about
every aspect of his living. The more tightly he could weave one
strand with another, the better he was pleased. He recognized
clearly that his presence as a national celebrity at Warm Springs was
an asset to Peabody, as the banker intended it to be, as well as a
dramatic benefit to Father's recovery. He quickly responded to
Loyless' idea that a way must be found to restore the moribund
resort to prosperity as a health center for sufferers from polio and
kindred diseases. Loyless, in frail health himself, was the lessee and
manager of the Meriwether Inn. Father promised to have a long talk
with Peabody as soon as he got to New York again, whenever that
might be.

He passed on the thought to Louis, who was handling all affairs at
Fidelity and forwarding daily packages of correspondence and
newspapers for Father's attention. Missy kept up with the letter
writing as part of her responsibilities, before they settled down for
quiet evenings reading and playing endless games of rummy by the
fire.

Louis' immediate reaction was to stir up publicity, his initial
approach to any public relations problem. The handful of people in
the village of Warm Springs, a mile away, had already planned a
reception for Father in the town hall there. In Manchester, with its

two or three thousand citizens, Father was invited to another ham-and-hominy supper as the principal speaker.

The hand of Louis could be discerned when Major Cohen sent the star feature writer of the Atlanta *Journal* to spend five days in Father's company, swimming with him, chewing hot dogs bought from a stand near the pool washed down with bottles of beer. FRANKLIN ROOSEVELT WILL SWIM TO HEALTH, said the headline on the published story, which was promptly picked up by newspapers all over the country.

By the time Father and Missy left in November inquiries from other polio patients had started to arrive in the mail at Loyless' hotel. The challenge now was how to capitalize on the situation. Warm Springs, in Father's agile brain, spelled health, potential profits and perhaps a permanent haven for himself and Missy. The result at the polls turned out as he and Louis had anticipated: Coolidge, 15,719,921; Davis, 8,386,704. But Al Smith was returned as governor, grateful for the help that Mother had given him.

2

The most pressing need, as always, was money. The bills for our family's highly complicated life-style had a habit of piling up, accounting for a sizable share of his correspondence. He was dunned for overdue contributions to the Church of St. James. "You promised to give $500 to the endowment fund," complained George Bilyou, the treasurer, who happened to be the village drugstore clerk in Hyde Park. "You will greatly oblige me if you will send me your check for $300 so I can turn it over to Mr. A. Rogers."

Father's reply was both bland and frank: "I had entirely forgotten. . . . In fact, I had not thought of it at all for six years. I will send you $100 this spring. I could no more send you $300 than $3,000,000." Attending meetings as a vestryman had become too big a drain on his time and energy.

He hired a Vassar girl, Mary Hellyer, to work for him at a dollar an hour and expenses some afternoons, helping him collect copies of land titles for a slender volume he started writing in a still shaky hand while he first convalesced at Hyde Park. She waited half a year to be paid her final $58.46. The book did not go to the printers until

1927, when one hundred copies of *Records of the Town of Hyde Park 1821–1875* came off the press. "We didn't have the money to prepare the index, anyway," said Father.

His inability to refuse an invitation made him the official local historian, complete with that imposing title. A state law spelled out his duties: "to collect and preserve material relating to the history of the political subdivisions for which he or she is appointed, and to file such material in fireproof safes or vaults in the city, town or village offices."

He wrangled with a Pleasant Valley stonemason who complained that his bill of $280 was overdue after he had repaired "eighty rods of wall at $3.50 per rod." The agreed price was only $3.00, replied Father. "From this there would be, of course, a material deduction, as there was a good long stretch of wall which you did not build from the ground up but merely straightened out the top stones." He sent a token $100 and asked for a corrected statement.

Watching expenses like a hawk, he shopped around until he found a painter—a loyal campaign worker, of course—who agreed to Father's terms for a job on Granny's rambling establishment with its uncounted windows and doorways: "Painting house two coats with apple green trim and furnish materials, $205, and painting roof, gutters and chimneys two coats and furnish materials, $50. I think a light grey is the best color for the roof and chimneys."

He kept Moses Smith on his toes by having him compile a complete record of woodcutting in an orange-covered school exercise book, while he happily reported to William Plog, after a second visit to Warm Springs, "I have walked two blocks with the right leg brace off."

He cited reasons of health when he made up his mind to sever connections with Marvin and Emmet and find a new partner with whom to practice law. "There is no question that I shall have to spend the greater part of the next four or five years in devoting my primary attention to my legs," he told Grenville Emmet. The truth of the matter was that the safe-and-sound business of settling estates and drawing up wills bored him to death. He was too busy with a hundred and one other things to bring in new clients, which meant that he earned nothing whatever in fees. His old partners were not sorry to see him leave. They had been as disappointed as he was, but Father's deft handling of his departure left the taste of friendship in his wake.

He wasted no time entering into partnership with a tough-fibered young Irishman whose offices were in the same convenient building with its low front step as Fidelity and Deposit. Basil O'Connor was ready to guarantee him $10,000 a year in expectation of the business that Father's name was likely to attract. O'Connor was patient with his partner's months of absence in Warm Springs and, for the time being, aboard the *Larooco*, but he turned out to be a stern taskmaster.

When Father, in his search for quick profits, involved himself with a certain glib-tongued promoter as a director of something called the International Germanic Trust Company, O'Connor cracked the whip. "It has all the earmarks that [he] thinks he can 'kid' you and that you're easygoing and won't mind," he told his partner bluntly. "This annoys me (if I'm right) more than anything else. Of course, I'm with you—even if you're wrong."

He wanted Father to bring the promoter to see him personally, to "make proper arrangements." Otherwise, "your next move should be to hand in your resignation! Heretofore I have been able to say we had no banking affiliations. That was strong. I can't say that now." Father, weighing O'Connor's advice like everyone else's, resigned and sold for $50 apiece shares which he had bought at $170. The company eventually went into receivership.

Van-Lear Black was every bit as patient as O'Connor with Father's prolonged leaves of absence. He knew that his part-time vice-president's political know-how would bring "world beating" results, as Black said, "if you can hold expenses." Certainly in the five years that ended in 1928, the bonding company's New York volume grew from $2,000,000 to $5,000,000. A sizable hunk of that came from Fidelity and Deposit's share in a New York State issue after Al Smith got back to Albany in 1923. Father's influence—and the press releases Louis wrote for the State Treasurer—boosted Fidelity's allocation from $7,000,000 to $10,000,000 worth.

Father demonstrated his style again when Al's candidate for mayor of New York, the devil-may-care Jimmy Walker, beat Hearst's man in office, Mayor John Hylan. Jimmy was a neighbor of ours, with an apartment in Mayfair House on the opposite side of East Sixty-fifth Street. I could see down into it from the window of my front bedroom in Granny's house, where I sometimes sat marveling at the way the liquor flowed and Jimmy and his friends cavorted with their girls.

Mother took a dim view of the new mayor, who occasionally dropped in to see Father, but she was handed one job which Louis told Father about during one of his vacations. "Wine, women and song are playing the very devil with Jimmy Walker, and your missus has been asked by some very distinguished Democratic ladies to reason with Jimmy. This is easier said than done in my judgment." Louis turned out right again.

But Father appreciated the importance of Walker to Fidelity and Deposit. He found jobs in the firm for the sons of two Tammany leaders, in the time-tested tradition of political patronage.

Louis operated on a different level. While he wrote to naval contractors that the former Assistant Secretary had other irons in the fire these days, he concentrated on his old wartime contacts in labor unions. A bottle of whiskey placed here and there often helped, he knew. He had instant access to William Green, chief of the American Federation of Labor. Some half dozen trips to Washington won a promise from the AFL to let Fidelity handle its bond issues. But the hopes of the team of Roosevelt and Howe were dashed when Black's home office in Baltimore refused to meet the low rate which Green and his colleagues wanted.

From their wedding day until he died, Father's financial affairs were a closed book to Mother. Granny never told him just how much money she had or what her income amounted to. In the same tradition, he told Mother no more about the ups and downs of his finances than he did about his plans in business or politics. In her opinion, of course, he was as reckless about his investments as he was about everything else.

In his role as a kind of public-relations counsel for Fidelity and Deposit, he seldom failed to preach the merits of conservative investing. The absence of "that element of speculation which enters into so many classes of business" made his job attractive to him, he told one interviewer. His advice to young men, other than his sons, was to deposit their first thousand dollars into a savings account.

Yet as a result of being pressed for cash and as an inevitable consequence of his nature, his handling of his own finances was like the draw poker he liked to play, with one-eyed jacks and deuces wild. He firmly believed in his luck. That was part of the broad streak of superstition in him. He was apt to be careful about what he did on any Friday the thirteenth. He had his private lucky numbers;

lucky days; lucky clothes like his campaign hat, an old fedora he wore for years; lucky shoes that he had bought in London twenty years earlier.

Promoters were drawn to him like bees to honey, both before and after his fascination grew with Warm Springs. Pat Homer, big-mouthed and irrepressible, was a persistent caller for years after his fiasco of a scheme to build a wartime oil refinery at Fall River. The Compo Bond Corporation was typical. That was a company set up to raise capital by selling, through various banks, low-cost bonds similar to United States Treasury savings stamps. Louis and Father helped launch the plan just before the polio attack. Homer was urged to pick up the franchise for his home state of Massachusetts.

Even he was skeptical. Louis wrote him sharply, "What do you mean 'what is Compo doing besides catching suckers?' You've got it all wrong. . . . Compo is doing everything in the world except catching suckers. They have built enough castles to fill all Spain. . . ." Four years later, the company sagged into gradual bankruptcy. Father, who was a member of the board of directors, resigned before the inevitable end came. His personal losses amounted to no more than $2,500, but a lot of time had been wasted, and he had risked his good name.

He and Louis both were lured by Homer, whom Louis regarded as something of a financial genius, into the lobster business, another disaster, which finally put a stop to their association with the supersalesman. The idea was to buy mass quantities of the creatures, keep them alive and penned up until prices rose, then sell them to hotels and markets. Louis got along famously with Homer, to the extent of being able to kid him, "If I were your Missus, I would keep you tied up around the house for a week." This was a reference to the promoter's not unknown weakness for chorus girls. Louis fancied that he was being as shrewd in business as he was in politics when he contrived to obtain for Father majority control of Witham Brothers, Incorporated, lobster fatteners.

But prices stubbornly refused to rise, and their catch had to be fed and maintained in captivity. More and more thousands of dollars had to be poured into the company until majority interest became the major responsibility for debts running close to $26,000. Louis, as ever, was unrepentant. When a Texas women's organization asked Father to donate some sort of white elephant for sale at a fund-raising tea party, Louis promptly suggested, "Why not send them your stock in the lobster company?"

One venture followed another, none of them producing the kind of gains which Father counted on now that politics took second place in his thinking. He hoped somehow to profit from the boom times which, however spottily, continued under canny Cal Coolidge. He dabbled with two thousand shares of a wildcat Wyoming company, whose drilling produced only gas. "If the Montacal Oil Company should happen to strike oil," he told John Lawrence, "it would be a considerable help to yours truly." It never did, and by 1929 Father's dreaming had switched to the possibility of piping natural gas into Salt Lake City, a valid enough concept except that it was a couple of decades ahead of its time.

In retrospect, many of the notions spun out by his imagination fell into that category. One of them was to sell advertising space in taxicabs. Another was Photomaton, a system of quarter-in-the-slot camera portraits taken in booths installed in railroad stations, department stores and public washrooms. Father and Henry Morgenthau were both directors of the company. The Depression ultimately killed it, but not before Henry, acting on Father's behalf, bought and resold five hundred shares at a profit of $3,000.

His bounding, personal enthusiasms colored many of his adventures in finance, often at the cost of cool-headed judgment. Ships and shipping magnates were equally appealing to him. He spent a year and more trying to arrange a merger of small lines and arrange backing to buy ten 9,000-ton surplus vessels from the United States government at $30 a ton. They would run cargoes between the Pacific and the Atlantic by way of the Panama Canal, Uncle Ted's creation, which Father had greatly admired upon inspecting it as Assistant Secretary.

He would serve as general counsel of the new company, Twin Coast Navigation, until he was fit enough to take on its running as vice-president. Literally hundreds of hours were put into detailed analyses of potential business, to be wrested from eleven established competitors. On capital of $2,000,000, he calculated, earnings after payment of taxes and operating expenses would top $700,000 a year.

The Skipper, as his associates liked to call him, set up luncheons, teas and dinners at our house to lure prospective investors. Banks and trust companies were pessimistic about his chances. Cargo hauling was a cutthroat business. The existing shipping lines would drive out a newcomer. Father lowered his sights, to drum up $6,000 as expenses for fund raising. "The project ought to be worth that much of a flier if it is worth pushing at all," he told one financier whom he approached. "I should gladly do this underwriting myself if I did not have so many unusual demands to meet just now."

The capital of $2,000,000 proved impossible to raise. This particular dream came to a close with a note written by Missy to one of the shipping executives involved: "Mr. Roosevelt is cruising . . . and will not be back until September 1." As the result of a minor investment made along the way, Father's time did not go entirely unrewarded. He received one-third of the proceeds from twenty shares bought at $2,500 and sold at $4,400. In other words, $633.33.

His deep-down dislike and distrust of airplanes dated from the day he was given his maiden flight aboard a Navy NC-4 seaplane off Campobello when he was Assistant Secretary. Like most people in the twenties, he thought that dirigibles were the safe, sure way to travel in the future. A week or so before polio struck him, he was writing, "I wish all my friends . . . would keep out of aeroplanes. I was horrified to get a cable from London the other day saying that my mother also had flown across from London to Paris. Wait until my dirigibles are running. . . ."

He and Louis were using every maneuver they had learned in their Washington days to drum up government support for an airship service linking New York and Chicago for a start, then expanding into other major cities. But the airplane won out, and another scheme leaked away, like helium escaping from one of the dirigibles that General Air Service never got around to building.

At Hyde Park, his fascination with the art and craft of forestry kept him constantly having seedlings planted to grow into tomorrow's trees. He bought thousands at a time from nurserymen and begged even more from the College of Forestry at Syracuse University. Red pine, yellow pine and Scotch pine; European larch and Japanese larch; Norway and Sitka spruce; tulip poplar— William Plog took care of the planting of nearly five thousand young trees a year for more than fifteen years.

This was one more activity which Father's imagination turned into elusive profit. His scratch-pad figuring indicated that on working capital of half a million dollars, up to 15,000 acres of forest could be planted and operated along the lines of similar state-owned tracts in Europe. The American building boom was resulting in trees being cut faster than they could regrow. As a keen conservationist, that alarmed him. It did not, however, alarm any moneymen to the extent of putting up the necessary cash.

He kept his investment accounts meticulously handwritten on sheets of long columnar paper, locked away out of sight in his office safe. They invariably showed more losses than gains. Lack of cash compelled him to set a limit of $5,000 on most of his investing. He was too far away for months on end to watch the rise and fall of the market at every opening and closing. Louis' telegrams helped somewhat, but he often had to make decisions for Father, and he had only a newspaperman's background for handling finance.

Sometimes, they did strike it right, but not rich. Germany was a country that intrigued Father more than any other except England. He had briefly been in school there before he entered Groton. When the Weimar Republic, set up after the war, had trouble maintaining the value of its currency, Father joined in a Canadian corporation, United European Investors, which used cheap marks to buy stock in nineteen German corporations involved in electric power, machinery making, dyes and chemicals, and other basic industries.

As soon as the period of wild inflation was over, United European Investors Limited was wound up, at a profit of more than 200 percent. In 1930 the Republicans attempted to turn that incident into a specter haunting Father with the claim that he had been an evil exploiter of Germany's distress. As a firework designed to alarm German-American voters, it proved to be a damp squib. During the three years he was involved to "save from further losses the foolish Americans who bought German marks at much higher prices," Father personally profited to the extent of roughly $5,000.

Money in these amounts would be chicken feed when it came to buying Warm Springs. Oil wells, lobsters, airships, automatic cameras, advertisements in taxis—there had to be some way the cash could be found.

3

Coinciding with Mother's first *Larooco* cruise in March, 1925,

Father's thoughts began to focus on parting with the boat. The expense was getting out of hand. New canvas and a new engine had been installed while she was laid up in Miami. When Father and Missy arrived in the first days of February, they discovered that stateroom furniture had been stolen while the work was being done.

Selling the "floating tenement" which had stood for most of the personal pleasure that living held for him would be a wrench. It was easy to tell what Mother's views were when the subject came up between them. As soon as she had left at the end of her brief stay, she wrote him in words which signified the precise opposite of their surface meaning: "Don't worry about being selfish, it is more important that you have all you need and wish than anything else, and you always give the chicks more than they need, and you know I always do just what I want!"

He could understand those messages better than anybody else. He proposed almost immediately to Lawrence, the absentee co-owner, that they try to find a buyer for the *Larooco*. "There is now no question," he said, "that this Warm Springs pool does my legs more good than anything else. Last autumn I added at least ten pounds to the weight I could put on my knees."

He had gone straight to Warm Springs with Missy after seeing the houseboat put out of commission for another season. They found trouble of a special, unexpected brand waiting. Thanks to the publicity of the previous fall, the place was already attracting polio patients set on "swimming back to health" like Father.

They had only just arrived and were sitting talking with Tom Loyless when one of his helpers interrupted them. "Two people have been carried off the train down at the station. What shall we do with them? Neither of them can walk."

The solution seemed to be to find accommodations in the village overnight. In the morning, Loyless could get to work fixing up one of the empty cottages for them. But before that could be done, eight more cripples had arrived there at the desolate ruin of a resort five miles from anything that rated halfway to being a town. A challenge of that order was something that roused the best in Father.

The first priority was to send to Manchester for Dr. James Johnson, who was no polio expert, but he had attended Louis Joseph in that young man's sensationally successful visits to the pool. The doctor checked out the new arrivals and, in Father's words, "guaranteed that they did not have heart trouble or something else from which they would suddenly die." For his prompt services, Dr. Johnson was eventually to become consulting physician to the Georgia Warm Springs Foundation.

At the moment, though, the place had ten unexpected polio patients with varying degrees of muscle damage and no one in residence to care for them—no doctor, no physiotherapist, no nurse. Father gleefully took on the first two jobs, Missy the other. "I sometimes wish I could find some spot on the globe where it was not essential and necessary for me to start something new," he told Livy, only half jokingly, in a long letter. "A sand bar in the ocean might answer, but I would probably start building a sea wall around it and digging for pirate treasure in the middle."

Missy, as was her custom, said very little. She was a genuinely modest woman, self-effacing by nature, until Father invited her opinions on something. "Loyalty," she considered, "is to me the first virtue." "Speak up, Missy" became one of Father's bywords.

Of the ten men and women in "old Dr. Roosevelt's" first class, he taught one man how to swim and all the rest how to exercise by playing around in the water. One workout method of his own invention he labeled "the elevating exercise": from a sitting float position, you forced both feet to the bottom of the pool, then attempted to stand, buoyed by the warm mineral-laden water.

"I remember there were two quite large ladies," Father recalled. One of them had trouble getting both feet down. "Well, I would take one large knee and I would force this large knee, then I would say, 'Have you got it?' "

"Yes," she panted.

"Hold it, hold it!" cried Dr. Roosevelt, grabbing for the other knee, though before he got it down below the surface, the first knee would be popping up again. "This used to go on for half an hour at a time, but before I left in the spring, I could get both those knees down at the same time."

With Missy's help, he drew rough anatomical charts on cardboard, putting to use the detailed knowledge of muscle structure he had acquired over the past four years from Dr. Lovett. They set up an informal clinic, with Dr. Johnson as the visiting physician. Every morning, Father dressed in his loose-fitting black tank suit and a floppy linen hat to protect his head, with its thinning hair, from the Georgia sun. Then he would be wheeled to the crumbling concrete dock, to lower himself over the edge and stand waiting for his followers in hope of health. "You would howl with glee," he said, "if you could see the clinic in operation at the side of the pool, and the patients doing various exercises in the water under my leadership—they are male and female of all ages and weights." More often than not, Missy worked with the man whose side she seldom left through all those Warm Springs years.

He liked to label himself "consulting architect and landscape engineer" for the Warm Springs Company, which Peabody controlled. Father was already looking ahead to the day when by some means or another he could take over the place as his own. Hours a day went into conferences with Tom Loyless, who grew more frail with every month that passed. Where the buildings should be moved; where new roads should be put in; what trees to plant; how to remodel the inn.

They mapped out a new water system, a new sewage plant, a fishing pond. They started the Pine Mountain Club with plans for a dance hall, a restaurant, picnic grounds and a golf course. Each of their dreams was ultimately realized, but only for Missy and Father. Tom Loyless was slowly dying of cancer. "You are just bound to get on those legs of yours sooner or later," he told Father before the end, "because the world, the flesh and the devil can't beat the sort of fight you are making."

By the close of that year seventeen patients, uninvited and uncared for except by the improvisations of "Dr. Roosevelt" and his nurse, showed up at the inn, wracking it with turmoil. The handful of regular guests objected to the "IP's" using the pool, fearing contagion. They refused to share the dining room with them, so Tom had to provide separate quarters for the paralytics. Father's temporary solutions were to build a small new outdoor pool some thirty yards from the public one and to fix up the other vacant cottages in order to reassure his followers that neither they nor he were social lepers.

In New York and at Hyde Park, Mother pursued her own vision of a completely separate life. She wanted locks installed on each of the connecting doors between our town house and Granny's. She pressed hard for the building of the Val-Kill cottage for Nancy Cook, Marion Dickerman and herself. She, too, was seeking something approximating her own home, not Hyde Park, where she felt like a lodger living in a spare room, or Warm Springs, which was strictly the domain of Father and Missy.

Louis persuaded Father that, no matter how short family funds were, he should let her have the money for the cottage. Father's part in drawing up the plans with Henry Toombs, the architect, stopped short with the exterior. In keeping with the Dutch traditions of Crum Elbow, it had to be of fieldstone, like the early settlers' houses. To make the interior entirely hers, Mother sketched out the clutter of tiny rooms which were as different as it was possible to make them from the sunny spaciousness of Granny's house.

In his sympathy for her melancholy existence, with the sense of duty fulfilled as her only real reward, Louis brought her closer and closer to understanding that if she could not be a complete wife, she had to learn to allow Father to have other outlets for himself so that he could lead a normal sexual life. She needed a haven, too, to share with her friends. Rosy, in his seventies now with his gout growing worse, jeered at the lot of them. "Hope your Parlor Socialists are not living too much on the fat of the land with you against their principles," he wrote to Father.

At first, Mother insisted on obtaining bids from contractors for building her new refuge. The figures they came up with struck Father as exorbitant. "If you three women will go away, Henry and I will build the cottage," he told her. She reluctantly allowed him to take over supervision of the job, at a saving of $4,000. She also got her swimming pool. A stream ran from behind the place into a swamp in front. The stream was dammed and the swamp cleared, but it was an abortive effort. The little man-made lake constantly silted up and water lilies flourished. When we went to swim there, we had to cut out the vegetation before we took a dip.

Granny actively disliked the idea of Val-Kill and made her feelings clear to Mother with scathing references to the place and the two women who would be its permanent tenants. She kept up her use of Sis as a thorn to be driven into Mother's side. Sis was in a hurry to be married to escape the cold war which promised no armistice between Granny and Mother, Mother and Father.

That Christmas, my sister arrived at Hyde Park and announced that she was in love. She brought her prospective husband, Curtis Dall, with her. Curtis was a stockbroker, a Princeton graduate, twenty-nine years old. Jimmy and I doubted whether he was the right man for our tomboy sister, who came back from her Arizona vacation on the Greenaways' ranch convinced that there was nothing finer than outdoor living and work with animals. She had been talked into taking a course in animal husbandry at Cornell and, as a warm-up for that, some six weeks of study at the State Experimental Station at Geneva, New York. On the drive up there with Mother, they spoke not a word to each other. Of all the worries on Mother's mind, Sis ranked number one. From college, she wrote seldom, if at all, to Mother, only to Father, whom she adored.

Her two oldest brothers undertook to knock some of the starch out of Curtis by inviting him to play pickup hockey on the ice at Hyde Park and also up at Barrytown with us and the Delano boys. We thought he was a bit inclined to boast about the prowess he had achieved in the game at Princeton. At Barrytown, when Jimmy and I had heard enough, we tripped him. Blood was streaming from a cut made by a skate slicing into his chin when Sis took him into the house, raging at us for damaging her beloved.

He still bore the scar on their wedding day the following spring. Granny secretly offered to buy an apartment for them as her wedding gift. Sis was not to tell Mother, since, said Granny, she would argue them out of accepting it. Sis did, in fact, let Mother in on the plot, leading her to fire off an angry outburst to Father on the day before his last aboard the *Larooco*.

". . . It is all I can do to be decent," she said. ". . . Sometimes I think constant irritation is worse for one than real tragedy now and then. I've reached a state of such constant self-control I'm afraid of what will happen if it ever breaks." Perhaps the message was intended for Missy, too.

In any event, Granny had her way as usual, ignoring Mother's fears that misplaced generosity would trap the newly married Curtis Dalls into living beyond their means, thereby driving them into perpetual reliance on the grandmother. "I did not think I *could* be nasty *or* mean, and I fear I had too good an opinion of myself," Granny professed to Mother. "Also, I love you, dear, too much to ever want to hurt you. I *was hasty*, and of course I shall give them the apartment."

Once again, with no great expectation of success, Mother tried to draw Father into the ruckus by forwarding Granny's letter to him, along with a few contrite words of her own: "I've been thoroughly nasty, but I'll try to behave again now for a time." Since the day of Sis' marriage was approaching, she nudged him with a reminder that perhaps he should buy a new suit. By this time I had provided what seemed to be a fitting finale to the *Larooco*'s checkered career by hooking the record-making jewfish. Missy had left for New York a couple of weeks before, tearful as usual that the cruise was over and the future of the old boat uncertain. I rode with Father on the evening train from Miami to Warm Springs. He declined to take sides in the dispute over the proposed apartment.

Not long before the wedding, Mother was following her custom of sitting up waiting for Sis to come home. There was a sofa in my sister's bedroom which Mother used for the purpose. In the early hours one morning, she told Sis something of Lucy Mercer and the circumstances of her own failed marriage. Mother and daughter had never been so close.

If Mother had expected to shock Sis, she was disappointed. Sis was her father's daughter, as Jimmy and I were decidedly his sons. We felt completely at ease with him, much less so with Mother. Lucy Mercer or Curtis Dall notwithstanding, Sis' feelings for him were unchanged. She told him, for example, about a night when she and her new husband dropped in at East Sixty-fifth Street with nothing to wear to bed. "So I stole (borrowed) your best pair of pajamas from one drawer and a pair of B.V.D.s from another! The pajamas were a good fit—but Heaven help the B.V.D.s! They wouldn't stay on, so I spent a good half-hour tying him into them with tape!"

Father tinkered with plans to keep a foothold in Florida before he put the boat on the market. What he had seen in his meanderings around the keys impressed him. He smelled opportunities there, especially in Boca Chica, if it could be developed as a winter resort. With Missy doing the legwork, he had obtained an option on 109 acres of land there with a mile and a half of beachfront. The arithmetic looked roseate. Subdivided into some six hundred lots, the property would bring in $146,100 for a purchase price of $53,500 (minus a 10 percent reduction for cash, as Father happily noted). He was ready to put in $15,000 himself, which represented a major investment for him. Perhaps Henry junior could interest his father, "Uncle Henry" Morgenthau, the aged angel of the Democratic Party, in the deal. Unfortunately, he could not. "My Father," said young Henry, "feels that at his time of life, it is a mistake to make this kind of investment." Father accordingly had to see one more scheme lie waiting for some future speculator to grow rich on.

Fifteen thousand dollars was the asking price when the *Larooco* first went on the market. When there was not so much as a nibble of interest from any prospective customer, Father came up with a different idea. Why not have four or five patients with the necessary cash join together and run the houseboat as a floating hospital, all sharing the expenses? That did not work out, either.

The hope of raising cash toward buying Warm Springs by selling the boat faded fast when a September hurricane swept Florida's east coast. Captain George Pilkington's boatyard up the Fort Lauderdale River, where the *Larooco* was laid up, lay close to the heart of the disaster area. The two palm trees to which she was made fast were uprooted as the river flooded, and the boat took off on her last voyage. She brought up in a pine forest four miles inland, a mile from the nearest waterway, nestled on a bed of pine needles.

Captain Pilkington's letters went unanswered for a year. "I have tryed to sell your boat," he wrote in a wandering hand, "but thear has not been any sales for any kind of boat in this country property as every thing has been flat. . . . I can not lay out any more money to protect the boat unless I am payed for what I have all ready spent. I do not know how you expect me to."

Three weeks later, he obtained a marshal's order to put the boat up for sale. "I do not believe that the boat, furnishings etc. will sell for more than the amount of the bill together with interest, costs etc.," declared the captain, "which will amount to in the neighborhood of six hundred dollars."

Father took the occasion to add a postscript to the ship's log, which, squirreled away with ten thousand other souvenirs, looked as good as new: "So ended a good old craft with personality. On the whole, it was an end to be preferred to that of gasoline barge or lumber lighter." Missy, who could be sentimental at times, must have shed some tears over the outcome.

4

Something about his early experiences at Warm Springs impelled Father to speed the pace of his drive for recovery. After serving as "Dr. Roosevelt" to the first batch of polio patients, he spent three months in and out of his New York offices, saw Missy off on a vacation with her family in Potsdam, then departed with Louis to try out a brand-new treatment.

Our family scattered to all points of the compass that summer.

Father had been supervising the building of the Val-Kill place. Jimmy and I took off for the dude ranch in Wyoming that Uncle Hall had recommended. Mother would soon be suffering the chaos of her trip to Campobello with Franklin, Johnny, Miss Cook and Miss Dickerman.

With the family chauffeur at the wheel, Father and Louis crowded into the back seat of a car with "several score suitcases, braces, crutches, canes, sandwiches thrown in for good measure," as my parent cheerfully reported. "However, it saves eleven dollars for each person to travel thus to the beach!"

They were headed for Horseneck Beach, where Mother was to follow, to spend a few days in a rented cottage similar to the Howes' and reasonably close to it, before she left on her camping excursion. Father had heard from Uncle Fred of yet another approach to the challenge of how to walk again. Dr. William McDonald, a stern-faced neurologist who had turned to specializing in polio, preached the benefits of strenuous exercise, hours a day on a "walking board," having the patient drag himself around an oblong of wood with a handrail circling it. With no one to assist him in treatments at the little clapboard house he had taken at Marion, an hour or so's drive from Horseneck Beach on Buzzards Bay, he accepted only four patients at a time in general, but he had stretched a point and added Father to his roster.

Granny thought it was a "grand plan." She told Father, "I feel so hopeful and confident . . . now for the first time in more than a year I feel that *work* is to be done for *you*, my dearest."

Father refused to let her forget that her original ambition was to keep him a permanent invalid. "Braces are, of course, laid aside," he replied. "He is hot against them and confirms what I have told you for two years, and you would not believe."

Compared with the shanty in which Father at first found himself, the Howes' place was a palace. Indoor plumbing was primitive. Going to the toilet involved dragging himself through soft sand to an outhouse a dozen yards away. Getting from the weather-beaten shack to the road and a waiting car could be done only when the tide was halfway out.

Yet he considered the sheer relief of freedom from braces to justify extending what he had foreseen as a few weeks' stay into a punishing daily workout which lasted until it was time to go to Hyde Park for Christmas. The only interruption came about when Dr. McDonald strained his heart carrying one of his patients to see a football game. Jimmy and I spent a few days with Father on our route back from Wyoming. Missy began visiting Marion off and on as soon as her vacation was over, then joined him again at Key Largo for their last cruise together.

After opening negotiations with Peabody, he was assured that he could buy Warm Springs. The banker's philanthropy did not extend to business transactions. The price would be stiff, far more than Father could afford. He wired Loyless that "at last you and I will see our dream carried out." He knew he would need Granny's moral as well as financial support. "I want you to take a great interest in it," he said, "for I feel you can help me with many suggestions, and the place properly run will not only do a great deal of good but will prove *financially* successful."

Mother, who sometimes found that there was not enough money in the household account to pay the New York servants' wages, was understandably cautious. "It was good to hear about you from Louis," she wrote him in the middle of the negotiating, "and you seem to be moving along in Warm Springs. Don't let yourself in for too much money and don't make Mama put in much, for if she lost she'd never get over it! I think you ought to ask her down to stay for a week. She's dying to go and hurt at not being asked. I'll bring her if you want, and Missy could move out while she stayed."

He was not to be deterred. On April 29, 1926, he acquired the derelict property, where Loyless was running ever deeper into debt. At the peak of his obligations as the new proprietor, Father had precisely $201,667.83 invested in the place in the form of a demand note, which was not completely paid off until after his death, and then only from a life insurance policy he had taken out in Warm Springs' favor. The $200,000-plus represented more than two-thirds of everything he owned. It was the only time he took such a monumental risk. Mother was terrified that if this went the way of so many of his business ventures, none of us boys could go to college, a fate which I, for one, was more than ready to face. "Mama will always see the children through" was his calm reply. Jimmy, in fact, entered Harvard that fall.

Basil O'Connor took care of the legal work involved in the purchase, as concerned as Mother that Father this time had bitten off more than could be chewed. Louis, to whom doubt was disloyalty, scurried around New York as an unofficial fund raiser, buttonholing friends and associates in the new cause. Granny, who suspected that her son was on the road to bankruptcy, did her part by arranging a dinner party for possible angels and, when the summer was over, went to Warm Springs for two weeks.

The new owner's first thought was to get medical accreditation for the spring water. The American Orthopedic Association happened to hold its annual convention in Atlanta. It was hard for a layman to convince these specialists that Warm Springs deserved investigation, but Father had the charm of a supersalesman. A committee of three experts was set up to study reports which would be prepared by a physician on the spot.

To carry out the actual tests of patients in the pool, Father engaged Dr. Leroy Hubbard, orthopedic surgeon of the New York State Department of Health, with years of experience in the aftercare of polio. With a trained physiotherapist and a swimming instructor, the doctor checked the progress of twenty-three patients over a period of seven months. In every case, there was improvement to be reported. When the three specialists of the association read his findings, they put the stamp of approval on Hubbard's work and recommended that a hydrotherapy center be established at Warm Springs. The first important milestone was passed.

Father had not waited to celebrate the founding of his own domain, a permanent home away from Mother and Granny, where he could enjoy Missy's love and companionship. "You needn't worry about my losing a fortune in it," he reassured Granny, "for every step is being planned either to pay for itself or make a profit on."

He wanted some means of getting around his 12,000 acres without a chauffeur—Missy could not drive. He had the village blacksmith, Tom Bradshaw, fit out an ancient Model-T Ford with pulleys and levers so that he could brake and change gears with his hands. In it, they sometimes dropped in at the Cove, where the moonshiners hung out, to sample a little white lightning from a fruit jar with the rest of the company. The old flivver carried them all over Meriwether County, exploring the sun-drenched countryside, striking up friendships with anyone whom Father took a fancy to. He made sure that every one of his interests would be provided for by buying a farm of nearly 2,000 acres near the peak of Pine Mountain. His main purpose there was to raise cattle, as a demonstration to his neighbors that cotton and peaches were not the only crops Georgia was good for. He laid plans for constructing a scenic highway on his property, which stretched for miles, an estate bigger by far than Hyde Park. In the guest cottages and in the houses of their new friends, a floating poker game was started that lasted on and off long after Father entered the White House.

When Tom Loyless' failing health made it impossible to continue writing a column he supplied to the Macon *Daily Telegraph*, Father stepped in with a dozen or so articles dictated to Missy under the title "Roosevelt Says." His first effort lightheartedly explained that Loyless was "out picking wild flowers, and I have returned to my former profession—I used to edit the college paper in the old days." His thought was to syndicate these articles nationwide as a useful platform for his opinions. Only the Atlanta *Constitution* expressed any interest. The publisher of the Macon *Telegraph*, a last-ditch white supremacy sheet, expressed his appreciation later by demanding Father's impeachment as President.

He drew up plans with Missy for a new cottage, the first of a colony of similar small houses to be subscribed for by a long list of well-wishers whom Louis was already working on. Granny was persuaded to donate $3,000 to build one of them, which turned out to be the full extent of her giving. Their first home, when it was completed, was "really very good in every way, the woodwork covering all walls and ceilings a great success," said Father.

The little pine-paneled house was usually filled with laughter. He joked about their dime-store "silver" when the table was set for meals. He installed an old icebox, serviced by the iceman, because "A long, tall, cool drink always tastes better with real ice." The two of them took turns cranking an ancient ice-cream freezer. "It makes the only really decent ice cream."

Once again, he returned to New York in time to be at Hyde Park for Christmas, as all the family were. He had seldom looked better, tanned from the Georgia sun, bubbling with enthusiasm for Warm Springs. With the orthopedists' seal of recommendation, he set about transforming his private enterprise into a nonstock, nonprofit foundation. Besides himself, the principal incorporators were Peabody; O'Connor; John Raskob, the General Motors tycoon who was to be the chairman of the Democratic National Committee; and, of course, Louis Howe.

The occasion was commemorated at home—Father virtually never dined out—with a dinner of wild duck sent by Hall. "I cannot tell you how much they were appreciated by everybody," Father told his brother-in-law in a thank-you note. He was speaking strictly for himself, as a matter of fact. His idea of perfection was to hang game birds in the larder until they fell off the hook, then have them barely warmed in the oven by the cook. Nobody but he could stand the thought of eating more than a mouthful or two out of politeness. Mother this time was spared the duty of doing even that. She had just been to the hospital to have her tonsils out. On the same day, Johnny fell and broke an arm, and Jimmy came home from Harvard with a heavy case of influenza.

A few days later, our parents took the train together to Warm Springs, Mother to help Missy shop in Atlanta for a stove and other equipment for the new cottage, Father to lay out more money for land to add to the farm he had bought. Most of the new furniture was handmade as the product of a business which Mother had just got herself into.

She was reconciled to the fact that, for the present, nothing equaled the importance of Warm Springs to Father. After he bought the tumbledown resort, she had been appalled by the cost and the sheer magnitude of the task he was taking on as promoter, innkeeper and amateur physiotherapist. "I know you love creative work," she told him at that time, "my only feeling is that Georgia is somewhat distant for you to keep in touch with what is really a big undertaking. One cannot, it seems to me, have *vital* interests in widely divided places, but that may be because I'm old and rather overwhelmed by what there is to do in one place, and it wearies me to think of even undertaking to make new ties. Don't be discouraged by me; I have great confidence in your extraordinary interest and enthusiasm. It is just that I couldn't do it, but then I couldn't contemplate what Nan is proposing at Hyde Park!"

"Nan," of course, was Nancy Cook, whose brain came up with the notion that she and Mother should go into the furniture-manufacturing business, Nan to provide the organizing and designing talent, Mother the working capital. For the sake of her friend, Mother used to say that her earnings from writing magazine articles and talking on radio went toward the little factory which they built. That was a polite deception. At the time she took up furniture making, she had only what she had inherited from her parents to put in as capital. When she became First Lady, she earned comfortably more than $100,000, principally from her "My Day" column syndicated by the

North American Newspaper Alliance and from her lecturing. She gave most of it away, a portion toward keeping the factory going.

Nan fired her interest originally by taking her around any number of museums, inspecting early American antiques. The idea was to see whether a market existed for expensive, authentic reproductions of fine pieces, chests, tables, chairs and so on, all finished by hand so that the wood looked and felt as if every piece had a past. Mother was out to test her own abilities as a manager simultaneously with Father's challenge in making a success of Warm Springs.

His interest in furniture production was minimal at best, but he humored Mother in his customary fashion. What stirred his imagination was the potential for finding something like a cottage industry that might be developed around Hyde Park to provide occupations for young men who would otherwise drift away from farming. He knew of a community in Vermont which had raised its standard of living, and held on to farms that were too poor to support a family, by the expedient of turning out wooden handles and saucepan knobs during the winter months.

Nancy Cook was shrewd as well as talented. She hired Norwegian and Italian cabinetmakers to teach their craft to local youngsters. Father's curiosity began to grow, though nobody could convince him to put any money in the business, whose stationery listed her as president and treasurer, with Mother and Marion Dickerman as vice-presidents.

Their initial project was the strange fancy of making the furniture for Father's new cottage at Warm Springs, including, if I remember correctly, a bed of extra length for him. He was delighted to be their first customer, though as time passed, Mother was their best, buying various pieces as wedding presents and other gifts. Some of us in the family still have some chairs and desks, beautifully finished with a gleaming patina, which will last for generations to come. The factory itself never paid its way.

Father's move with Missy and McDuffie into his new home prompted Mother to spend days at a time in her own Val-Kill hideaway with Nan and Marion. She often took Franklin and Johnny with her, in spite of memories of the Campobello excursion, to keep them out of Granny's orbit. Sis and Curtis, waiting for the apartment, spent occasional weekends at Hyde Park, in one of Granny's guest rooms.

Mother regarded herself as having three jobs in looking after her two youngest sons, managing the furniture factory, and working for the state Democratic organization. She felt that there was room for still another to fill the emptiness of her living. The more she saw of what other women, less sheltered and more secure within themselves, could achieve, the more clearly she came to appreciate some of her own inadequacies. "If I had to go out and earn my living," she said with a touch of bitterness, "I doubt that I'd even make a very good cleaning woman."

The answer to the question of where to find something more to do lay with Marion Dickerman. She served as the assistant principal of a very correct Manhattan private school for one hundred uniformed girls aged five to eighteen, founded and run by an English spinster, Miss Todhunter. Mother yielded to the persuasions of Miss Dickerman and started work at the Todhunter School as a teacher, uncertificated but desperately anxious to make up in enthusiasm what she lacked in qualifications.

Ingrained doubt about her success as a young mother in bringing up her own children prompted her to choose teaching only older girls American history and American and English literature. She dug out the old notebooks she had kept from her school days in England thirty years ago and put them to use again. She carefully monitored her own performances in front of her classes and set homework for herself as well as for her pupils.

A few months later, Miss Todhunter took it into her head to retire to her native land. Would Miss Dickerman care to take over the school? She, in turn, wondered whether Mother and Nancy Cook would like to join her in buying the place. A letter was hurried off to Father in Warm Springs, posing a question to which she knew the answer in advance. "I ought to plan to be freer . . . yet . . . as you know I'm not keen to get into W.S. life at all as one would have to do if one stayed long or often. It is very hard to decide, so please write me at once how you feel."

She was out of sympathy with her absentee husband's pursuit of the rainbow that would enable him to walk, and she was still skeptical about the chances of Warm Springs being made profitable. Her feelings had seldom shown more nakedly than in the lines she scribbled on a letter addressed to her by a manufacturer of surgical appliances, who offered to make a lightweight brace for Father "without any obligation" if only he could "hear from Mr. Roosevelt personally concerning his health."

She forwarded that letter with her own comment: "This man talked to me for *hours* on the plane and feels hurt that you haven't written him. Please do. I don't want to talk to him again."

The decision concerning Todhunter School was simple enough, reached without argument on either side. Mother would pursue her activities in and around New York. Father would spend as much time as he could spare in Warm Springs. They would meet when their paths converged, certainly at Christmas and during summers at Hyde Park.

5

What Warm Springs stood in need of more than anything else was customers and funds for expansion. Louis accepted the main responsibility for rounding up both, employing his customary mixture of cajolery and high pressure, laced with a liberal serving of cynicism.

His personal finances remained as shaky as ever. His Fidelity pay had to be stretched perilously thin to cover the running around he did for Father, who doled out precious little in the way of extra cash for Louis. "I may want to hit FR Friday instead of Saturday this week," Louis mentioned on one occasion to Mother, "as next week looks like hell."

He was sensitive about asking. "I may remark," he wrote to Father, "that your check arrived in the nick of time, as I was busted. I hate like hell to take a cent from you when you need so much for W.S., but when you come back, I hope to go on the war path myself and bring you more than the amount from sources you wouldn't otherwise reach."

They continued to keep their eyes peeled for additional means of raising cash to pour into the health resort, which was slowly beginning to take shape in Georgia. Their old campaign teammate, Charles McCarthy, Missy's original boss, served as a scout for them in Washington. There was a chance, he reported, of making as much as $300,000 on an investment of roughly one-third of that amount by buying a building on F Street. He and Father could split the commission of $20,000.

Louis scuttled to and from the capital to keep in touch. "I have a bill for nineteen plunks . . . for certain viands furnished at the dinner in Washington," he told Father. "It had a narrow escape from falling into the Missus' hands. I sent him my check, and we can adjust it next month."

He bird-dogged Father's stock in such fliers as a company formed to sell postage-stamp slot machines, which merged as part of Camco, the Consolidated Automatic Merchandising Corporation. Plans called for a chain of automated stores, banked with machines dispensing cigarettes, candy, razor blades and other items. Trouble developed in the frequent failure of the mechanisms to deliver anything at all and the fact that slugs fitted the slots. When the Depression developed, the Republicans tried to accuse Father of contributing to "technological unemployment" by replacing men with vending machines.

He faithfully followed his policy of finding paying jobs for Louis to do on behalf of other employers to fatten up his income. Louis landed an appointment as assistant to the chairman of the Crime Commission, a private organization formed to check into the causes of a rising national problem and offer solutions for it. For $400 a month, the little giant of a man raised money for the group, pushed out a barrage of propaganda, and became something of an expert on the crime wave. He gave Father the credit.

Father tried, and failed, to pick up an extra $5,000 a year for Louis by appointing him secretary of the Taconic State Park Commission, of which Al Smith had made him chairman. He was blocked in that attempt by a granite-faced politician, Robert Moses, who as president of the New York State Council of Parks had the whip hand.

Louis calmly told Moses that he could work only part time, since he had other irons heating in the fire for Father. Moses exploded. If Father wanted a secretary and valet, he stormed, he would have to pay his salary out of his own pocket. "It is an absurd and humiliating position to be put in," Father protested to Smith in an oblique reference to the rebuff from Moses. That gentleman proceeded to rub salt in the wound by channeling almost every dollar of available funds into building a parkway system for Long Island, forcing the abandonment of Father's hope of getting a highway into Dutchess County. But the day was coming when Father and Louis could settle the score.

For the present, the world had to be told about Warm Springs in words and pictures. The foundation was no more than a few weeks old before Louis was begging Father for publicity photographs, "particularly if any part of the golf links can be dressed up to look like golf links."

Better yet, some before-and-after pictures of some child patients. "I am not at all certain," Louis said, "whether a still photograph would show the improvement after some months' treatment, but you are an ingenious cuss and might think of some way in which this could be done. Perhaps just one photograph showing them doing a hundred-yard dash or shovelling coal or something another after treatment, together with the statement that when they arrived, it required two stretchers and an ambulance to get them down to the pool, might do the trick. (As every patent medicine faker has discovered, nothing lures the 'come on' like a before and after photograph. Why, God only knows!)"

Whenever his string pulling with old newspaper contacts resulted in the appearance of a favorable account, he milked it to the last drop. "The papers certainly gave you a grand play on the I.P. [infantile paralysis] story," he scribbled in a penciled note. "Have not got over the shock of seeing it on the front page of the *World* yet! Now to capitalize the publicity. Suggest you send clippings of the *World*, *Times* and *Tribune* to both your traveling salesmen at once, telling them to show it to the people they talk to as evidence of the need of funds to put the Foundation on its feet."

The "traveling salesmen" were professional fund raisers, hired to augment the personal efforts of Louis and Father at the top end of the social scale. Louis made a sterling effort to reach John D. Rockefeller junior, but it did not come off. Father dashed off dozens of letters to his millionaire friends without receiving much more than good wishes in reply. "My one fear," he joked, "is that this gentle charm will appeal to some of our rich friends who are suffering from nervous prosperity and that they will come down there and ruin the atmosphere. Cousin Susy Parish talks of a visit there, but I am not certain that she could endure our Southern cooking."

He did succeed in getting Edsel Ford, old Henry's son, to visit Warm Springs with his wife, Elizabeth. She was a polio victim who had undergone nerve grafting, which was sometimes resorted to in a desperate attempt to regain muscle control. Hers was one of many cases where the surgeons failed, and Father privately congratulated himself that he had never been tempted to try the operation. The

Fords' response marked a real turning point in fund raising. Edsel subscribed $25,000 to the foundation, spent on enclosing and roofing the new patients' pool with glass.

One ambitious scheme for making a fortune died from Father's neglect. It called for making Warm Springs the headquarters of a chain of health resorts extending all the way north to Lake Placid. "My idea," Louis said cautiously, "would be to talk about the therapeutic project and carefully conceal the fact that you are going to run a competitive social resort on the side."

The moribund resort colony was coming back to life with new cottages, new lawns, new pathways where the "push boys," as Father named them, wheeled patients to and fro. The whole atmosphere was as congenial and relaxed as he could make it, matching his own mood. One of his favorite true stories about the place centered on the ornamental fountain that played in the middle of the front lawn. In their off-duty hours, push boys took to sitting around there in wheelchairs. One day, a push boy convinced some visitors that he had been cured of polio by a dip in that fountain. A second boy, in on the plot, groaned that he was still waiting for his treatment to begin.

"Why don't you start right now?" said the first, picking up his workmate and tossing him into the water. The second boy splashed around for a minute or so under the bemused gaze of the onlookers, then leaped out, yelling, "I'm cured, I'm cured!"

By the middle of the first full year under Father's overall management Warm Springs' hydrotherapy facilities were booked to capacity. "Sixty-one patients is grand," Mother noted in a letter, "but I don't see where you put them." As extra space was built and the staff passed the hundred mark, that, too, was taken up by crippled men and women who found that, in greater or less degree, there was something like magic in the water.

With the essential help of Louis, Father kept himself posted on every turn in state and national politics no matter where he was living. The intricate task they set themselves was to maintain Father's reputation at exactly the right temperature while he waited for his own cure to be effected—not cooling off to the point where he was forgotten, not heating up so fast that he would be nominated again for public office. The second was the greater risk, as Georgia party leaders demonstrated when they responded to his fondness for making speeches in Manchester and elsewhere by inviting him to run for the governorship now that he was a resident of the state.

He had a stock answer for everyone who urged him to get back into the game and quit sitting on the sidelines as a middle-aged elder statesman showering advice on Al Smith: "My legs are coming back in such fine shape that if I devote another two years to them I shall be on my feet again without my braces." It seemed constantly to be "another two years." There was no question in his mind that he would manage to do it, though sometimes months went by with no noticeable further progress.

His reluctance to say no to anything or anybody worried Louis when Al Smith telephoned Father, asking him to be temporary chairman and make the keynote speech when the New York State Democrats convened in September, 1926. The governor was after a fourth term, and he wanted Father to strike sparks for him again. Louis smelled the danger of a draft. "I have been warned of plans to get you up to make a speech and then demand you to accept the nomination by a stampeded convention with everybody yelling, 'We want Franklin!' This is, of course, a possibility, but I hope your spine is still sufficiently strong to assure them that you are still nigh to death's door for the next two years. Please try to look pallid and worn and weary when you address the convention so it will not be too exceedingly difficult to get by with the statement that your health will not permit you to run for anything for two years more."

Father looked anything but "pallid and worn and weary" when he appeared on the platform at Syracuse to see Al voted in as the party's choice and, in November, into the Executive Mansion once more. For the first time, radio listeners across the country heard the rolling voice lash out at the political enemy. "Calvin Coolidge would like to have God on his side, but he must have Andrew Mellon.... The people of the East have well learned, through months of struggle to get coal for their furnaces and stoves, the hard meaning of the slogan 'Keep cool with Coolidge.' "

Louis, for once, had underestimated the machinations of Tammany. The party slate had been settled weeks in advance. Even before Al was nominated, the billboards already carried posters summoning New Yorkers to vote for Smith as governor and Robert Wagner as United States Senator.

The following spring, some of the financial pressure on Father eased when Rosy's will was read. The massive, bearded half brother, plagued by asthma now as well as gout, took to his bed on his return with Aunt Betty from a vacation in Bermuda. He never again left it, to sit, as we remembered him, in his study with a throbbing leg propped on a hassock made from an elephant's foot, one of his trophies of his African days. One May morning, soon after six o'clock, with Granny and Aunt Betty at his bedside, James Roosevelt Roosevelt died of bronchitis, himself a memento of an earlier age when a gentleman could take his ease undisturbed by politics and independent-minded women, devoting his attention to good works of his choice. He left Father $100,000 in securities and, as a sentimental mark of his faith in Father's ultimate recovery, all his hunting gear and fishing tackle.

"In so many more ways than I had realized," Father said, "I depended on his companionship and on his judgment." The bequest was not discussed within our family. It made no difference to us, because the money was simply earmarked as funds for Warm Springs if it should be needed there.

A tangible consequence of Rosy's dying showed in the closeness which grew between Granny and Aunt Betty, who remained distinctly a London Cockney in spite of now being a millionairess. She was delighted to lend Granny her best china and be invited to dinner to meet King George VI and Queen Elizabeth of England when they spent a June weekend at Hyde Park with Father in 1938. She was unperturbed by the thunderous crash that we heard from behind the screen set up outside the pantry door just before the first course was to be served.

She turned a quizzical glance on Granny. "I 'ope that was *your* china, dear, not mine," she said.

6

Two families less alike than the Franklin Roosevelts and the Al Smiths would have been hard to find. As personalities, Al, who liked everyone to call him that, and Father, who winced when Smith persistently called him Frank, were incompatible. But their politics, like Artemus Ward's, were of "an exceedin' accommodatin' character."

Father, perennially wrestling with Tammany, was leery of Smith's unfailing support from that stronghold of unscrupulous power. He felt that the four-term governor was too often hasty in his judgments, based invariably on intuition since he refused to open any book, while Father was an addicted reader. Father's method of toying with any idea, no matter how apparently impractical so long as it glittered for him, seemed to Smith to be the mark of a man with his head in the clouds, dominated by the Machiavellian Louis Howe. Smith's response to the barrage of suggestions from Father on how to run New York State affairs was to insist that he knew exactly what he was doing without gratuitous advice. "I will not get into a fight with you for anything or for anybody," the governor once told him. "But that does not stop me from giving you a little tip, and the tip is don't be so sure about things that you have not the personal handling of yourself."

Both men were moving into new territory in their thinking. The heir to Hyde Park felt more at home now with workaday people of broad down-to-earth experience than with his old friends among the social elite. That was Louis' doing, with Missy's eager aid. Smith, conversely, grew more and more fascinated with the company of the rich. Money equaled power in his book. He quietly despised anybody who had not made his way in the world, as Smith believed he had done. Father was still a playboy and a hopeless visionary in his eyes. If he had thought differently, he might have done much more to block Father's ambitions.

Mother found less to criticize in the governor than Father did. The fact that he had women in key state jobs, like Frances Perkins in the Department of Labor and indomitable Belle Moskowitz as his closest political adviser, impressed her as much as his social programs, which treated men and women as equals. He had, she thought, "certain shortcomings," chiefly his firm opposition to Prohibition and his personal fondness for hard liquor. He liked to sit with a glass in his hand, replenished as he talked, when he conferred with anybody. Mother's refusal to cater to him in that respect limited the calls he made on the Roosevelts. She had doubts, too, about his vehement religious faith, which led him to visit the Pope and have one of his daughters married in high style by a cardinal that spring. Mother, mindful of Lucy and now Missy, had some reservations about Catholicism.

In his role as a loyal party man, Father did what he could from Warm Springs to persuade the anti-Catholic South that Governor Smith did not sport horns and a tail. "Is it true," he was asked one day, "that if Smith becomes President, my marriage will be invalid and all my children illegitimate?"

Father roared with laughter and told his questioner, as Mother reported it, "that he considered himself safely married even though he lived in New York State. . . ."

In May, he spent ten days in the Midwest, speaking to party leaders on Al's behalf, and as the 1928 Democratic convention approached, Smith tapped him once again to be his floor leader and make the nominating speech for him. Louis forecast that Smith's enemies would cooperate to make him the party's Presidential candidate, then work for his defeat on election day. Father could see no end in sight to Republican rule so long as national prosperity continued. "But there is just the possibility," he considered, "that if Smith is elected, he will prove equal to the task of new leadership. In my judgment, it is at least a gamble worth taking."

When the Democrats gathered in Houston, Texas, that June, my job was the same as Jimmy's had been four years previously, to lend an arm in getting Father into and out of the Sam Houston auditorium and run messages for him. Missy, of course, came with us to the steaming city. Mother stayed in New York.

The Democrats had learned the sordid lesson of Madison Square Garden. Al's nomination on the first ballot was a foregone conclusion. Father devoted much of his time to polishing his speech, the first of its kind on nationwide radio. He and Louis smelled the importance of this mushrooming new medium. Smith derided microphones as "pie plates," aware that his Bowery accent alienated radio listeners who could not see him in action. Father sensed that microphones would be a mighty ally for him.

"Sometimes," he said, "I think that we are driving so wholly into a radio future that we shall get even our detective stories over the air instead of through the printed page." He deliberately wrote his speech with 15,000,000 listeners in mind, not the 15,000 delegates in the hall.

There was no thought of wheelchairs and no need for crutches as he made his smiling way to the speaker's stand. Warm Springs was working for him. With a cane and my right arm, he *walked* to the platform, no longer crippled, merely lame. Louis had sent advance copies of the speech to newspaper editors everywhere.

The New York *World* ran a tear-jerking eyewitness account of Father's appearance: "A figure tall and proud even in suffering; a face of classic profile; pale with years of struggle against paralysis . . . most obviously a gentleman and a scholar. . . . Hear the nominating speech; it is not a battery of rockets, bombs and tear-drawing gas—it is not shouted, it is quietly read; there is hardly a gesture, hardly a raising of the voice. This is a civilized man. . . . For a moment we are lifted up." According to schedule, Smith was nominated on the first ballot as the Democrats' hope for the Presidency.

The subject of all the high-flown newspaper prose took an objective view. "The only remark of the convention which will live was that of Will Rogers," Father thought, "who said that in trying to mop his brow in the Rice Hotel mob, he mopped three others before he reached his own." Smith told "Dear Frank" that the speech had "brought tears in the Mansion when you spoke it." Mother, busy at the party's state headquarters, had nothing special to say personally, but "everyone was talking of your speech and feel you did untold good to the Governor's cause." As for herself, "I'm doing just what Mrs. Moskowitz asks me to do and asking no questions, the most perfect little machine you ever saw and after the National Committee meets and they appoint permanent people I'm going to get out and retire."

Father's conviction that the "people's choice" of the Democrats was headed for defeat at the hands of his old friend, Herbert Hoover, whom the Republicans had nominated in Kansas City on June 12, intensified when Smith doggedly pushed the "repeal Prohibition" issue in his acceptance speech. The certainty grew when Smith chose John Raskob, another Catholic Wet and one of the country's wealthiest industrialists who listed himself as a Republican, to be the Democrats' national chairman. Father left Louis to deputize for him at party headquarters in New York and took off for Warm Springs with Missy in September. So far as he was concerned, Belle Moskowitz was welcome to run Smith's campaign with the help of General Motors' public relations staff, volunteered by Raskob.

Mother plowed on with her job at national committee headquarters, flattered to be heading up the work of women in Al's campaigning under Belle's direction. "I have always been grateful to her for the opportunity," said my mother, who tore herself away from her desk only to keep up with her classes at Todhunter.

Apart from the inevitability of presenting herself at the party's state convention in Rochester that September, Mother had a telephone call from Smith personally urging her to do so. Louis' trained political sense, as keen as a truffle hound's nose, sniffed a cageful of rodents. Reason told him that Hoover would be elected as boom times continued undiminished and go for two terms in the White House. Given four more years of Warm Springs, building up his legs and the investment in the place simultaneously, Father would walk again unaided, except possibly for a cane, by 1932. That would be the natural year for him to run for office again, and the governorship of New York was the obvious winner's choice. On his record, he would be ready for the White House in 1936, when the odds were that the golden twenties of Republican prosperity would be over at last.

Louis' strategy called for Father to be kept out of any race at any level. Before the convention, Southern Drys had tried to make him the party's choice instead of Al. Louis, as he said himself, "threw enough cold water on the idea to extinguish the Woolworth Building." During the summer, newspaper editorialists, as well as good party men concerned about impending defeat in November, pleaded with Father to run for the governorship as the best available means of helping Smith. He answered them all with polite but firm refusals.

Al's campaign was on a breakneck course toward disaster. The South was hostile over his avowed intention to make America "wet" again. Liberals were antagonistic because of his declared admiration for big business, as exemplified by Raskob. When Father tried to communicate some of this to the stubborn Irishman he had declared himself for at three conventions, Belle Moskowitz blocked him. Yet party strategists expected the contest with Hoover to be so close that New York's forty-five electoral votes would spell the difference between Smith's victory and defeat.

Father remained with Missy in Warm Springs, standing clear of party plots and counterplots. "The pool is lovely," he wrote to Granny, who was spending a week on Campobello, "and I'm getting a real rest. . . . I am borrowing the money for the foundation to put in a new water supply. It simply has to be done." He set up a schedule of speechmaking on Smith's behalf: Atlanta, September 26; Columbus, October 4; Cleveland, October 5; then, with the Rochester convention safely over, back briefly to New York on October 7.

New York State leaders meantime closed in on the man within their reach, Louis. They were prepared to accept only Father as candidate for the governorship. Louis wired a summary of their arguments to Warm Springs on September 25; telephoning there was a chancy business, subject to long delays and interruptions. He mentioned that Mother shared his belief that Father should not run. "THERE IS NO ANSWER TO THE HEALTH PLEA BUT ANY OTHER REASON WILL BE OVERRULED BY THE GOVERNOR HIMSELF," said the telegram.

The party strategists came back to Louis the following day with a proposal designed to answer the health problem: They would nominate a lieutenant governor as Father's understudy to do all the hard work. Louis snorted that the boss was not the kind of man to take on a job and leave it to someone else to perform. His telegrams to Father that day included another astoundingly accurate prevision: "I DO NOT BELIEVE YOUR RUNNING WILL REALLY INDUCE ANYONE TO VOTE FOR AL BUT ON CONTRARY SOME OF YOUR FRIENDS NOW VOTING FOR AL FOR YOUR SAKE WILL VOTE FOR YOU AND NOT FOR AL."

Father would not budge. He was enjoying himself too much. Now the plotters talked about sending an emissary down to smoke him out. Smith, out West on a campaign trip, ordered Ed Flynn, the Bronx party boss, to keep working on Father by telephone. Ed was a friend, but Father told him no. On September 28, in answer to a plea from Louis, he issued a statement to the New York *Sun* to underline the fact that he was turning down the governorship.

Ed fancied he had detected a chink in Father's defensive armor. Instead of citing only health reasons for his refusal, he had mentioned to Ed that Warm Springs needed his time and attention to be put on a paying basis. Smith grabbed at this as a crumb of comfort. A financial problem could be taken care of somehow. He ignored the statement in the *Sun* and telephoned Mother from Milwaukee. Would she intervene with her husband? Mother studiously avoided the issue and told him to call Father direct. She would be available to meet Smith at the convention.

She dropped a note to Father before she left. "I have to go to Rochester, but I wish I didn't have to, for everyone makes me so uncomfortable. They feel so strongly about your running, and even good explanations can be made to sound foolish." She counted on being away for no more than an overnight stay. Todhunter's summer vacation ended on the following Monday, and duty demanded that she be there for classes on Tuesday, October 2. Miss Dickerman and Miss Cook, who would be with her in Rochester, had to return, too.

Her letter was dated Sunday, September 30, the day Al made his first telephone call to Father, who flatly refused to yield to the governor's entreaties. "Well, you're the doctor," snapped Smith as he hung up. He left Milwaukee that night for the Hotel Seneca in Rochester. Father emphasized everything he had said in the course of their conversation by sending a telegram to await the governor's arrival there.

Two more years of Warm Springs, it said, would see him rid of leg braces. "I OWE IT TO MY FAMILY AND MYSELF TO GIVE THE PRESENT CONSTANT IMPROVEMENT A CHANCE TO CONTINUE." Besides, Smith did not need him. "MY NOMINATION WOULD MAKE NO DIFFERENCE TO YOUR SUCCESS ON THE NATIONAL TICKET." A note to Granny went off at the same time. "I have been perfectly firm," Father wrote. "I only hope they don't try to stampede the convention tomorrow and nominate me and then adjourn."

A torrent of letters and telegrams poured into Warm Springs, many of them certainly planted by party leaders to urge a change of mind. Sis sent one, eager to share in the glory: "GO AHEAD AND TAKE IT." She received one of the few replies: "YOU OUGHT TO BE SPANKED."

By sticking to Louis' strategy, Father had at last satisfied Smith that he was not available in 1928. Louis confirmed that with a wire: "THE REAL PRESSURE COMES FROM LEADERS AND JOBHOLDERS WHO FEEL YOU WILL BE ELECTED GOVERNOR AND PATRONAGE MADE SECURE. . . . GOVERNOR DOES NOT REALLY CONSIDER YOUR NOMINATION VITAL TO HIS PERSONAL SUCCESS." From his fifth-floor suite at the Seneca, Al sent word to the nominating committee that a new eleventh-hour candidate must be found. Nominations would have to be postponed until tomorrow. "There is no alternative," the committee replied. "Roosevelt has to be the nominee." The plotting started over again and lasted through the morning.

Smith bowed to pressure and tried again to reach Father, who was taking his daily workout in the new pool when the call came through. Through Missy, he sent back word that he was off on a picnic and after that would be going to a meeting—"Don't say where"—so he would be gone all day. Missy was happy to tell white lies for him. He had no word to transmit to Louis. When Father got back to the cottage, a terse telegram was waiting for him: "IF YOU CHANGE YOUR MIND AND RUN PLEASE WIRE ME—LUHOWE."

In the afternoon, Smith and Raskob asked Mother to come to see them. They put the key question to her. "They told me how much they wanted him to run and asked me if I thought it would injure his health," she related afterward. She chose to ignore the reply that Louis had always urged on Father, the impenetrable defense that health reasons kept him out of any race. "I said I did not know," she remembered. ". . . My husband himself once laughingly said that if he lived long enough he might be able to walk again, but progress was slow and I sometimes wondered how much more could be achieved."

An account of the meeting by the governor's daughter, Emily, put a different complexion on the conference with Al. "He found," she wrote, "that Mrs. Roosevelt was entirely willing to have her husband nominated."

Boss Ed Flynn had the same impression. It appeared to him that "she was anxious that he should run and that she would be happy if he would consent to it." Her great friend Esther Lape believed that "the most wonderful thing Eleanor did was to encourage him to run in 1928 when most people thought he was not up to it."

I believe that Mother could easily have prevented the Smith forces from naming Father. She decided not to, even though she knew that he and Louis were dead set against it. Stubbornness was one factor in her action. Another was her conviction that Father was frittering away his time and his money in Warm Springs in a life with Missy in which Mother had no part.

She felt that Father owed Smith whatever sacrifices were necessary, to prove that he was 100 percent behind him in his efforts to become President. She had no more faith in Al's chances than did Father and Louis, and she rated Father's chances of winning to be no better than Al's. He should make the gesture, that was all. It was a small loss, in her opinion.

The governor and the automobile tycoon together persuaded her to place a call to Father and ask him to run. "I insisted that he must make his own decisions," she recalled, "but I said I would be willing to try to get him on the telephone. We parted for a few hours." If the thought of consulting Louis crossed her mind, she did nothing about it in that interval. Neither did she attempt to put in an advance call to Father on her own behalf.

The Rochester operator made the formal call that evening. By this time Father had gone off with Missy to the deliberately unspecified meeting—to make a speech for Smith, delivered in the Manchester High School auditorium, three flights up, where the aisles were jammed with Roosevelt admirers and party members. A messenger whispered the word that Mother was on the line at the nearest telephone, located in the drugstore a block away. Father instantly guessed what was afoot. Even if he had wanted to—and he did not—he could not possibly take the call. During the next hour, further messages came for him. Mother was still waiting. He impishly stretched his speech for half an hour beyond its planned time, showering praises on Governor Smith.

He finally reached the drugstore telephone. He would not have answered then, he said cheerfully, if anyone else had been calling but Mother. Frances Perkins, who was in the Seneca suite with Mother, Smith and a group which included Raskob, overheard one end of the conversation.

"Yes, I know, Franklin," Mother said, "I told him that, but—" She looked helpless.

Smith grasped the telephone from her hand. "I need you, Frank. This is why. The program which the Democratic Party has made in this State must go on. We've got to carry on our program. You've got a great name. We believe you are the man to carry the State for the ticket. We need a big vote to swing New York. It all depends on you."

A prolonged pause, then Smith put Mother on the line again. "I've told them all that, but the Governor is very insistent—" At about this point, the connection broke. Mother's concern was starting to turn to the matter of catching the overnight train to New York, so that she and Marion Dickerman would not be late for school in the morning. Father left Manchester for Warm Springs. The connection was restored when he arrived there a little later, at the Meriwether Inn.

If a variety of accounts of what happened next is pieced together, none of them coinciding with each other, it may be said that Mother again spoke for a minute or two with Father, then broke off to hurry to her hotel room, pack her bag, and catch the train. Raskob took over from her, to deal with Father's objections from a financial

viewpoint. "Damn the foundation," he said. "We'll take care of it."
Taking care of it meant a check in the mail for $250,000 as a
twelve-month loan. When Father got back to New York, he handed
it back; if Raskob was willing to underwrite Warm Springs, that was
enough, he said.

Smith's roar sounded next on the line. A couple of radio speeches
would be all it would take for Father to win the governorship. Then
he could spend two months in Warm Springs before returning
briefly to Albany, where Herbert Lehman would fill in for him
meantime as lieutenant governor. A month of work in the Executive
Mansion would free Father for the rest of the summer.

"Don't hand me that baloney," Father said.

Smith's parting shot was carefully planned. "I just want to ask
you one more question. If those fellows nominate you tomorrow and
adjourn, will you refuse to run?" The split second that passed while
Father put together in his mind another way of saying no was all
that Al wanted. "All right, I won't ask you any more questions," he
snapped and hung up.

The following afternoon, while Mother taught her Todhunter
girls, a wire arrived in Warm Springs from Louis: "JIMMIE WALKER
NOMINATED YOU AND IT WAS CARRIED UNANIMOUSLY DESPITE DIS-
PATCHES FROM ATLANTA SAYING YOU DID NOT INTEND TO RUN BEING
SHOWN SMITH IN ROCHESTER. HE MADE THIS REPLY QUOTE THE CON-
VENTION HAS THE CONSENT OF MISTER ROOSEVELT TO DO WHAT IT DID. IT
NOMINATED HIM AND HE WILL RUN UNQUOTE MESS IS NO NAME FOR IT. IN
ANY EVENT I WOULD NOT CHANGE PLANS ABOUT RETURNING BUT CLEAR
UP THERE. . . ."

When it came time to tell Uncle Fred what had happened, Father
said, "You got caught off third base in a squeeze play and were run
down and tagged just as you were sliding for home plate."

Louis was outraged that they had been foxed. "We are much
upset," he told Grace, "and are praying that we get licked, but it
looks bad."

Mother read about the nomination in the newspapers, then sent
Father a wire: "REGRET THAT YOU HAD TO ACCEPT BUT KNOW THAT
YOU FELT IT OBLIGATORY." To inquisitive reporters she said, "I am
very happy and very proud, although I did not want him to do it, he
felt that he had to. In the end you have to do what your friends want
you to. There comes to every man, if he is wanted, the feeling that
there is almost an obligation to return the confidence shown him."

Father never told her whether he regretted what had been done to him, by him and for him. "I sometimes wonder," she mused some twenty years afterward, "whether I really wanted Franklin to run. I imagine I accepted his nomination and later his election as I had accepted most of the things that had happened in life thus far; one did whatever seemed necessary and adjusted one's personal life to the developments in other people's lives."

There was no doubt in Missy's simpler way of thinking about whether she wanted Father to be governor. She was beside him at the inn when he spoke with Mother, Raskob and Smith. "Don't you dare, don't you dare!" she repeated as he listened to them wheedle him into getting into a race he did not feel that he was ready to run. She prayed that he would lose the election. She knew as well as he did that if he won, he could never have time again to succeed in his struggle to walk.

Albany

1929

1

Looked at from its surrounding lawns, deep in snow, the Executive Mansion seemed as if it might have been haphazardly assembled to serve as the classic house on haunted hill, popular in any number of Hollywood spine tinglers now that the talkies had arrived and you could actually hear the screams. When we moved to Albany on New Year's Day, 1929, it appeared to my adolescent eyes that our new home showed obvious signs of paranoia in its confusion of turrets and towers, balconies and chimney stacks.

In bitterly cold weather, I had driven up in an open car, recently repainted fire-engine red in a Poughkeepsie garage, to join Father's motorcade on Inauguration Day. After Hyde Park, where we had spent an exuberant Christmas following his hairbreadth victory at the polls, the latest family residence was no more inviting than a reform home.

The coals blazing in the great fireplace of the downstairs hall did nothing to warm up the atmosphere. The twin chandeliers, the stucco walls, the impersonal furniture and color scheme running heavily to red and gold—all this had been prescribed for the Smiths by a decorator at Bloomingdale's New York department store; it could have come straight from a high-class hotel. The layout of the rooms—morning, music, reception, breakfast, library—strengthened that impression. The dining room rivaled the Vanderbilts' in size if not in style, with space for thirty-two. A lot of the original china and glassware had, in fact, seen service at the New York State pavilion at the San Francisco Exposition, which our parents had formally visited in 1915.

At the top of the massive main staircase lay the upstairs hall, where most of our trunks were piled. Like the Smiths, we made use of that area, where another coal fire was burning, as a living room. On some evenings, Father liked to sit there and watch the movies he could not get out to see. They did not have to be particularly good movies, though he preferred a good blood-and-guts Western to anything else.

The second floor contained most of the nine bedrooms, each with its private bath, in the governor's official home—I do not remember ever proceeding beyond that to the servants' quarters above. Every room in the house had a push button for summoning the staff of fifteen servants, which by some quirk of state budget did not include either a cook or a chauffeur. These had to be paid by the governor personally. Since Father's job at Fidelity and Deposit had come to an end and he was on a salary of $10,000 a year, Granny stepped in to make up the difference and more, overjoyed, as she said, "now that Franklin has grown up and is the Governor."

Mother allocated a back bedroom as her own. Around the corner and down the hall on the second floor, Father had the imposing master bedroom with big windows on two sides, next to Missy's. These two rooms were joined by a little door with clear glass panels, curtained on her side. Mother thought that this was a perfectly suitable arrangement in view of the role Missy played in Father's life.

It was not unusual to enter his sunny corner room and find Missy with him in her nightgown. There was no attempt to conceal their relationship. Everyone within the family had come to accept the fact that Missy was a special part of our family.

I would go in at the start of the day, and the three of us would talk with no embarrassment between us. It was no mystery. Mother had not shared life with Father for more than twenty years. We kidded Mother about her public support for Margaret Sanger when she still had not the least understanding of the practice and techniques of birth control.

Mother rarely traveled anywhere with Father in those days. Only when she was present did the routine vary, out of respect for the public image. Otherwise, Missy sat with him in the back of the car, with a lap robe tucked in around them. Mother simply did not care what Father did.

Missy had recently turned thirty. Her black hair was already developing a silvery sheen. Her gray eyes had a look of disarming candor under their arched brows. She kept her weight down and her figure trim by breakfasting on black coffee and eating only a snack for lunch. "I get fat so easily," she would say gaily, "and if I hold off during the day, I can eat what I like for dinner." She sat down to dine with us, of course, as a member of the family.

"I was terribly independent," she liked to remember about her indecisiveness about coming to work for Father some ten years earlier, "too independent, I would say." She had gladly surrendered all physical independence, but her mind remained her own.

"Missy is my conscience," Father used to say, with no sense of irony.

I do not think she ever felt that she was his great heart's desire. She was too honest with herself for that. But she could serve him as only a devoted woman was able to. Her motives stemmed not from pity but from generosity and understanding. She sought no special status except the satisfaction of a dedicated servant. I am certain that she had no fear of sin in their relationship, in spite of her Catholic background.

Perhaps, however, there was tension concealed by her calm, and his running for the governorship destroyed some cherished secret hope of a different life. Shortly after the long October night of plotting that resulted in his nomination, she fell ill. She took no part in the frantic four weeks of his campaign.

He was in no hurry to get started. Accepting Louis' advice, he lingered for a day or so in Warm Springs, then adhered to his previously planned timetable for making "Vote for Smith" speeches in Atlanta and Cleveland en route to Hyde Park, which he reached, as he had told Granny to expect, on October 7. A crowd of neighbors met him at Poughkeepsie railroad station with a motorcade to follow him to the house. A few jealous Dutchess County Democrats sported Hoover buttons in their lapels. Louis icily suggested that they should be lured to a picnic on the banks of the turbulent Wappingers Falls on the Hudson close by. "Then I would invite them, one by one, to a private conference behind the bushes and drop them into the creek with a weight about their neck like so many sick kittens. This would do a world of good for the Democratic Party in your county—think it over."

The next day, Louis set up headquarters for the boss at the Biltmore Hotel in New York, a stone's throw from the Yale Club, where Father and Nigel Law had once joined in a midnight serenade. "Obviously I am not in condition to run," Father said, grinning, "and therefore I am counting on my friends all over the State to make it possible for me to walk in." The odds on a victory for State Attorney General Albert Ottinger, who had been expected to win handily for the Republicans in the governorship race, fell dramatically. Wall Street now gave him no more than an even chance, discounting his appeal to Jewish voters in New York City.

The battle-scarred team of Roosevelt and Howe went into this fight as if they had sought it from the beginning, not had it thrust on them. They divided the job along accustomed lines, Louis to serve behind the scenes, Father to barnstorm at hundreds of meetings, talking sometimes at more than a dozen a day. "Too bad about this unfortunate sick man, isn't it?" he liked to joke with his followers.

Both of the old campaigners appreciated the fact that somehow they had to win, if that were humanly possible, no matter what happened to the national ticket. One more defeat, now that they had been pitchforked into the contest, could wreck Louis' timetable for getting Father into the White House or, worse yet, ruin every last chance of the Presidency.

Louis, in point of fact, had two overlapping tasks on hand. Besides running Father's Biltmore headquarters, he headed Smith's Business and Professional Division. Form letters flowed out by the thousands. News releases extolling the virtues of the candidates were prepared every day. Scrapbooks and digests of newspaper editorials and all incoming mail, prepared to Louis' morose orders, kept him and Father posted on the political climate. Louis' cough got worse as his Sweet Caporal intake increased. The gap between his neck and his greasy stand-up collars seemed to widen on his lunchtime diet of an apple and a glass of milk gulped at his desk.

He boasted that he gave the men and women who worked under him "unshirted hell" for their least mistakes, but the vast majority of them were inspired by the cantankerousness of the impossible little man with the gleam in his eyes whom they nicknamed Felix the Cat after the silent-movie cartoon. For the girls who attempted to mother him, he had his own caustic labels. Lela Stiles, who became one of his White House secretaries, was "Chief Inspector of New Speakeasies." Margaret Durand, whom he chose as his personal assistant, was "Rabbit."

With her unkempt clothes and straggly hair, Rabbit came half-way to matching Louis in sheer physical unattractiveness, but she had a twinkle in her eyes and a steel-trap mind. A closeness of exchange developed between them which called for no words on either side, but Louis was no womanizer. Neither his mind nor his body equipped him for romancing, though some women found him fascinating, dirty fingernails, cigarette ashes and all. High on any list of those who did not stood the name of Belle Moskowitz, Smith's Girl Friday-through-Thursday. They detested each other on sight. She was as jealous of anyone trying to break through to her boss as Louis was about Father. At the moment, she had the power. She exercised it to make Father beg to see Al and to let memos from Louis sit unanswered on her hero's desk.

Mother's role was limited almost entirely to the national race. "Comparatively speaking," she acknowledged later, "I knew very little about the 1928 campaign for the Governorship." Her influence had pushed Father into the contest. Now, she said, "Franklin felt I was obligated" to continue working at Smith's national headquarters under Mrs. Moskowitz's arrogant eyes. There was speculation at first that Father would make only four or five speeches and leave Mother to stump the state on his behalf. "You don't have to cross bridges until you come to them," she said oracularly.

She went occasionally to hear him speak and joined him on his final swing through the Hudson Valley. By this time he had covered something approaching 1,200 miles on his travels, following the route of his 1920 fight for the Vice Presidency, wearing his beaten-up brown fedora, the same hat, we fancied, that saved him from concussion when he was running for the State Senate ten years before that and he fell on his head from the steps of a Lexington Avenue trolley.

His constant campaign companion was a nimble young attorney, Sam Rosenman, who kept him supplied with drafts for fresh speeches in every city they touched, typing them overnight while Father slept. Sam, who had performed a similar job in the past for Smith, had been led to expect Father to be an ineffectual playboy. He was stunned by the reality, and a friendship began which put Rosenman among the men dearest to Father's heart.

Sam gathered the facts, Father garnished them with drama, which gave Louis the ammunition he needed to make headlines every day. He was beginning to feel the interior tingle of victory ahead. A single week of fund raising for the campaign had brought in $100,000, a healthy portion of that from Republicans. "I am horribly afraid," he jeered two weeks before voting day, "you are going to be elected." The betting odds were now two to one in Father's favor.

He persistently thrust on four main issues: progressive government, reform in administration and the law courts, aid to agriculture, and the development of rural electricity. To those, he was compelled to add the unsavory subject of bigotry. He had already publicly repudiated the Klan and lambasted Protestant party leaders who equated a Catholic with an antichrist. His Bible knowledge helped him there. "Let him who is without sin cast the first stone," he quoted. He turned that knowledge to good use, too, in a stinging attack on Ottinger's dealings with utility companies in the state. "I preach from the Old Testament," Father told a Syracuse audience, "and the text is 'Thou shalt not steal.' "

The simple words—always written with Moses Smith in mind —and the calm voice made it almost impossible to notice that he was lame in both legs. "If I could campaign another six months," he exulted, "I could throw away my canes." In fact, he had to be carried up a fire escape into one meeting hall, and Jimmy, who came back from another trip to Europe with Granny to help in the campaign, came close to tears again when he saw Father being lifted over obstacles "like a sack of potatoes."

"No movies of me getting out of the machine, boys," he said when he swung himself out of the car in front of Hyde Park Town Hall on election day before a crowd of newsreel cameramen and press photographers. Mother spent the day working at the polls in New York. They appeared together at a buffet party for friends and party workers at his Biltmore headquarters that evening. At nine o'clock, Smith stopped by, carrying his brown derby, wearing a white carnation in his lapel, with a sheaf of cigars behind his breast-pocket handkerchief.

"Let's go down and hear the verdict, Frank," he said. He and Father drove to the Seventy-first Armory on Park Avenue, to sit for hours on folding chairs, listening to the returns. From the beginning, it was clearly another Walpurgis Night for the Democrats. Hoover was steamrollering Smith even in New York State, where Al was 100,000 votes behind. Father, it seemed, must be flattened, too.

At midnight, Smith dictated a telegram to Hoover conceding the election, then returned to his suite in the Biltmore. Granny and Mother went home from there and then to bed, certain that Father was defeated. Louis sagged into black despair. Missy, convalescing beside a radio, did not share that mood. According to her creed, once you were in a fight, you had to win it. She was furiously angry when it seemed that Father had lost.

Father's jaw remained set, though the smile came only seldom now. Upstate, Ottinger was so far ahead that the early editions of the morning newspapers went to press with stories that he was the winner. Back·at the Biltmore, Father refused to concede. He remarked to Sam that maybe some upstate Republican leaders were playing their traditional game of holding up returns until they knew how many votes would need to be stuffed into the ballot boxes to compensate for his lead in Manhattan. At one o'clock, Ed Flynn projected victory by an eyelash for Father, who picked up a telephone and began calling county sheriffs, insisting that they watch for ballot stuffing.

An hour later, Ed in a press statement charged the Republicans with fraud. The calls to sheriffs continued until six o'clock, fortified by telegrams sent in Father's name to Fidelity and Deposit agents in every county, asking them to check results with the local county clerk and report by wire to him. When dawn came, he was confident that he had won. But Jim Farley, the New York Athletic Commissioner who had become secretary of the state Democrats, stayed up for three days, terrified of an upset when all 4,000,000 votes were accurately counted, and Ottinger refused to concede until a week later.

"Well, the time just hasn't come yet when a man can say his beads in the White House," said Al, loser in the state by 103,481 votes.

"I have just heard from my *late* opponent," Father wrote on November 19, "and since he is going to permit me to go to Albany, it looks like I will have a man-sized job on my hands for the next two years." He had succeeded to what most people thought of as the second biggest task in America by a razor-thin margin of 25,574 votes.

He scorned the thought of hanging around New York, waiting for every last ballot to be checked and rechecked. Warm Springs was the place to be, with a stream of visitors scheduled for appointments to begin discussing exactly how he was going to run the state now that the speechmaking was over and done with for the time being.

Once more, he had a victory to celebrate, and he bubbled over with sheer good humor. It seldom showed itself more typically than in his penciled notes, scribbled for Missy's amusement, on a remarkable letter addressed to him by another manufacturer of surgical hardware, this one located in Rochester. Louis seemingly sent it down to him, reluctant to follow his old practice of having Father's signature forged on correspondence.

To each sentence of the letter, Father added his comment: "Can you walk without a cain or some assistants? (*I cannot walk without a cain because I am not abel.*) Does both your shoes fit you even? (*They fit me even unless by accident I put on an odd shoe.*) Are you inclined also to have a weakness in the ankle? (*I have my little weaknesses like anybody else.*) Are you sure of your step? (*We all have to watch our step with so many prohibition agents around.*) Have you any pain below the hips? If so, tell me where. (*My principal pain is in the neck when I get letters like this.*)"

During those idyllic weeks, which lasted until he came up to Hyde Park for Christmas, he also took up some proposals from Mother concerning domestic arrangements for our move to Albany, including her suggestions for where Missy should be accommodated in our new home. "We can talk that over," she wrote Father early in December.

Meantime, she related, the chauffeur's wages were overdue. She had been compelled to spend her own money to pay him. Would Father please reimburse her? She could get free laundry equipment installed in the New York house "if we will let them photograph it here and use as an ad." Would he wire her if he were willing for that to be done? Would he lend Jimmy fifty dollars? Jimmy, by the way, had just become engaged. "It is to be a secret!" Mother wrote.

2

Her delight with her teaching job at Todhunter made it impossible for her to give it up and devote herself simply to being the chatelaine of the Executive Mansion. The company of her own sex, the compliant students, and the appreciative teaching staff held an irresistible appeal for her. It proved that she was capable of leading a separate, satisfying existence of her own, with no need to lean on Father, Granny or anyone else. Serving merely as the governor's lady would mean that she was still within the shadow of the man for whom she had a certain amount of respect but no great admiration. She felt that she was a good influence on him. She was as much interested in his future career as he was. But the cold war continued.

Every Sunday evening, she caught the train back from Albany to Grand Central Station so that she would be at school sharp on time on Monday morning. Her last Todhunter class ended at 11 A.M. on Wednesday, allowing her to be aboard a noon departure that brought her back to the mansion in time for her "at homes," which began at 4:30. Only school vacations interrupted the schedule.

"I realize now," she said twenty years later, "that it was a foolish thing for me to have done, since while I probably fulfilled all the obligations that went with my position as the wife of the Governor and hostess in the Executive Mansion, I did not have much time to make real friends or to see much of the Albany people outside of the official routine."

Missy filled in for her. She was the accepted hostess on those days when Mother was pursuing her own interests as a teacher or as manager of Val-Kill Industries. Missy worked along with Father in converting the barnlike mansion into the resemblance of a typical, friendly, cluttered Roosevelt establishment, with some of the old furniture from our Washington days. She handled the details of demolishing the Smiths' three fancy greenhouses and installing in their place a swimming pool, which she and Father shared, along with other guests.

She was too shy then to admit that swimming was no great pleasure for her. "I don't like exercise," she confessed later, "but for years I hated to say so." She accompanied Father to the new pool whether or not she wanted to swim. This degree of docility lasted through his first Presidential term. Then she stopped exercising. Talking about it made a little crumb of gossip to offer reporters, who usually tried in vain to pry any information whatever from the smiling woman who was seldom seen anywhere but at Father's side. With a glibness acquired over the years, she told a woman columnist, "The Roosevelts can't imagine it. I think they think I must be ill and bravely concealing it, but the fact is I don't like exercise."

The fact was, too, that getting away from the Executive Mansion to Warm Springs with Father was important for her health as well as his. "Albany was the hardest work I ever did," she said afterward in Washington. She was on call twenty-four hours a day. Instead of having three secretaries and a trained staff to help her as she had in the White House, there was only one assistant, pretty young Grace Tully, who subsequently brought her sister, Paula, in as an assistant.

Grace had been Cardinal Hayes' secretary before she worked briefly for Mother during the campaign for Al Smith. With her deep-dimpled Irish charm, Grace was a key member of what Father labeled "the Irish Mafia." Missy, Grace, Paula—they were Catholics all; it was no coincidence that as President, Father appointed Myron Taylor to be his personal representative to the Vatican. Or that Cardinal Spellman, with whom Mother always had an arm's-length relationship, could invariably find Father to be an attentive listener.

Missy liked a five o'clock drink as much as Father did. Albany saw the beginnings of the "children's hour," as he called it, when his handful of intimate associates gathered in his office to talk over the day's business and exchange the day's best jokes. Officially, of course, liquor was not served in the mansion until Prohibition ended, but Father saw no reason in the world to interrupt any good adult habit, governor or not.

Making a martini was a ritual for him, involving a shaker filled with cracked ice, two parts gin to one of dry vermouth. Then Sis, now mother of a baby named for his father, persuaded our parent that three-to-one was more stylish. Jimmy, still at Harvard but engaged to be married to Betsey Cushing, convinced him that one jigger of vermouth required four of gin. When my turn came to join the drinking club, I protested, "My gosh, Father, you've got to change this. Everybody makes them five-to-one nowadays." Franklin and Johnny got the proportions a notch drier, and he eventually became a seven-to-one martini mixer, which resulted in a pretty high-powered drink.

He took great pride in his manhattans, too, but his other specialty was "my Haitian libation," concocted by a formula which he said he picked up on a visit to the riot-torn island as Assistant Navy Secretary. He perfected it when we were aboard the *Larooco* and then at Warm Springs. Into the frosted cocktail shaker he poured dark

Haitian rum, brown sugar, orange juice and white of egg. The smooth, frothy mixture went down like cream, not much of a drink at all, his guests imagined, until two or three of these libations really got them on their way. Father often reserved these specials of his for women companions when he wanted them to feel frivolous. But he frowned on drunkenness in anybody. I saw him relaxed after two or three cocktails during the children's hour, never drunk.

He used to tell each of his sons as we grew up, "A gentleman learns his capacity and tries not to exceed it. If he must drink to excess, he does so when he has no call to be in touch with anyone else. I am going to assume that you're a gentleman."

One parent a Wet, the other an almost fanatical Dry—that was just one more difference between them that could not be bridged. When Al Smith was clearing up at the mansion, so the story went, he sprinkled our newly arrived trunks with champagne. "Now, Frank," he said as though he were addressing Father, "if you want a drink, you'll know where to find it."

Granny was on Mother's side on this question. At Hyde Park she outdid Mother in dropping broad hints. She would lift Father's martini to her lips and flinch. "Now, Franklin, haven't you had enough of your *cocktails*?"

When King George and Queen Elizabeth arrived late one afternoon in 1938, he had the shaker ready for them on a card table set up by his governor's chair in the library. "I thought you might like a drink before dinner," Father said, "though my mother here says you would prefer some tea."

The king smiled appreciatively, the son of another resolute woman, Queen Mary. "That's just what my mother would have said," murmured our royal guest, who happily took a glass from Father's hand.

When Franklin junior and Johnny were old enough to have drivers' licenses—Father's rule was that a boy reached driving age as soon as he was strong enough to crank a car—Mother bombarded her husband with peremptory notes. "Will you speak seriously and firmly to F. jr. and J. about drinking and fast driving? I really think it's important." Her last two children, she realized, were heading away from her control.

With Louis to teach her the techniques, she gradually developed another skill which served as a consolation of sorts; she began to write and sell articles to magazines. She was thrilled when they were accepted. The few hundred dollars each of them earned was more desperately necessary evidence to her that she could go it alone. For Louis, it was a strange, secondhand satisfaction, too. As a struggling racetrack reporter in Saratoga, he had dreamed of earning his living as a free-lance writer. Thirty dollars apiece was as much as he earned for the features he pounded out on his typewriter then.

She developed a unique and mystifying ability as a writer. In the hundreds of thousands of words, possibly even millions of them, which she ultimately set down on paper, reaching her zenith with her "My Day" column started in 1936, she managed to conceal her personality completely. She pictured herself as a calm, contented woman deeply concerned with the world and her family. We read her articles and marveled how she created the image of a total stranger, not the detached, harried, fault-finding wife and parent we knew. Only deep below the surface of her careful prose could be found an occasional clue to her conflicts. "I have always wanted to try to write fiction," she said, "but I never have had the time."

As she took on a steadily increasing list of jobs, she hired a part-time secretary of her own in Malvina Thompson, another graduate of Smith's campaign headquarters, a retiring young woman with a firmly expressed New England conscience, whom Mother considered "a wonderful person to keep one living up to one's obligations." When the Val-Kill furniture factory failed, the building was converted into a bizarre cottage, which Mother and "Tommy" eventually shared.

When Father moved into the governorship, Louis and Mother kept each other company in New York, a rejected woman and a morose little man who suddenly had nowhere else to go. A guest room stood waiting for him every weekend in Albany, but there was no full-time work for him there. In the early days of the takeover from Al, he threw himself, with his habitual mixture of disdain and devotion, into putting together a scratch team of new talents to replace the men and women whose first allegiance was still to Smith. This had to be a new regime, under Father's control, not his predecessor's, no matter how eager Al was to remain a power behind the scenes in the apartment in the Biltmore, where he had retreated to heal his wounds.

Belle Moskowitz was among the first to depart. Al urged Father to retain her, but neither Father nor Louis could tolerate her. Mother, too, had no illusions about where Belle's loyalties lay, much as she admired the lady's professional know-how. "Don't let Mrs. M. get draped around you for she means to be," she told Father. Nothing was further from his mind.

"You don't want me to stay on, do you?" Robert Moses asked. A noncommittal answer covered Father's deep dislike for the man whom Smith had promoted as his Secretary of State. When he offered his resignation, it was accepted, though Father, who liked to keep a string even on his enemies, persuaded him to remain as head of the Park Commission. That settled the score so far as Moses' turndown of Louis six years earlier was concerned.

Louis was still number one in the long-range planning for the Presidency, the only man allowed under the screening process devised by Missy to contact Father day or night. Nobody else could scarify the governor as he did. "I hope to God you drown!" he would yell into the telephone to the other half of the team who, after seventeen years of Louis' exclusive management, had of necessity begun to pull away from him. "Can't you get anything into that Dutch skull of yours?" yelled the gnome, like a schoolmaster berating a pupil, never caring who overheard him.

"Dear old Louis," as he remained to Father, did not change. He was hostile, grouchy, contemptuous of politics and politicians, but then he always had been. As circumstances changed around him, he looked more and more like a figure from an earlier age, before the inescapable problems of running the biggest state in the Union descended on Father's debonair head. Louis, unable now to climb a flight of stairs without gasping for breath, looked darkly on the people whom Father brought closer to him—Henry Morgenthau, Jim Farley, Ed Flynn, Lieutenant Governor Herbert Lehman, and, in particular, Sam Rosenman. The master schemer, in his unspeakably cluttered cubbyhole on the third floor at East Sixty-fifth Street, focused his whipped-up energies on the plot to make Father the President. That demanded winning two more years as governor at least. A second term would carry him safely into 1932, when they both counted on seeing the beginning of an end to the golden age on Wall Street. None of them imagined that chaos lay just around the corner before the year was over.

Depression was the word for a mood, not an economic condition which it would take a war to end, when Mother began preparing for another trip with Franklin and Johnny, this time to Europe. She still had not realized her old desire to show any child of hers the places which had once represented happiness to her. As before, on the disastrous camping expedition, Miss Cook and Miss Dickerman would complete the party. Mother was nothing if not resolute in her convictions about the kind of company that would be good for our younger brothers.

The major problem was whether our overstrained family budget, which meant little to Father, could stand the expense of the vacation. Granny, who had very definite ideas about what was or was not suitable style for a governor and his lady, came to the rescue once again. Her immense pride in what Father had achieved made her happy to subsidize her son to whatever extent proved necessary. She was much more willing to give than he was to ask, then and later.

Without Granny's largesse, neither of my parents could have survived those years sufficiently insulated from real financial stress to spread their wings and learn to fly. It was a matter of honor for her to accept nothing from anyone or any source, individual, group or government, in her bankrolling of Father. The life-style which he established at Warm Springs and Hyde Park was paid for largely by her. The pattern he set as a country squire has been emulated and enlarged upon by every President since, with the possible exception of Harry Truman. The difference was that Father used no federal funds and accepted no benefactor's gifts other than Granny's.

Truman would go to the Key West naval station on vacation as his retreat from the White House, a humble-enough hideaway for an unassuming man. That followed along the lines of a sturdy American tradition. Ulysses Grant made no money from his high office; he was flat broke until, dying of cancer, he wrote his memoirs to pay off most of his debts. Wilson did not feather his nest; neither did Harding, rogue that he may have been. The most cash that Coolidge earned in his entire life was the $100,000 he received for his autobiography. Hoover, a millionaire to start with, added nothing to his personal fortune during his White House years.

Yet after Father the style changed, for the worse. Camp David, which he christened Shangri-La, was an unimpressive cluster of wooden cabins when it was built in the mountains of Maryland as a World War II retreat, where he recorded events in a ship's log not unlike the *Larooco*'s—and Mother could not count on getting her telephone calls through to him as she traveled the world under the code name he chose for her, Rover.

Under Eisenhower, Camp David blossomed into something fancier, paid for from federal funds; his elaborate Gettysburg, Pennsylvania, estate was built with donated money as a necessary part of a life-style that the young United States Army major of 1939 could not have imagined even as a fantasy. Jack Kennedy's possession of huge funds, and his power over the direction of government, guaranteed that he never lost a nickel in manipulating his private wealth. Lyndon Johnson was a poor schoolteacher with scarcely a dime to his name when he entered public life; when his years as President came to an end, he had piled up far more in the way of gross assets than could be acquired by saving every dollar he had earned from the day he first went to work in Texas.

Presidential tastes for extravagant living on a Superman scale beyond the reach of the average man and woman reached a new level with Richard Nixon's White House in Florida and its counterpart at San Clemente, California. The trend carried the nation one step closer to the megalomania of long-departed European monarchies and the grandiosity of Versailles.

Every President from Father on increased his wealth. He lost $100,000 a year for every year he was in the White House. It was Granny's money. In 1933 her estate stood at $3,500,000. By 1945 it was down to $2,300,000. So she left two indelible marks on history, only one of which she understood and gloried in. She made it possible for her dearly loved son to be President. And because his successors copied the style in which she set him up as befitting his office, every American taxpayer has reason to remember her.

Granny's harping on *noblesse oblige* only irritated Mother, who accepted her role as the governor's lady as just one more change to which she was reluctant to adjust. She planned to take both the family cars for the trip this time, to avoid the previous horrors of overcrowding, which frayed everybody's temper. She and her two friends would share the driving and perhaps try camping in England, Germany and France. Granny would not hear of it. "The *Governor*'s wife does not usually drive herself or sleep in *tents*," she said. "It would be undignified."

One more stormy scene was added to the score, with Mother in tears, Granny standing fast on her principles, and Father remaining on the sidelines. Franklin, fast approaching fifteen, shared the reservations which most of us had about Mother's driving. She hired a chauffeur-driven Daimler to meet her and my brothers in England, while Miss Cook and Miss Dickerman tagged along in our

Buick. Our Chevrolet, whose fenders bore evidence of Mother's steering abilities, remained in the garage.

This trip turned out no better than the hegira to Campobello. She had not been overseas alone since her school days, and her forty-fifth birthday was coming up next. She shuddered at the thought of her two sons roughhousing in hotel rooms in the fashion which Father encouraged at home, so she made a point of taking them climbing every bell tower in the guidebooks and walking them for miles every evening to tire them out before bedtime. Of course, she was the one who grew exhausted first.

She fretted over the responsibility of guarding their passports, keeping Franklin and Johnny out of harm's way, and making plans for their sight-seeing. Above all, she worried about spending more money than her tight budget allowed. "I realized," she said, "that I was a poor person to be taking on a trip two youngsters who needed good, hard physical exercise daily. . . . I put in a good many anxious hours wondering if I would come out with enough to get us home." If she failed in that respect, it would mean wiring for emergency funds, which would probably entail borrowing from Granny. Mother would have cringed with shame and burned with anger. Fortunately, it was not necessary. "On landing I breathed a sigh of relief," she remembered, "and made a vow that never again would I take a trip on which I had to be responsible for the young."

So far as my brothers were concerned, the highlight of the vacation came in a *pension* at Mont-Saint-Michel, where she grew so tired of their squabbling that she went off without them to see the sights. When she got back, she found Franklin dangling Johnny by the heels from an upstairs window, with a crowd watching from the street outside.

The scale of Granny's gifts to her grandchildren kept pace with Father's increasing importance as a national figure. Drawing on his and Louis' experience in government and politics, he was trying out more than a few of the measures which were to lay the foundations of his policies as Chief Executive—farm relief, an old-age pension system like the one he had talked about to Moses Smith after the winter of death on the Wilkes farm, a law covering working hours and wages.

Jimmy's wedding brought him a check from Granny for $2,000 and an undertaking to give him an allowance until he settled himself in a career after leaving Boston University Law School, which he had entered from Harvard. She had already made him a "loan," which brought Father down on him like a ton of bricks. "I do realize," Jimmy wrote to him abjectly, "that you are absolutely right about borrowing and the lesson is well learned and will be remembered."

Father had stipulated that my brother, in his Harvard days, must save enough to buy his first car, a spluttering Ford roadster. But a winter snowstorm wrote finish to it, and that Christmas his present from Granny was a new Chrysler runabout. She did much the same later on for Franklin after he wrecked the little car which Father and Mother gave him on his graduation from Groton.

Granny liked her grandchildren to mix with the people who, in her judgment, still made up society, winters in New York, summers at Newport and elsewhere. It was not hard for Franklin to convince her that he would be unable to go partying that summer because Mother, as punishment, had refused to let him have a replacement for his ruined automobile.

"You may go to the showroom and order a new one," Granny told him. "It is to be charged to *my* account."

Mother was on the front terrace when Franklin drove back from Poughkeepsie in a new Buick convertible. "Whose car is that?" she asked suspiciously.

"It's mine, Mommy." How did he get it? "Well, you see, Granny gave it to me."

Mother stalked in to see Father, fuming. "Franklin, you have got to talk to your mother and tell her that she must not do these things. The car must be sent right back, now." He wanted no argument with the woman whose money made his career possible. He never did raise the subject with Granny, but she and Mother feuded for weeks over this thwarting of control over my young brother.

In his never-fulfilled desire to retain close contact with his children, Father had a way of drawing each of us into his life by turn from time to time. It was a compromise made necessary by both circumstances and choice, one of a hundred compromises which he designed, and we accepted it as such. I had balked at the idea of going to Europe with Mother, so I passed a good part of that summer with Father.

More than any other single issue, Father was set on making cheap electric power the cornerstone of his program for the state. The prospect of generating millions of kilowatts from the flow of water had fascinated him ever since he piloted sailboats in the Bay of Fundy. He put Louis to work comparing rates charged customers by private interests in New York with the cost of public power in Ontario.

Louis dramatized his studies by coming up with a hypothetical family who, for identical service, would pay $19.50 in Albany and less than $4 under the Canadian system. Uncle Fred, a conservative in his business thinking, heard of Father's demand for government development of public power of the Saint Lawrence River, marking the New York-Ontario border. Father answered his relative's counterarguments sharply: "Where there is government operation the household consumer pays less in monthly bills."

He wanted to open up talks with officials on the Canadian side. There was no more fitting means of traveling to see them than aboard the good ship *Inspector*, a freakish small craft with a glass roof, used by state functionaries for making inspection trips of New York's canals. Plans were formulated for Mother's group to sail with Father and myself as far as Buffalo, then, while he went down the Saint Lawrence to discuss the business of constructing hydroelectric systems to harness the river's tremendous flow, they would embark from Montreal for the Atlantic crossing to Liverpool.

To while away the monotony as we dawdled along in the *Inspector*, I played cards with some of Father's party, notably with a muscular young roughneck who had been a circus acrobat, among other things, before becoming a state trooper and boxing coach at the State Police School. I was down twenty-five dollars to Corporal Earl Miller before we got to Buffalo.

His muscles were the prime qualification for his new job with Father, lending an arm whenever one was needed, lifting him into and out of corners which he could not negotiate alone. Miller had been Smith's bodyguard, but with his brash, barrack-room manner he soon made himself more than that within our susceptible family. He was shortly promoted to sergeant, and before Father left Albany for the White House, this vigorous gymnast was director of personnel of the Department of Correction, dropping such intimate notes to the governor as "Cheerio, and may your coming trip be most profitable as ever—Your Sergeant Miller."

At first, he operated in Father's orbit exclusively, accompanying him virtually everywhere. Miller was an expert horseman who performed trick riding at the state fair. He persisted with his arguments until Father agreed to try horseback riding again at Warm Springs. Earl included Missy in the class and Mother, too, on her rare visits to the place.

In his prime, their instructor was a handsome enough man of abounding energy. His first marriage ended in divorce, so he turned his eyes on Missy. He was no believer in unwarranted subtlety; he simply made passes. She did not actively discourage him; neither did Father. Theirs was a highly special relationship in which Missy was given complete freedom to enter into whatever friendships she pleased. Father felt no possessiveness about her, appreciating that one day, to fulfill herself, she might find a man to marry. The fact that she did not possibly surprised him, but not her.

If Mother shared some of Missy's natural pleasure in the attentions of a husky male, that explained her decision to take riding lessons from him, perhaps from a deep-rooted drive to compete, woman against woman. Only Father could have recognized the subliminal contest, if that is what it amounted to. With no false hope of ever again being able to balance himself in a saddle, he went along with the classes, trailing along through the woods and over the mountains, watching Missy blossom as a rider, while Mother's courage failed her. "Missy was a much better pupil than I" was Mother's summing up of the episode, which did more harm than good to Father's legs.

He went back to relying on a hand-controlled automobile to take him anywhere he wanted to go, no matter how rough the road. It was always a Ford, following Edsel's gift to the foundation, and invariably blue, which was the color Father and Granny both favored for a car. But Mother continued to suppress her fear of horses running out of control, to the point where she went riding at Hyde Park now and again. When our family left Albany, Miller gave her his horse Dot; Mother gave up horses when Dot died.

"I never again could find a horse in whom I had the slightest confidence," she said. "Also, I had fallen off Dot three times, and each time it had taken me longer to recover from the slight effects of the fall."

Miller moved closer into the family circle, striving to act as a buffer for Father. He took great pride in his own physical fitness and in his new importance, as he saw it, to my parents, though he may have deceived himself where Father was concerned. But people like Moses Smith had the clear impression that a letter to Earl was one way of gaining Father's attention on Hyde Park affairs. "Please tell the Governor he had better make the check for at least $250 as there will be two weeks payroll," Moses wrote to Miller on one occasion, for example. And a week or so later: "May I please ask you to be so kind as to deliver this memorandum personally to him?"

Because of Mother's poor driving record, Earl was assigned to travel with her. She encouraged the friendship which developed between them, absorbing from him a touch of the self-assuredness which she still lacked. Louis had done all that he could for her. Earl, as different as night from day, gladly took over the task of instilling courage in her. There was no question that she admired his strength and felt obvious affection for him. In the growing circle of women with whom she shared similar bonds, he stood out like a tiger among kittens. He was the only close male friend she made in those years.

Where Father insisted on Missy as part of his rare pattern, Mother could follow with Earl, but more as a doting aunt than anything else. She helped pay for a house for him out of her earnings in later days. She kept a guest room ready for him in the converted cottage at Val-Kill. On visits to New York in the nineteen thirties, he stayed in the crowded little apartment which Mother and Tommy kept in the house owned by Esther Lape and Elizabeth Read in Greenwich Village. When Mother's memoirs were serialized in 1937, she had sets of the *Ladies' Home Journal*, in which her story had appeared, bound in leather for presentation to Father, Sis, Tommy—and Earl. The gesture was intended for all of us. The previous Christmas, Father had given copies of his "I Hate War" speech to Mother, Granny, his children—and Missy. Now he was told where the score stood, without an unnecessary word being said. Mother liked to get even, to show that she, too, could inflict pain if she had to.

Sis was a bridesmaid and I was best man when Earl took as his second wife a cousin of the first Mrs. Miller. Mother had the ceremony conducted at her Val-Kill cottage. Father was in Warm Springs with Missy, whose heart was scarcely broken. That marriage did not change Sergeant Miller's relationship with Mother. Neither did the subsequent divorce nor the third wedding ceremony he went through sometime later. Throughout these years, he played up his intimate friendship with Mother, with the result that by the time of his final divorce it became almost credible that his devotion to her was the cause of his lack of provision of a home for his wife. Of course, this was grossly untrue.

3

Winning two more years in Albany turned out to be no problem at all. The strategy worked out with Louis, Sam Rosenman and Basil O'Connor succeeded beyond their wildest expectations. It took aim at Republican "incompetence" on a national more than a mere state level, a plan designed to lure GOP votes away from GOP leadership.

Louis pulled a stunt, which was repeated in 1932, of squelching the tired old rumors that Father was a sick man by arranging for a quarter of a million dollars' worth of life insurance to be taken out on him. Then he released the doctors' reports, certifying the candidate to be in glowing health.

As chief coordinator of the campaign, Louis checked out the audience figures of the major radio stations, to haggle with them over prime time. He set up movie coverage of Father's official tours and produced a documentary, *The Roosevelt Record*, which ran in some two hundred theaters, with sound trucks covering outdoor rallies. Mother took up her old assignment at the women's division, without Mrs. Moskowitz breathing hard over her this time. "Politics does not excite me," she told one interviewer. "It never did. I take things as they come. . . ."

In the past two years, Father had surrounded himself with a smooth-running team of professionals that even included old "Uncle Henry" Morgenthau senior as a money raiser for the campaign. My parent had no worries on that score, and he showed no fear then or ever that his peculiar domestic arrangements might somehow be brought to the notice of the voters by anyone among the dozens of people who sensed something strange in his married life. The gambler in him counted on their silence, their ineffectiveness, or both.

His luck held firm, just as it had in the matter of Black Tuesday, the October day when the boom on Wall Street broke and the economic fabric of the country began to disintegrate. He did not appreciate the significance of what, just before Christmas, he had still airily described as "the recent little flurry downtown." When Frances Perkins' statistics revealed that unemployment in the state was spreading like a contagion, he forecast that the Depression would soon be over and urged employers to keep the faith as men of goodwill safeguarding the American way. As an analyst, Louis was no less naïve. What the situation called for, he felt, was "to point out that wicked Wall Street is paying the freight to excite three cheers from every farmer."

Banks across the country were already starting to fold, but the earthshaking crash of the Bank of the United States, where a quarter of a million New Yorkers had their accounts, did not stun the state until the campaign was concluded. Louis, however, smelled opportunity in the air. Father had not only to run for another term as governor; he must emerge as the only possible candidate for the White House, two years ahead of schedule.

Hoover's dithering refusal to recognize the growing crisis, much less come to grips with it, played straight into Father's hands. In his speeches, he hinted that massive public works programs would be important in making jobs; businessmen warmed to that idea. He paraded his endorsement by the American Federation of Labor and appealed for unemployment relief "as a matter of good citizenship and good Americanism." Millions of voters, with or without jobs, applauded that. He denounced Prohibition as a tragic failure, which proved to be worth 181,000 votes to him.

He had seized the tailor-made opportunity that radio provided for a man with a voice like his by instituting a series of "classrooms," as he called them, to tell listeners about his achievements as governor, as well as making a more formal "annual report" in March. Except as a powerful weapon in politics, radio did not particularly interest him. He much preferred reading newspapers, magazines, books—anything which his facile mind could absorb, with the pages flipped so casually that it was impossible to figure out how he could remember what he seemed only to have glanced at. Sitting before a microphone did not bother him in the least. He would spend a few days in advance quietly penciling changes in his scripts. But a radio day for him was like any other, relaxed, chatty, good-humored. He would be helped by one of us into his little Hyde Park study, and then, with perhaps only an engineer beside him, he would talk to the impersonal electronic box as if it were his best friend. As a politician, he knew it was precisely that.

Weeks before election day, Father was confident of victory. His own guess was that he would win over his almost anonymous opponent, Charles H. Tuttle, by 437,000 votes. Jim Farley thought that was an underestimate and put the figure at 600,000. The electorate astonished everyone by returning Father to Albany with a 725,000 majority, twice the size of any plurality Al Smith had ever achieved. Now there was no one left to doubt that he would be nominated for the White House in 1932. No one, possibly, but Mother, who insisted, "Franklin did not tell me when he decided to run for the presidency, but I knew from Louis Howe. . . ."

The question no longer was whether Father would be President—that was taken more or less for granted—but whether Louis would live to see it happen. He had been looking forward to taking another of his increasingly frequent vacations, his "drying out" periods in his words, the next spring when Father put aside all other business to hurry to Paris, where Granny was ill with pneumonia.

At the age of seventy-seven, she saw no reason to vary the lifelong habit of going to Europe at the time of year when she considered the Continent to be at its best. But now it seemed that the gallant grand dame had overreached herself. Louis unfailingly put Father's needs ahead of his own. He stayed on in New York, where he had just opened up offices for a new propaganda letter-writing organization known as the Friends of Roosevelt, to free my parent to sail on the Cunard Line's *Aquitania* with McDuffie and myself as traveling companions.

It was my first trip outside the United States, and I had only one complaint to make: Father was even more flirtatious than I was. My shipboard romance was with a girl not yet twenty who had danced in the chorus of Charles Cochran's London revues, then gone into Fleet Street newspaper reporting. Sheilah Graham was due to be a leading Hollywood columnist, but right now she was the sudden object of my affection, and Father's, too. He was, I decided, about the most flirtatious character I had ever known.

I was used as a kind of understudy in his flirting with another charming passenger, Rosa Ponselle, the buxom opera singer. The one thing Father could not do was dance with her, so I was brought in as his deputy. One night, the ship rolled so badly that, while we danced together on the deck, Rosa and I slithered against the rail, with Mademoiselle Ponselle pinning me against it, every pound of her, so that I fancied my spine was fractured.

After we had seen and consoled Granny in Paris, he and I spent hours together, shopping for books at the little stalls along the Seine,

browsing in art shops and galleries. He said it was unfortunate that
I could not afford to buy a small bronze of a mare and foal that I
rather desperately wanted to own. Four months later, on my
twenty-first birthday, it arrived as a present from my father. By
then, of course, Granny's iron will, together with some help from her
doctors, had restored her to good health. Mother remembered a
remark he made when friends questioned the wisdom of a woman of
Granny's age traveling alone overseas. "After all," he said, "the
place where you die and where you are buried is of little importance."

What was important to him was the companionship of attractive
men and women, the accent being on women. Between his close
companions and Father, there was always an implicit understanding: There must be loyalty on both sides. Anyone who failed to
appreciate everything implied by this was certain to find that Father
had somehow drifted out of the relationship and become a stranger.
He was more brutal in cutting off any man or woman if he suspected
that he was being used by them, which was something he refused to
tolerate. Among his entire team, the people allowed to know him
totally amounted to two: Louis and Missy.

Where those two represented the core of the target of Father's
intimates, the inner ring contained only a handful of close friends
and members of the family. He was slow to make friendships
because, once entered into, they were expected to last. Some unlikely
people came into this category. Gus Gennerich was one of them, a
New York City policeman promoted to detective for the single-
handed capture of a mob of gangsters in a 1925 gun battle. He was
assigned as a bodyguard in Father's 1928 campaign, went with him
into the White House, and seldom left his side.

Gus was "my humanizer" to Father, the bluff, gum-chewing
ex-cop whom Father trusted completely. Everybody, from the
shopkeepers, laboring men and saloonkeepers he brought in to see
the governor, was "Pal" to Gus, including Father when strangers
were not around. I was proposed by Gus as a Free Mason in his lodge
in 1931; he performed the same service for Jimmy and Franklin
later. In every case, Father, as governor and then as President, was
the honored guest. Gus also acquainted us in turn with the
remarkable ways of New York speakeasies, with Father's complete
approval.

Aunt Polly enjoyed a charmed life in the inner circle. Father often visited her at her 200-acre estate in Rhinebeck, to pass hours on summer evenings on her cool terrace, with its uninterrupted view of the Hudson and the Catskills beyond. Louis and Polly had a great rapport, too, but Louis never figured in the long list of her romances. As children, we always insisted, whenever we were in Rhinebeck, that we stop at the little exchange shop which she ran there. We were not interested in the handmade linens and woolens that she sold but in her raspberry syrup, put up in bottles; added to water, it made a deliciously sweet drink.

We were not too much older when Aunt Polly started serving us different kinds of drinks at her house parties. Once or twice, Jimmy and I would drive down from Rhinebeck with girls we had taken up there. Two or three would be feeling the effect of Polly's liquor, which aroused Mother to a fury. She could see the whole dire story of the Halls' problems with Vallie and her father's illness coming back to haunt her and her own children.

Polly simply laughed at her. "Oh, you can't be so stuffy," she would say. "This is a modern day and age. Children all see their parents drinking at home. You've got to let them express themselves. Let them get used to it."

Laura Delano had no patience with Mother or with anything she did. She believed that Mother had been the wrong choice as a wife for her cousin. Our tiny, bejeweled aunt felt sure that Lucy Mercer and Father should never have given up each other. She saw no reason why they should not begin to meet again.

In her scheming over the years, Polly found an unlikely ally in another friend of Father's, his distant relative Margaret Suckley, whom we knew as Daisy. Two more different women would be hard to imagine. Polly looked like a Dresden doll; Daisy was as homey as an old cardigan with her hair drawn back tight in a bun. She gave Father the succession of Scotties which reached a peak of publicity with Fala, and she was devoted to this man, the idol of her eyes. Mother approved of Daisy Suckley.

With Daisy's knowledge and active assistance, Polly connived to keep Lucy Mercer Rutherfurd more than a faraway memory for Father. I believe that they met at Warm Springs. I know that they met at the great Rutherfurd estate at Aiken, half a day's drive away, before and after Wintie Rutherfurd died there at the age of eighty-two in 1944. I am certain that Bernard Baruch, the financier who hired publicity agents to picture him as a kindly old gentleman addicted to park benches, was the host of Father and Lucy at his South Carolina hideaway, Hobcaw Barony. Bernie Baruch made it his business to ingratiate himself with Presidents.

Mother was unaware that, for his first inaugural in 1933, Father provided a private limousine for Lucy. There is no way that Missy would not have known about that.

En Route to Chicago

1932

1

EVERYONE in the cabin felt queasy most of the time as the plane burrowed its way west through swirling gray clouds. Only Father and I had no need to replace the little brown paper bags thoughtfully provided by American Airways, from whom he had chartered the three-engined Ford. Sitting at the folding desk which had been set up for him, he gulped hard now and then when we bucketed into an air pocket, but the smile flashed on and off around the cigarette holder clenched in his teeth.

Beside him in a front inside seat on the starboard side, Missy's airborne misery went beyond gulping. Soon after we bumped over the grass for the takeoff from Albany, she had been well enough to scribble a telegram from him to Granny, noting our flying over the home of a relative: "I AM WRITING THIS AS WE PASS OVER 'HENDERSON HOUSE.' ALL WELL. MUCH LOVE. F.D.R." But now Missy was suffering too much from the jouncing to tackle even a Lucky Strike, which she normally smoked at the rate of two or three packs a day.

Gus Gennerich and I took up our positions across the aisle from Father, the two of us serving as his bodyguards and physical handlers on the trip. Mother sat nearer the front of the cabin, pale and wan, her pride in having overcome motion sickness long ago completely shattered by this flight against strong head winds which kept tossing us around like a leaf in a gale. Earl Miller was with her as her companion in misery, the last time he ever traveled with Father. Elsewhere in the rear of the cabin, Johnny had turned a sicklier shade than anybody else, and he stayed that way until after we had landed. Missy's assistant, Grace Tully, tried to cope with a typewriter that refused to stay put.

We all had started the day bravely enough, bustling out of the Executive Mansion bright and early in two limousines with an escort of police squad cars and motorcycles, ready for our seven-thirty takeoff. Dozens of Albany friends and neighbors, who had heard on the radio of Father's nomination for the Presidency, had been up since this Saturday dawn, too, to see him off to Chicago. Their cheers gave us a mild foretaste of what lay ahead before November, when most of the country seldom ceased roaring out applause for the man to whom the voters turned as their savior from despair and the chaos of impending revolution.

Only Mother isolated herself from the rising tide of elation, which the snappily upturned brim of Father's Panama symbolized for the rest of the family. "From the personal standpoint," she said afterward, "I did not want my husband to be president." She realized there was nothing to be done about it when he had worked and schemed with Louis toward that goal for better than twenty years. "It was pure selfishness on my part, and I never mentioned my feelings on the subject to him," she said.

Flying to the Chicago convention to accept the challenge of running against Herbert Hoover to end a dozen years of Republican rule was Father's idea, much as he detested planes in those days when commercial aviation was in its infancy and Amelia Earhart made headlines as a pilot simply by crossing from coast to coast. His chartered plane, rented from the company which became American Airlines, had been sitting for a day at the Albany airport. He turned aside reporters' questions by joking that he planned to visit the convention on a five-seat tandem bicycle, with himself steering and his four sons doing the pedaling.

Weeks earlier, he decided to fly so that he could deliver his acceptance speech in person, not dawdle across the country by train. Courage was part of the decision—overcoming his fear of travel by air. He also wanted to demonstrate by this gesture that he was a man of vigorous action, not the semi-invalid depicted without fail by his enemies in both parties. Above all, he knew that by smashing precedent by accepting on the spot, he could thrill the voters with a sense of decisive leadership and get his campaign off to an instant start.

None of us had caught more than a few hours' sleep during the past two days. We had been up with him through Thursday night far into Friday morning, with the blare of oratory crackling in our ears from the radio in his little sitting room. Granny, Mother, Missy and Gus sat with him, while Sam Rosenman helped him revise his acceptance speech for the umpteenth time. In shirt sleeves, Father chain-smoked cigarettes, which he liked to keep in most of his pockets and every convenient desk drawer.

The garage at the rear of the mansion had been converted into a temporary press room, where telephones pealed and reporters hammered at their typewriters, updating the running story. Mother had them supplied with pots of coffee from the kitchens and at one point made them the one and only dish she could cook, scrambled eggs, which were her standard token of hospitality.

Father concentrated on every word coming out of the speaker, nodding approval or frowning his objections, chuckling with derision when some platform orator poured on the platitudes to add to the flood which was drenching the sweltering Chicago Stadium. That afternoon, his own name had been put into nomination by old Judge Mack, who on an August morning twenty years earlier had been one of the group that whisked off Father to the policemen's picnic, where he had his first taste of politicking, with side orders of sauerkraut, clams and real beer.

When Mack finished, an enormous portrait of his candidate was unfurled from the balconies and delegations lugged their state placards out to shuffle through the steaming aisles while the organ blasted out "Anchors Aweigh," chosen by Father as his theme song. Louis was already installed in Room 1702 in Chicago's Congress Hotel, which was Father's headquarters. He was too feeble to involve himself in the vicious infighting for delegates, which was in Jim Farley's capable hands this time. He stayed away from the convention floor, spending his nights racked with coughing and his days by the open window of his room, propped against pillows in the breeze of two electric fans.

As the demonstration for Father roared on, Louis' disgust with the racket he heard on his radio burst into anger, focused on "Anchors Aweigh." He whispered hoarsely to Ed Flynn, who sat by the telephone, "For God's sake, tell 'em to play something else." Okay, but what? Louis recalled something a secretary of his liked. "Oh, tell 'em to play 'Happy Days Are Here Again.'" Father had a new theme song, which stuck to him for the rest of his life.

The hours of Thursday dragged along. If sheer racket had determined who the candidate would be, Al Smith would have walked in on the first ballot. His obsession was to beat down the man who had humiliated him with his victory in 1928. Father had gone beyond that, Al thought, by driving him away from the seat of power in Albany and flouting his ideas about how to handle state government. "The Sidewalks of New York" thundered out endlessly from the organ as the demonstrators whooped and screamed for Al in a whirlwind of confetti.

Every preliminary count by Father, Louis and Jim Farley had indicated nomination on the first ballot. Big Jim Farley had worked like a demon all week to win delegates for Father, until now he was close to exhaustion, aching to catch some sleep on the cot set up in his convention hall headquarters. The technique had been to usher key delegation men in to see Louis, who sat by an open telephone line to Father in Albany. Always impressed by what telephone companies could be nudged into doing, Louis had a microphone attached to the line so that he could put Father on to talk to a roomful of visitors. With his prodigious memory, he could usually address any delegate by name and, as often as not, recall some personal detail to amaze him. No decisions of any consequence were made without reference to my parent. No orders came from him for anyone except through Louis.

But no Roosevelt bandwagon had as yet begun to roll. Smith stood firm, predicting that Father's support would fade right after the first balloting. The party machine in Chicago, steered by Mayor Tony Cermak, had packed the stadium galleries with a claque that rooted only for Al. "Cactus Jack" Garner, the Speaker of the United States House of Representatives, held tight to the Texas delegation, which, like the California delegates, was controlled by Hearst. Father's managers dangled every kind of bait to get more fish on their lines, but whatever they tried brought no bites.

"I would have given anything in the world to have been there too," Father said a few days later. "It was the most difficult thing for me to sit here with the telephone and get everything secondhand."

Throughout Thursday night, the nominations of favorite sons, followed by unending seconding speeches, deluged the littered, sweaty stadium with oratory blatting over the sound system. Friday morning brought a crucial question. Should Farley press for a ballot now or call for adjournment to give him time to scrape up more votes? Louis could not answer that. He got on the open line to Albany. "Go ahead" was, of course, Father's order.

At a minute or so before 4:30 A.M. the roll call began. When it was over an hour and a half later, Father had 666¼ votes, 464½ more than his closest rival, but 104 short of the needed two-thirds. A second ballot followed immediately. Without a few more votes, Father's chances would crumble. With desperation in his dark-ringed eyes, Farley rounded up just half a dozen more. The "Stop Roosevelt" forces pressed their advantage and demanded a third ballot, certain that they would crack him this time around.

In his sitting room, a telephone rang with a call from "Kingfish" Huey Long, the demagogue who was then a Senator from Louisiana. "You're a gone goose," he said, chuckling, to Father. News of the third impending ballot outraged Granny, who declared her intention of returning to Hyde Park later that day. "Who *is* that horrible man?" she asked in a penetrating whisper the first time Father brought Long there to lunch in the years ahead. Father's views on Long were sharp as a knife. "That man," he once told me, "is an influence for evil in the entire structure of our country."

It was 9:15 by the time the third count was completed. Disaster had been averted by a whisker. Father's total had inched up to 682. Smith had lost only 10 votes. Cactus Jack had picked up 11. Before the yawning, crumpled delegates met again on Friday evening, Farley, with Louis' gasping help, had to find 100 more votes or Father would be finished on the fourth ballot. Laboring over the draft of the acceptance speech, Sam Rosenman wondered if he was wasting his time.

Friday was a strange, aimless day for most of us in the Executive Mansion. We dozed when we could, picked at our meals, started to do a dozen things, then dropped them as soon as they were begun. Father had an hour or so of unbroken sleep, then returned to the telephone and Louis. Farley had taken a cab to confer with him. He stretched out on the floor beside him. Jim wanted to stake everything on Texas. Louis had to be persuaded that the Garner forces might conceivably yield, contrary to his own conviction that Cactus Jack would hold out to the end. Farley convinced him that the job could be done.

Telephone calls went to Hearst at San Simeon, California. The newspaper tycoon was no friend of Father's, though he had softened his antagonism when, four months earlier, Father spoke out against America's joining the League of Nations—and thereby infuriated Mother and most of her friends. But Hearst nurtured an irrational hatred of Smith after a series of feuds with him in New York. Between the two candidates, Hearst preferred Father. If Garner would swing California, which was pledged to him, into supporting Father, the Lord of San Simeon would not stand in the way.

Garner proved willing. "All right," he said, "release my delegates and see what you can do. Hell, I'll do anything to see the Democrats win one more national election." But the Texas delegates struck a bargain before they would go along with California: Cactus Jack must be nominated as Father's running mate. That was agreed.

A few minutes after leaving Louis, Farley returned to Room 1702 with the news that Texas would switch, the war was won, and Father was sure of the nomination. "That's fine," Louis muttered, picking up the telephone to call Father. We were sitting down to dinner when the call came through. Missy, as usual, was there as an acknowledged member of our family. By some devious working of her mind, Mother accepted her almost as one of her children, often going shopping to buy clothes for her when Missy was too busy to do that for herself. "F. D.," Missy said, laughingly, when she saw Father's face, "you look just like the cat that swallowed the canary."

"I'll fly to Chicago first thing in the morning," Father told Louis as Missy flung her arms around Mother in a spontaneous embrace and Johnny and I ripped up scratch pads to hurl in the air by way of celebration. We went our separate ways to start throwing clothes together for the trip.

Louis had his son, Hartley, with him. Rabbit, Hartley and Louis' personal staff joined with the little wizened man who had waited twenty years for this in drinking champagne from paper cups. The secret of the deal that had been struck remained unknown to all but a handful of delegates when they filtered back into the hall, where the reek of cigar smoke still lingered. Everyone but the insiders expected another long night on hard chairs, waiting and wondering as the ballots were tallied.

On the first count, it was over. William Gibbs McAdoo, leader of the California delegation, heard the claque in the galleries hoot disapproval when he announced that the state was for Father. The bandwagon was rolling at last. By the radio, Father beamed. "Good old McAdoo," he said, a politician who recognized that in the extraordinary game at which he had proved himself a master only a hairline distinguishes an enemy from a friend. By 10:30 he had heard himself proclaimed as the nominee. But Smith clung to his 190½ votes to the end and left Chicago before we got there. That night, posters of Father were defaced on the billboards of the city.

Louis had no real faith in the ability of anyone else to follow his example of controlling any situation by constant attention to every detail, large or small. As a speech writer, Rosenman struck him as a poor second to himself. He had no higher opinion of Raymond Moley, the saturnine Columbia professor whom Louis had met in his part-time functions for the Crime Commission. Moley, introduced as something of a Howe protégé to lead Father's brain trust in 1932, had drawn up the original outline for the speech. Louis insisted on having the entire text of it dictated over the open line to Rabbit. He snorted with contempt when he read it and struggled to a desk to rewrite it in longhand on his favorite sheets of lined yellow paper before Father landed.

The flight plan for the trimotor Ford called for us to touch down at the municipal airport in time to reach the stadium, 20 miles away, by 2:30, to hear Garner nominated. The winds we ran into for close to a thousand miles changed the schedule. The pilot had to put down twice for fuel, in Buffalo, then in Cleveland. The crackling radio in the cockpit picked up a flow of messages from Chicago. Cactus Jack's name was already in nomination. Time was being killed with one seconding speech after another. But delegates were growing restless and beginning to leave. Father calmly went on working over the text of his speech, cutting paragraph after paragraph to tighten the impact of his words. At first, he dictated his few changes to Missy. When the roar of the motors and the swaying of the cabin overwhelmed her, Grace Tully took over.

We descended through a rain squall and billowing cloud cover two hours late. By then Father had put his leg braces back on after trying to doze for a few minutes. As the silvery plane touched down on the gravel runway, the crowd of ten or fifteen thousand that had waited all afternoon broke through the flimsy barrier and streamed toward us. We taxied cautiously toward a ramp decked with bunting.

Mother was the first to leave the plane, looking remote and a little dejected in a plain helmet of a hat, white blouse and plaid tweed suit. Father came last, making a conqueror's appearance in the doorway, with a hand on my shoulder and his other arm linked in Gus'. Farley struggled through the cheering mob. "Good work, Jim," said Father. Mayor Cermak, with perspiration beading his gold-rimmed spectacles, followed close behind. "I was a good sailor," Father told him contentedly.

Then came the moments we had feared and tried to guard against ever since he reentered public life. The crowd pressed irresistibly around him, threatening to force him off balance. Once he was down, he might well be trampled on. We thrust back at the adoring, dangerous throng to squeeze a few inches of space for him. He suffered nothing more serious than having his hat knocked off and his glasses dislodged but not broken. His smile faded only for a second or two. He said something about "returning the country to the people," but his words got lost in the din.

Seven months later, Tony Cermak was in another milling crowd that greeted the President-elect when he drove in an open Packard to Marine Park, Miami, to address twenty thousand American Legion men. From a bench a few feet away, Joe Zangara, a psychotic Italian bricklayer, sprayed the car with bullets from a .32 caliber revolver bought in a pawnshop for eight dollars. "I hate all Presidents," he confessed afterward. "I kill them."

Father's driver instinctively started the target car moving forward. "Mayor Cermak's shot!" somebody shouted; four other people had been hit or grazed, too. Father had no means whatever of protecting himself. He was physically incapable of ducking to the floor. He said, "Stop the car. Bring him in here." There was no knowing whether or not the firing was over. Panic threatened to turn the crowd into a milling mob. He said later, "He was alive, but I didn't think he was going to last. I put my left arm around him and my hand on his pulse, but I couldn't find any pulse." The slug had grazed Cermak's liver and lodged in his spine. "I remember I said, 'Tony, keep quiet—don't move. It won't hurt you if you keep quiet.' "

Cradling the stocky little mayor in his arms, Father was driven to Jackson Memorial Hospital. He waited until Tony was settled in bed, then went in to comfort him. Three weeks later, just after Father was sworn in as the thirty-second President of the United States, Cermak died. Father took the oath on the Dutch Bible published in Amsterdam in 1686 and handed down from his great-great-great-grandfather, Jacobus. It lay open at the thirteenth verse of the thirteenth chapter of First Corinthians: *And now abideth faith, hope, and charity; but the greatest of these is charity.*

As the Chicago airport police struggled to restore some semblance of order, Jimmy and his wife Betsey stood waiting for us with Sis. Miss Cook and Miss Dickerman had come out to greet Mother. Louis was out of sight, biding his time in the terminal, until he would sit next to Father in the motorcade of sixty automobiles that would follow a roundabout route to the stadium. Father took a few minutes to telephone Granny in Hyde Park, where she had been telling reporters her reaction to his nomination: "Of course, I am glad . . . but I was not very much surprised."

The moment their big white car began to roll, Louis thrust the typescript of the acceptance speech he had written into Father's hands, arguing that it was a far superior effort to the now drastically cut original. With one hand waving his battered hat at the thousands who lined the route, Father flipped over Louis' pages with the other. Out of the corner of his beaming smile, he tried to cope with Louis' objections, until he snapped at him, "Damn it, Louis, *I'm* the nominee."

Applause exploded in the auditorium when he appeared on the platform, where two typed speeches lay side by side on the lectern, which he gripped with both hands so that he could stand up as straight as a Marine. With the country and much of the world listening, he scanned the first page that Louis had written and decided that the old newspaperman's opening paragraphs were better than the words he, Rosenman and Moley had devised. Father used that lead as a tribute to the man who, more than anyone else, was responsible for his standing there in triumph. Then, imperceptibly, he slipped into the speech which he had trimmed and polished in the bouncing plane.

In essence, it was a rallying cry, aimed at drawing the entire nation together to restore prosperity and to share the national wealth more fairly between rich and poor. There were appeals in it to politicians, businessmen, farmers, workers and workless. Almost casually, there appeared in the final paragraph a phrase which he had borrowed from Mark Twain's *A Connecticut Yankee in King Arthur's Court*: "a new deal." But he struck magic from it when the clear, ringing voice declared, "I pledge you, I pledge myself to a new deal for the American people. . . . Give me your help, not to win votes alone, but to win in this crusade to restore America to its people."

In almost everyone's opinion, the outcome of the election was a foregone conclusion; Hoover had no chance of reelection. But Father started campaigning before the cheering ended, shaking hands on the platform with supporters who rushed up to him, then continuing the process for hours afterward in the Congress Hotel. When he took off on the campaign trail which Louis had laid out for him months in advance, Ray Moley and Jim Farley divided the bulk of the behind-the-scenes work between them.

One or more of us children went along with Father on the trips which carried him virtually everywhere in the country. "I did not work directly in the campaign," Mother recalled, "because I felt that that was something better done by others, but I went on many of the trips and always did anything that Franklin felt would be helpful."

He traveled 13,000 miles before election day, most of them aboard the governor's train, which could be pulled into the private siding down by the Hudson River, a memento of Grandfather's days as a minor railroad magnate. Missy covered many of those miles with him. At his personal headquarters, Louis stage-managed the biggest direct-mail operation known to date, with hundreds of girls and a handpicked group of ghost-writers under his command. More than 3,000,000 personally addressed letters went out from his command post, 65,000,000 pieces of literature, and 5,000,000 buttons.

On election eve, Father drove to Hyde Park, then back down the Post Road to Poughkeepsie to make his final broadcast. In the course of that talk, he spoke from the depths of his inscrutable heart: "A man comes to wisdom in many years of public life. He knows well that when the light of favor shines upon him, it comes not, of necessity, that he himself is important. Favor comes because for a brief moment in the great space of human change and progress some general human purpose finds in him a satisfactory embodiment."

He sat up late that night by the crackling fire in the Hyde Park library, pondering, perhaps not for the first time, whether he would have the strength to do the job ahead, praying to God that he would be able to do it right according to his standards.

After voting the next morning at the town hall, he was driven back to East Sixty-fifth Street. Following dinner there, he made his way to the Biltmore, to sit at a long trestle table where twenty telephone girls waited to gather returns from every state. Louis sat alone in his own cluttered den, morose and ridden with fear beyond reason that some incalculable disaster would still strike.

That day, Father received 22,800,000 votes, Hoover 15,750,000, which exceeded by less than 2,000,000 the total of the country's unemployed. In front of a microphone in the hotel ballroom, Father said, "There are two people in the United States more than anybody else who are responsible for this great victory. One is my old friend and associate, Colonel Louis McHenry Howe, and the other is that splendid American, Jim Farley." "Colonel" as a courtesy title was a joke enjoyed equally by Father and Louis, who could not have passed an Army medical at any time in his life. At 1:40 in the morning on November 9, Father went home. Granny stood waiting for him at the door, weeping with pride and an overwhelming sense of fulfillment. "This is the greatest night of my life," he said as they embraced.

Louis' heart knew no rejoicing. Suddenly, now that his task appeared to be done, he felt uneasy. "I guess I've worked myself out of a job," he commented. Father only teased him. "The only job that Louis really wants is to be an Admiral. When we were in the Navy Department, he was furious because many navy officers made him stand back to let them enter the elevator first. He wants to be an admiral so he can go down there and push them all out of the way."

The appointment he received was something quite different. He became *the* secretary to the President and as such remained Father's principal troubleshooter for the rest of his days, forever with some fresh intrigue to occupy him, always jealous and suspicious of anyone who seemed more important to Father than himself. Louis moved into the White House when we left East Sixty-fifth Street and installed himself in suitable style in another cubbyhole across the corridor from the Presidential study.

Any visitor who knew the score paid a call on Louis after leaving Father. He changed only in appearance, never in nature. Brown spots marked the yellowing skin of his face. His eyelids drooped, but the gleam in his eyes did not dim. He spent more and more time lying on a cot, surrounded by disarrayed piles of documents and letters. On the walls, photographs of Mother outnumbered those of Father ten to one. A little radio stood on a weary-looking bureau. The top of the safe which served as a bedside table held an array of medicine and liquor bottles.

Everyone deferred to him. "Get word to Speaker Byrns and tell him he's got to push that bill," he would tell Steve Early, back on the team as one of Father's right-hand men. "Send Hearst a wire to say we will try to work something out," Louis would whisper hoarsely to Marvin McIntyre, another of the old retainers brought back into service. "Tell the President what I've said," Louis might add, unless he decided to telephone Father direct.

Missy had her own White House apartment assigned to her by Mother on the third floor—sitting room, bedroom and bath—and the only private office opening directly into Father's oval study on the ground floor. Her room was simply furnished, with bookcases, two little tables and a small, plain desk with a single telephone. "I can only use one at a time," Missy would say in her matter-of-fact way. The walls were decorated with pictures of Mother, Father and some of us children, together with two framed dollar bills, among the first printed with the signature of Henry Morgenthau junior as Secretary of the Treasury and presented by him to her.

Missy's job as private secretary paid $3,100 a year at first, until the 1938 budget increased it to $5,000, but she talked happily of buying a cottage on Cape Cod, and she owned a glossy mink coat. That was one of her luxuries. The only other was having her breakfast of black coffee and orange juice served in bed, a habit acquired from Father, while she read the Washington and New York newspapers.

She was on call by Father, and only Father, seven days a week, twenty-four hours a day. She took the elevator from the third floor down to the basement at nine thirty most mornings, then slipped out the south door, past the indoor pool and the rose gardens, through the French doors into her office. In her middle thirties now, she was always smartly dressed, in high heels and fashionably cut dresses of gray or Father's favorite blue, a contrast with Mother, whose taste invariably ran to sensible skirts and blouses and comfortable shoes.

She was in and out of his study throughout the day, not always waiting for the buzzer, solicitous if she heard him sneeze or cough.

She handled literally everything that Father wanted to keep genuinely confidential and personal, from matters of state to his income tax returns. As soon as he was wheeled into his office, Father's morning routine was to take a quick glance into hers and wave her a greeting. Then she would come in with Steve Early, Marvin McIntyre, and, at one time, my brother Jimmy to plan the working day with Father.

"I generally just listen," she explained once, "because I have the evenings to talk things over." She dictated to Grace Tully most of the personal letters he signed. Grace also took dictation directly from Father for an hour every afternoon before the inner team met again at five o'clock for cocktails and the "children's hour."

On Father's instructions, Missy was shielded from the pressure of appointment seekers who, unless the subject was urgent or especially confidential, were usually steered to Steve or Mac. She accepted incoming telephone calls only when she chose to. If anyone but Louis had questions about anything relating closely to Father, it had to be cleared first through Missy, the general manager and true hostess of the White House.

She presided at the tea table, checked the menus, handled the seating protocol at private dinner parties, kept Father and herself up to the mark in their dieting, which was not difficult on most of the dreary meals which emerged from the White House kitchens. The efforts of the housekeeper, Mrs. Henrietta Nesbitt, in whom Mother could see no wrong, were something of a standing joke between Missy and Father. Always handsome in a dinner gown and wearing chandelier earrings, Missy at her end of the table would catch Father's eye when some overcooked dish appeared, knowing how little it appealed to his gourmet palate, but they would dutifully eat as much as they could swallow. This was another facet of Father that Mother blandly ignored. "If I should give him bacon and eggs three times a day, he would be perfectly satisfied," she told herself.

She went with Missy to Somerville when Mrs. LeHand died at the age of seventy-seven ten days before Father was elected and he was in the thick of his campaign. She regarded that as a duty to the woman whom she treated as if she were a child in need of mothering. She resolutely refused to acknowledge to herself that Missy had any influence on Father politically, yet nobody in his inner circle would agree with that.

Missy was, as Father put it, his conscience. Most evenings after dinner, she would leave the table when he did, her blue eyes sparkling, with her innocent, wise smile. They would make their way together to his upstairs study, as they used to in Albany when he was governor, to go over the events of tomorrow and the days ahead. He used her as a sounding board for a host of his ideas. He employed her once in a telling gesture to humble Joe Kennedy, whom he had recalled from London as Ambassador to the Court of St. James's for his frequently stated opinion early in World War II that Hitler was likely to defeat the Allies.

Prior to that occasion, Father had urged the founding father of the Kennedy clan to end his long-term relationship with Gloria Swanson, with whom Joe had been close since his days as a motion-picture czar. Joe replied that he would be willing only "if you give up Missy LeHand." Father looked on that as a score to be settled. When Kennedy arrived back in disgrace, his President refrained from sending any ranking member of the Cabinet to meet him, as custom required. Instead, at Washington airport stood Missy, all smiles.

She took Father's admonition to "Speak up, Missy" to heart. If an idea turned up in the draft of a speech which she felt was inconsistent with the workaday ideals in which she believed so firmly, she would quietly prompt him to reexamine it because "It doesn't sound like you." She cared nothing about ideologies, but she interpreted politics and government as being essentially relations between people. She had learned that much from Father; she refused to allow him to forget it. From her own inner calm and good manners, she evoked the same response in Father, as the indispensable other half of the team that comprised only herself and Louis Howe.

Until she suffered a stroke, the probable price of a dozen years of overwork, in the summer of 1940, Missy was the unofficial, unrecognized hostess of the White House, filling the gap which Mother deliberately created. Mother wanted to continue the separate life she had made for herself at great personal cost in human happiness, as a schoolteacher, writer of magazine articles, amateur publicist and public speaker. She said as much after Father was elected in a letter she wrote to Miss Cook, which Louis urged Nancy to destroy as soon as he heard about it.

Mother tried only once at that time to keep in close touch with Father. The assignment she asked for can only have amazed him, when both of them lived with the memory of Lucy Mercer and the letters she wrote, which Mother came across as she searched his luggage. Perhaps, Mother said, "he might like me to do a real job and take over some of his mail." She pretended that to be no more than a tentative suggestion. It was much more. It was an unspoken reminder that she remembered what had gone before. And it was a last unavailing challenge to the influence of Missy.

"He looked at me quizzically," Mother said much later, "and said he did not think that would do, that Missy, who had been handling his mail for a long time, would feel I was interfering. I knew he was right and that it would not work. . . ."

One of the women in the steadily widening circle of Mother's friends was a newspaper reporter, Lorena Hickock of the Associated Press, fondly known as Hick. Mother, in a widely quoted interview, told her, "I never wanted to be a President's wife, and I don't want to now." But she did want power and influence, provided it was in her own right and her own name.

One more Christmas has come and gone, leaving as a timeless gift the well-remembered scene of childhood, when we settled ourselves by the library fire and watched the darting flames reflected in the lenses like wintry stars as he clipped his pince-nez to the bridge of his nose and turned to the opening page. *Marley was dead to begin with. There is no doubt about that. . . .*

It is hard to believe that nearly thirty years have passed since his voice was last heard, whispering of pain in his head, and he slipped into final unconsciousness in his chair in his little house at Warm Springs. It is easier to have memory hear him read to us again, while Mother's knitting needles click in accompaniment and the heat of the logs starts Granny's head nodding. Our family knew no happier moments than these.

The ghost of Christmas past would send shivers along our spines as he wailed at poor old Scrooge, but he has become a familiar spirit now, one of the host that grows in number every year. They all return unprompted in the sharp, clear light that the sentimental season can bring to the mind. This Christmas was no exception, though I was 3,000 miles away from the places where I grew up among them.

First, of course, there was Louis Howe, lying prone in a cot at Bethesda Naval Hospital with his face half-buried in a pillow, complaining from behind the beard he grew in the belief that it made him look more statesmanlike that the nurses kept him down "because if I started out I can't stop." He had been bedridden for two months by then, after nursing him in the White House proved to be well-nigh impossible. Much of the previous year had been spent under an oxygen tent on a diet consisting mainly of coffee and Cream of Wheat. But he insisted on an occasional turn around the halls in one of Father's wheelchairs, wearing pajamas of beach-chair stripes and defiantly dragging on a Sweet Caporal.

Toward the end, a truce was declared with Granny. For her eighty-first birthday, he wrote to her that "I probably know better than most people how much you have to be proud of."

Granny's reply showed that the personal style of both of them had escaped erosion by the twenty years they had shared with enmity on her side and courtesy on his. "I think I receive too much kindness," she said, "but I am proud to feel that my 'one and only' is the cause and I always hope his father knows."

When he was taken off to the hospital, Mother went to see that he was comfortably settled in. Father, whose visits brought a trace of the old gleam in Louis' eyes, saw to it that a special bedside telephone was installed, ostensibly to be used only during working hours. Louis, naturally, ignored any such restriction. Now and again, his calls still came for Father in the middle of the night.

Month by month, the little man seemed visibly to be shrinking, until he was no bigger physically than a wizened child. He fussed over plans for the 1936 campaign, issuing orders right and left for charts to be prepared and lists to be updated, but he had no illusions about his part in it. "Franklin," he said, "is on his own now."

With a wardrobe that bore the marks of being bought from a mail-order catalog, Grace arrived at the White House, so that she could read aloud to him again the tales of his boyhood—Kipling, Stevenson, rip-roaring adventures and detective stories. She was as intractable as the husband she had seen so seldom. If he did not look so pitiful, she remarked, she could wallop him with a book.

On April 19, the flags around the White House flew at half mast. Louis lay in state in the East Room. My parents and some of their sons rode the funeral train to Fall River. In the snow, the family members stood with Grace, her son and daughter as the remains of the man who had made a President were lowered into the earth.

Would Father's policies have been different if Louis had lived? The answer is, probably not. In the first hundred days of the crisis of 1933, Congress gave Father a blank check, to be written as he chose, to restore the United States to health. Neither he nor Louis had anything other than vague, unformulated ideas about what to do with it. No plan had even been dreamed of for the exercise of such unprecedented power as was pressed into their hands. Both of them were inveterate pragmatists, prepared to try anything to see if it would work. Between the liberals and conservatives of the brain trust—and Louis was a conservative—Father kept the balance and reserved his options.

When the mood of panic passed and Congress wanted much of the authority it had ceded so readily back where it belonged, it became fashionable for rich men to denounce Father as a radical who had sold out his class. Nothing was further from the truth. He had the inborn instincts of the rich, and he was careful to preserve the system in their interests. Granny was his eager accomplice. She would call him at the White House and say, "Franklin, I am bringing two banking friends of mine in to see you at eleven tomorrow morning."

"I am sorry, Mama, but I have appointments set up for that time. Perhaps we can make it another day—"

"They'll *be* there at eleven, Franklin." He would sigh and summon Missy to change his calendar. But the men introduced by Granny were among the most powerful in the land: our onetime tenant, Tom Lamont of the Chase Bank, and James Perkins of the National City Bank of New York. The bank holiday of March, 1933, was their idea; Father dictated cooperation with bankers as an ingredient of the New Deal.

Soon there was another gap beside the one left by Louis in the ranks of the extraordinarily few people who were truly important to Father. Gus Gennerich stood on the opposite end of the scales from Granny. But like her, he was as generous with his special brand of wisdom as with his money, which he would often lend to Father, who had a habit of forgetting to take his wallet along with him.

One December night in Buenos Aires, just after Father had been elected for a second term and was making state visits in Latin America, Gus saw him safely to bed, then went out to finish off the evening in a café with two other members of the Presidential party. Within minutes, he had a heart attack. He was "the kind of a loyal friend who simply cannot be replaced," Father said, moved close to tears. The loneliness which marred his later years was beginning to close in on him.

Mother felt little compassion for him on that score. She was much more concerned that Louis' absence would mean Father's getting out of touch with the kind of people whom she regarded as important: liberals, progressive thinkers, members of a dozen and one movements organized to change society for better or worse. "Louis Howe's not being on hand has meant that many people were not appreciated and had been forgotten," she thought.

Her sympathies and naïve acceptance of others made her an easy mark. She was flattered by the attentions of a variety of "forgotten" men and women, who used her willing services to give them entrée to the White House. Where Missy acted as a buffer to conserve Father's time and energy, Mother made sure that doors were kept open for her friends.

"I know I shouldn't bother you with these things," she would tell him over the dinner table, "but it's the only chance I have to talk with you nowadays."

"Let's fix a time for the morning."

"I would prefer to talk now, Franklin."

He would sigh and lift his eyes in pretended horror. "Fire when ready, then."

The American Youth Congress was a favorite cause of hers. On unnumbered occasions, she spoke up as its advocate, relentlessly urging Father to meet the leaders, pushing their complaints that since the establishment could do no right, the system had to be changed.

"Very interesting," he would say. "I'll think about it." Then he would discard what she had related to him. Yet with his ability to absorb everything said in his presence, he could keep her excited and dedicated, never discouraged by any lack of response. He had given her his close attention, which was enough to make her feel useful and happy.

Mother disclaimed having any influence over him, but somehow she created in the minds of various pressure groups, almost all of them left-wing, the idea that she could change the attitudes of the administration. She did not discourage them. They did their utmost to turn her enthusiasms toward their own ends, until they came to know the essential nature of Father, who could say no and leave the impression that what he had told you was yes. Under every kind of pressure, he retained his own identity.

She jumped into controversy while he invariably trod warily. On the subject of rights for blacks, she raced far ahead of Father. "You can't get too far in front," he would explain. "You don't just pass a law, and that's it. Only gradually can you create the impact that will get people to recognize that more has to be done for the downtrodden and for the education of the Negro."

What did interest Father were her personal reactions and opinions, not those of people who used her as a kind of usher. He listened to every word when she gave him eyewitness reports of what she found in an Appalachia mine or in the mountains of Tennessee. But he let his attention wander, without showing it, when she would say briskly, "I had luncheon with Bernie Baruch day before yesterday, and he told me to tell—"

"Well, that's certainly interesting. I'll have to give it some thought."

Her fascination with the American Youth Congress was decidedly dimmed when that organization's attitude toward Hitler Germany switched overnight from hate to sweetness and light on the signing of the Führer's short-lived pact with the Soviet Union in 1940. A year later, when the Germans invaded the USSR and the Youth Congress did another flip-flop, she was outraged. By that time the last of the men whom Father took to his heart as a boon companion had appeared on the White House scene.

Edwin Watson, nicknamed Pa, was cut to the same pattern as most of Father's dearest friends; he was a loyal, uncomplicated man with an ingrained sense of humor. He came as a military aide before he went on to the secretarial staff, and his rank rose from lieutenant colonel to major general. When a letter arrived from the Youth Congress asking for an appointment with Father, Hitler's armies were driving ahead toward Moscow. "Respectfully referred to Mrs. Roosevelt," said the note which Pa Watson attached to the AYC request. Mother's response signaled the end of a kind of love affair: She advised Pa to reply that "the President is too busy."

A week or so later, Father was anguished by another loss. He was engaged, for the second time in his life, in laying the groundwork for the United States to take the step which he considered inevitable and wage war again on Germany. Granny, close to her eighty-seventh birthday, had gone to Campobello that summer. We dismissed the fancy that she was growing frail, because we could only think of her as ageless. Doctors on the island, however, felt differently. They advised her to return to Hyde Park, and arrangements were made for her to be carried down the steep stairs to the waiting car. She refused help from anyone. Halfway down, she had to pause for breath. Then she smiled at the rector of St. James', Hyde Park, who had been visiting her. "You've never seen the old lady in this condition before, have you?" she said.

Not too long before, she had told another visitor, "Well, I know I am getting old and that I will have to die some time, but I hope it won't be while Franklin is in office. When I die, he will feel so bad, and if it is while he is in office, it will upset him for his duties, and I don't want to be the cause of that." Her hope was unfulfilled, but her forecast came true. Every day, the chance grew stronger that Hitler would overrun Europe and then, God forbid, try for the world. Cooped up in Washington, Father had been seeing very little of Granny.

He made time to spend a night at Hyde Park in the first week of September. She had a cold, but apparently nothing more serious. Two days afterward, she collapsed. Father and Mother were rushed to her bedside in the Hyde Park house which for so many years had spelled servitude to Mother. Soon after midday one Sunday, Granny's life came to its mortal close. She had not known that my parents were with her. "Mama had a very wonderful end," said Mother. In the sorting out of Granny's personal treasures, Father came across some carefully labeled packages containing his baby clothes and dozens of mementos of his childhood. He wept when he found them.

On the same night that Mother stayed by the dying woman whom she had simultaneously leaned on and rejected, respected and despised, her brother Hall was taken to Vassar Hospital in Poughkeepsie. Physically and mentally, he was a giant who towered over both my parents, yet he lent credibility to Mother's abiding fear that the Halls and their descendants were doomed to tragedy. He had turned into a monumental drinking man, who after a night of entertaining Jimmy or myself on the town would have us doing sit-ups on the balcony of his New York apartment, topped off with a double martini before breakfast.

On the day of Granny's funeral—she was buried next to my grandfather in St. James' churchyard—Mother had her brother moved to Walter Reed Hospital in Washington. She lived there for the next ten days, sleeping in her clothes, thinking, as she said, "He could have been so much and this is what he is." Something less than three weeks later, the service was held in the White House. My parents took the casket to the Hall family vault in Tivoli. "It was practically like losing a child," Mother said.

There was another funeral she attended, of which I heard her say nothing afterward. At a White House party during the summer before the Japanese attack on Pearl Harbor, Missy suffered a stroke. It was a direct consequence, as we knew, of the unending task she had set herself twenty years earlier in caring for the needs of the man she once addressed as "Your Majesty" at no matter what cost to her own uncertain health.

Now, in many ways, she was in greater need of care than he had ever been since his agonizing days of struggling to walk again. The attack left her partially paralyzed, with her voice slurred and her quick, assured walk painfully slowed. When she left the hospital to recuperate in the old cottage at Warm Springs, Father followed her, staying in the Little White House, built there in 1932. As soon as he arrived, he called on Missy and then again the following day, when his visit had to be broken off by news from Washington that the war was inching closer. She was in tears at his leaving.

She remained in Warm Springs on December 7, "a day which will live in infamy," as Father hurriedly wrote in pencil on the typescript of his speech to the Congress and the nation, declaring war. She tried to telephone him in the White House, but his line was forever busy. This was the result of the inexorable pressures of crisis, not lack of concern for her. When his will was filed for probate, disclosing a gross estate of $1,940,999, it provided that up to half the income should go to paying Missy's medical bills, with the balance earmarked for Mother.

Missy attempted to work for him again the following year, but it was out of the question for her. She retired to her family home in Somerville, but more and more time had to be spent in Chelsea Naval Hospital, Boston. On July 31, 1944, the almost unknown woman who had given her life to Father died of another cerebral thrombosis.

Father heard of her passing in Honolulu, where Admiral Nimitz and General MacArthur were haggling with him over the strategy for victory in the Pacific: Should the Philippines be bypassed, as the Navy commander urged, or occupied, as MacArthur successfully insisted? The statement from the White House on Missy's death bore no touch of his hand. "Memories of more than a score of years of devoted service enhance the sense of personal loss. . . ." Those were the pat phrases of a ghost-writer.

Her church's esteem for Missy produced a bishop, Richard Cushing, later to become a cardinal, for the mass at St. John's, Cambridge. Mother represented the family. In the eight months which passed before the end came for Father as he sat with Lucy, Polly, Daisy and the painter Elizabeth Shumatoff in the Little White House, he saw no reason to change his will. I believe he wanted the world to be given some clue to the importance of Missy in his life.

Mother at this time was "Rover," constantly in motion between one war zone and another, paying her nonstop calls at canteens, hospitals and military bases at home and overseas. Ever since Missy's first stroke, there had been jobs left undone in the White House which could be filled only by someone living there as an official hostess. The relentless strains of war leadership began to show in Father's face. He sometimes grinned apologies because his hands trembled uncontrollably. He had aged noticeably. His doctors continually urged him to cut down on cigarettes, but he was impatient with illness and any kind of pill taking, so he might try limiting himself to smoking only half a pack for a day or two, then quickly revert to the old habit of three or four.

Sis moved in to look after Father as Mother's substitute. After divorcing Curtis Dall, she was now Mrs. John Boettiger, the wife of a newspaper reporter turned publisher, and she brought her two children with her. We could not have guessed it, but the effect was to inhibit any chance of reconciliation between our parents in those few autumn years that remained.

Loneliness weighed as heavily on Father as did the responsibilities of being President and Commander in Chief. What he missed more than anything was someone dear to him with whom he could talk over every problem late at night or the next morning. He had depended on that camaraderie with Louis, that closeness with Missy. Now, with his four sons away in uniform and Mother roaming the corners of the earth, his immediate family had been whittled down to Sis. She delighted in the situation.

She took on the protection of Father, vetting his appointments, smoothing his personal arrangements, watching over his diet and his general health. Now it was Sis who talked with visitors Father was too busy to see, then passed on the gist of her conversations to him. She was the one now who really ran the White House as manager, organizer and protector while the rest of the family were occupied with the war.

Four years after Father's death, Mother wrote of Anna's role: "Everything she did was done capably, and she brought to all her contacts a gaiety and buoyance that made everybody feel just a little happier because she was around." Our mother, in the generosity of spirit which distinguished her by then, suppressed the bitterness she felt when she first learned that Sis, as mistress of the White House, had no qualms about concealing from her the fact that Father and Lucy had been meeting again.

Whenever the arrangements could be made, at Aiken, Allamuchy, Warm Springs or in the White House itself, the tired, gray man and the still beautiful woman spent hours together. Lucy was the woman he turned to for companionship in the afterglow of a desire that had been frustrated by Mother more than a quarter of a century ago.

The last of the men in the tight little circle of comrades died aboard the USS *Quincy* on the voyage home from Yalta. Pa Watson had been urged for some time by his Catholic wife to convert to her religion. In the hospital bay of the warship, Father, gaunt and exhausted from the struggle of maintaining amity between Churchill and Stalin, assisted the chaplain in the ritual of confirming his trusted friend in the faith of the Catholic church, Missy's faith, Lucy's faith.

In those last few months of his life, Father spoke to me about Mother in terms I had never heard him use before. We sat together in his bedroom one night when he said reflectively, "You know, I think that your mother and I might be able to get together now and do things together, take some trips maybe, learn to know each other again."

He talked at length of his appreciation of her as a person, her strength of character, her value to him. "I only wish she wasn't so darned busy," he said. "I could have her with me so much more if she didn't have so many other engagements."

I took it upon myself, without Father's urging, to pass on some of the things he had said to Mother. The estrangement between my parents had been of such long standing that a great part of their communication was through other people, such as myself and Sis.

Their crowded daily schedules left them with virtually no chance to break down into sentimental conversations with each other.

I was delighted when Mother expressed the same desire, that the day would soon come when their intimidating work loads could be rearranged to give them more time together.

"I hope this will come to pass," she said.

"You know that I do," I answered.

It was made impossible because Mother had surrendered the White House to Anna. They had not a single day when they might have talked away the pain of the past and come to an understanding that forgiveness is a necessary part of a full life, that neither of them could be blamed for what had happened when they were too young and too determined to know any better. Anna was the one who shared in Father's life during his last days, enjoying an easy intimacy with him that Mother was never to achieve.

Not long after his death, I sat again with Mother, talking about him. "He was a very lonesome man," she said. "I wish I had been able to be closer to him, to comfort him sometimes, but I suppose that could not be."

Another thought came to haunt my mind these past few days, along with the ghosts of Christmas. It was the season when sentiment is not out of place and memories may be given free rein. The lines of Whittier seemed to me appropriate:

> *For of all sad words of tongue or pen,*
> *The saddest are these: "It might have been."*

January–December, 1972

Index